Choice Modelling and the
Transfer of Environmental Values

NEW HORIZONS IN ENVIRONMENTAL ECONOMICS

Series Editors: Wallace E. Oates, *Professor of Economics, University of Maryland, USA* and Henk Folmer, *Professor of General Economics, Wageningen University and Professor of Environmental Economics, Tilburg University, The Netherlands*

This important series is designed to make a significant contribution to the development of the principles and practices of environmental economics. It includes both theoretical and empirical work. International in scope, it addresses issues of current and future concern in both East and West and in developed and developing countries.

The main purpose of the series is to create a forum for the publication of high quality work and to show how economic analysis can make a contribution to understanding and resolving the environmental problems confronting the world in the twenty-first century.

Recent titles in the series include:

Amenities and Rural Development
Theory, Methods and Public Policy
Edited by Gary Paul Green, Steven C. Deller and David W. Marcouiller

The Evolution of Markets for Water
Theory and Practice in Australia
Edited by Jeff Bennett

Integrated Assessment and Management of Public Resources
Edited by Joseph C. Cooper, Federico Perali and Marcella Veronesi

Climate Change and the Economics of the World's Fisheries
Examples of Small Pelagic Stocks
Edited by Rögnvaldur Hannesson, Manuel Barange and Samuel F. Herrick Jr

The Theory and Practice of Environmental and Resource Economics
Essays in Honour of Karl-Gustaf Löfgren
Edited by Thomas Aronsson, Roger Axelsson and Runar Brännlund

The International Yearbook of Environmental and Resource Economics 2006/2007
A Survey of Current Issues
Edited by Tom Tietenberg and Henk Folmer

Choice Modelling and the Transfer of Environmental Values
Edited by John Rolfe and Jeff Bennett

The Impact of Climate Change on Regional Systems
A Comprehensive Analysis of California
Edited by Joel Smith and Robert Mendelsohn

Explorations in Environmental and Natural Resource Economics
Essays in Honor of Gardner M. Brown, Jr.
Edited by Robert Halvorsen and David Layton

Using Experimental Methods in Environmental and Resource Economics
Edited by John A. List

Economic Modelling of Climate Change and Energy Policies
Carlos de Miguel, Xavier Labandeira and Baltasar Manzano

Choice Modelling and the Transfer of Environmental Values

Edited by

John Rolfe

Associate Professor in Regional Economic Development, Faculty of Business and Law, Central Queensland University, Australia

Jeff Bennett

Professor of Environmental Management, Asia Pacific School of Economics and Government, The Australian National University, Australia

NEW HORIZONS IN ENVIRONMENTAL ECONOMICS

Edward Elgar

Cheltenham, UK • Northampton, MA, USA

Published by
Edward Elgar Publishing Limited
Glensanda House
Montpellier Parade
Cheltenham
Glos GL50 1UA
UK

Edward Elgar Publishing, Inc.
136 West Street
Suite 202
Northampton
Massachusetts 01060
USA

A catalogue record for this book
is available from the British Library

ISBN-13: 978 1 84376 684 1
ISBN-10: 1 84376 684 1

Printed and bound in Great Britain by MPG Books Ltd, Bodmin, Cornwall

Contents

Contributors

Begona Alvarez-Farizo is a Senior Research Fellow at CITA in Zaragoza, Spain. She has used choice experiments to look at the environmental impacts of wind power in Spain, and at the benefits of Water Framework Directive impacts.

Jeff Bennett is Professor of Environmental Management, and Director of the Environmental Management and Development Program in the Asia Pacific School of Economics and Government at The Australian National University. His research interests focus on the development and application of environmental valuation techniques and the economics of nature protection incentives for the private sector.

Nick Hanley is Professor of Environmental Economics at the University of Stirling. His main research interests are in environmental cost-benefit analysis, the economics of sustainable development, and non-point pollution control. He has used the choice experiment method in a wide variety of contexts, including wildlife conservation, the environmental impacts of renewable power, and in recreation demand modelling.

Paula Horne is a senior researcher at the Finnish Forest Research Institute, where she leads a research program: Safeguarding Forest Biodiversity – Policy Instruments and Socio-Economic Impacts. She has published more than 60 refereed articles, research reports or popular articles concerning non-market valuation, forest and nature conservation policies, forest recreation, and valuation methodology. Ms. Horne is also leading the monitoring and evaluation of socio-economic impacts of the new nature conservation program in Finland (METSO).

Geoff Kerr is Associate Professor of Environmental Economics at Lincoln University, New Zealand. Dr Kerr's research interests have centred on understanding, measuring and managing extra-market effects of policies affecting water, recreation, wildlife, transport, local communities and fisheries. Geoff has established the New Zealand Non-Market Valuation Database, a comprehensive collection of New Zealand non-market valuation studies, as an aid to benefits transfer. Geoff has recently developed an interest in monitoring public perceptions of the environment and its management.

Adam Loch is a cotton grower at Emerald, in central Queensland, Australia. He has a Bachelor of Commerce from Bond University, a Masters in Marketing Management from Griffith University, and a Masters in Business from Central Queensland University.

John Loomis is a Professor at Colorado State University and Distinguished Scholar of the Western Agricultural Economics Association. He has published more than 100 journal articles and book chapters on valuation of non-marketed resources and benefit-cost analysis. His research focuses on valuation of recreation, wilderness, wetlands, rivers, forest fire management, and endangered species such as the spotted owl and salmon.

Mark Morrison is Associate Professor in the School of Marketing and Management, Charles Sturt University, Australia. He teaches and researches in both economics and marketing. His research areas include non-market valuation, technology adoption, market-based instruments, market segmentation and new product development. He is a Senior Research Fellow at CSIRO Land and Water, and associate of the Centre for the Study of Choice (University of Technology, Sydney) and the Institute for Land, Water and Society (CSU).

John Rolfe is a resource economist who is Associate Professor in the Faculty of Business and Law at the Central Queensland University, Australia. He has a number of research interests, but specialises in the use of non-market valuation techniques to assess community preferences for social, environmental and other impacts associated with resource development. He has been involved in a number of choice modelling studies that span agricultural, environmental and social tradeoffs.

Basil Sharp is an economist at The University of Auckland, New Zealand. His research career spans thirty years beginning in the 1970s with the economic analysis of water resource development in Canterbury, New Zealand. Basil was awarded a Fulbright Scholarship in 1974 and graduated from the University of Wisconsin-Madison in 1978. His PhD thesis received a national award from the American Association of Agricultural Economists. On returning from the US in 1980, he worked with a team of economists at Lincoln College that spearheaded the development and application of non-market valuation methods in New Zealand. His experience with non-market valuation methods includes the use of the travel cost method to estimate the value of recreation, contingent valuation to estimate the benefit of improved water quality, and more recently the application of choice modelling to environmental mitigation in the Auckland Region.

Martin van Bueren has a bachelor degree in agricultural economics and a PhD in environmental economics, both from the University of Western Australia. Martin is a leading Australian practitioner in the fields of agricultural and natural resource economics, and is a senior consultant with the Allen Consulting Group. He has spent time in the United States and the United Kingdom examining innovative market-based mechanisms for addressing externalities, including permit trading schemes and off-set programs. Martin regularly undertakes research evaluation projects for various research agencies in Australia. These projects involve cost-benefit assessments of various science and technology research programs, culminating in advice on whole-of-portfolio design to address research objectives.

Stuart Whitten is a resource economist with the CSIRO in Australia. He leads the Markets for Ecosystem Services project, which is focused on solving the obstacles to the practical application of markets for ecosystem services at the regional level in Australia through the development and implementation of pilot markets. Dr Whitten has extensive experience in environmental market and non-market valuation, having been involved in benefit-cost analyses as well as travel cost, contingent valuation, and choice modelling exercises. His research interests are focused on the design of robust, efficient and effective policies for natural resource management, with particular interest in designing institutions that reduce public and private transaction costs and effectively leverage community values.

Jill Windle is a Senior Research Fellow in the Centre for Environmental Management at Central Queensland University, Australia. She has a PhD from the University of Queensland and a broad research background that spans both the natural and social sciences. Her research interests are now focused on resource and environmental economics. In the last five years, her research has focused on extending the application of choice modelling to new and innovative areas of research.

Robert Wright is Professor of Economics at the University of Strathclyde, who now works mainly in the areas of population economics and migration.

Acknowledgements

The genesis of this book was a research project focused on understanding how environmental values for water resources could be transferred between sites and populations. The project was funded by the Australian Research Council, the Queensland Department of Natural Resources and Central Queensland University, and operated from 2000 to 2003. The results, together with the research available from other concurrent choice modelling studies, provided us with the depth of material to form the core of the volume. We would like to acknowledge those funding bodies for their support.

Benefit transfer is only possible when there are both demands from policy makers to include consideration of environmental tradeoffs in the assessment of resource use, and a pool of relevant non-market valuation studies from which value estimates can be drawn. In Australia and overseas there are increasing demands for benefit transfer in natural resource management policy studies, as well as a concurrent rise in the number of non-market valuation studies. We would like to express our thanks to our colleagues in the policy and environmental valuation areas for 'setting the stage' by stimulating both the demand for, and supply of, environmental value estimates. We hope the material in this volume helps these two key groups to develop and use the results of non-market valuation exercises more accurately and extensively.

Particular thanks and appreciation must go to Dr Jill Windle at Central Queensland University for her patient work in helping to assemble the material, and her efforts in guiding it through the preparation stages. Thanks are also due to Chris Ulyatt for his time involved in proofing the chapters, to Eve Humphries for formatting the material to a camera-ready stage, and to the staff at Edward Elgar who guided us through the process.

The research behind this publication could not have happened without the support of our families. We would like to express our thanks and love to Veronika and Ngaire, our respective spouses, as well as our apologies for being so immersed in our research work.

JR and JB

1. Choice Modelling and the Transfer of Environmental Values

Jeff Bennett

1 INTRODUCTION

Choice modelling is a non-market valuation technique that has been developed in the 1990s to estimate use and non-use values associated with options for resource use. It is a 'stated preference' technique in that it involves a sample of those likely to be affected by a change in resource use being asked about their preferences for the change. This is in contrast to 'revealed preference' techniques that rely on observations of peoples' actual choices as the basis for the estimation of values. The contingent valuation method is perhaps the best-known stated preference technique. It involves the presentation of a single trade-off scenario to survey respondents to gather information on the strength of peoples' preferences. In contrast, choice modelling involves giving a sample of people more detailed and repeated resource use scenarios to collect data about choices. As a consequence, the use of choice modelling generates substantial statistical data. A key question that emerges is how useful those data are and how much they can be extrapolated to circumstances beyond their immediate case study source. The extrapolation process, known as 'benefit transfer', has potential advantages in terms of making estimated non-use values more widely applicable, but there are some hurdles to overcome. To understand these, it is useful to begin with an historical overview of the development of choice modelling and the implementation of benefit transfer.

Methods designed to estimate environment non-market values — particularly the stated preference techniques — have been controversial both within the economics profession and amongst policy makers and their advisers. This controversy reached a head during the legal proceedings following the Exxon Valdez oil spill in Prince William Sound, Alaska in 1989. The contingent valuation method (CVM) — at that time, the most widely applied non-market valuation technique — was used to estimate the value of the damage done to the environment.

This estimate was used as the basis for determining the compensation to be paid by the Exxon Corporation to the people of the State of Alaska and the United States of America. Not surprisingly, with over a billion dollars at stake, Exxon challenged the technique and the value estimates it produced. Concurrently, the use of the same technique to estimate the value of environmental damage caused by a proposed mine adjacent to the World Heritage listed Kakadu National Park in the Northern Territory, Australia was being challenged by the proponents of the mine. At the core of both challenges was the prospect of the technique yielding upwardly biased estimates of the damage costs. The challenges brought into sharp focus the debate regarding bias that had been a feature of the environmental economics literature for at least a decade (Portney 1994).

A result of the sometimes acrimonious challenges was a reduced level of confidence with which policy makers held contingent valuation as a source of information regarding environmental costs and benefits. Despite numerous empirical studies designed to demonstrate the validity of those estimates, there was a distinct decline in the number of contingent valuation studies being commissioned for policy purposes in the time after the Exxon Valdez/Kakadu challenges.

In part as a response to the controversy surrounding the use of contingent valuation, researchers sought alternative stated preference, non-market valuation techniques. It was in this context that choice modelling began to emerge as an environmental valuation tool. Previously, it had been widely applied in commercial marketing to estimate the demand for products not yet on the market and in transport economics to determine potential market shares for alternative modes of transport. In both of these types of application, choice modellers were seeking to estimate preferences for goods and services that were, as yet, not being bought and sold in markets. Such tasks therefore were very similar to the task of estimating preferences for non-marketed environmental impacts. Researchers thus applied their attention to the development of choice modelling for application in environmental contexts.

Being a stated preference technique in which respondents to a questionnaire make hypothetical choices between alternative environmental outcomes, choice modelling has also been the subject of challenges centred on its capacity to produce unbiased estimates of value. However, its proponents argue that the choices presented in a choice modelling questionnaire are incentive compatible and can be designed in a way to provide realistic frames of reference for respondents (Bennett and Blamey 2001).

Policy makers steered away from the use of the contingent valuation method not just because of the risk of biased results. They were also reluctant to commission applications because of the time involved in work that required careful questionnaire design, extensive primary data collection and complex econometric modelling. Frequently, the policy decisions requiring environmental value information inputs were being made within time frames that did not permit contingent valuation — or for that matter, choice modelling — applications. Furthermore, because stated preference techniques require primary data collection, they are usually expensive to undertake when compared to 'desk-top' studies. This is especially true for studies that seek to be free of bias and hence require particular care to be taken in their application. Such care involves split-sample verification of results. Hence, for many decisions, the extent of the likely gain to be achieved from undertaking a non-market valuation exercise would be less than its costs.

It was in this context that the process of benefit transfer became more frequently used. Benefit transfer is the process whereby value estimates derived from a particular case study — called the source — are used to inform decision-making in a separate context — called the target. By employing benefit transfer, policy makers could avoid the costs and time delays associated with the commissioning of specific non-market valuation studies. This recognition led to the establishment of a number of databases of environmental valuation studies — notably ENVALUE in Australia and the Environmental Valuation Reference Inventory (EVRI) in Canada — specifically designed to act as repositories of source case data.

The superficial attractiveness of benefit transfer relating to time and money savings is, however, tempered by a recognition that the validity of the process depends on a number of conditions being fulfilled. First, the biophysical conditions applying in the source case must be similar to those applying in the target case. Second, the scale of environmental change considered in the source must approximate the target. Third, the socio-economic characteristics of the population impacted by the change investigated in the source need to approach those of the target population. Fourth, the frame or setting in which the valuation was made at the source must be close to that of the target. Finally, the source study has to have been conducted in a technically satisfactory fashion.

All of these conditions limit the use of benefit transfer, and studies have demonstrated that the 'one size fits all' approach is ill advised. In fact, one of the key tests of validity for stated preference technique applications is that different conditions can be demonstrated to yield different value estimates. If they did not, then accusations of 'hypothetical bias' might be accurate. In these cases, respondents are hypothesised to provide answers more or less at random because they are not willing to invest effort in determining their preferences, perhaps because they believe that the whole stated preference process has no foundation in reality.

Contingent valuation results have some specific limitations when used as source cases in benefit transfer. An individual contingent valuation application typically yields an estimate of the value of one specific environmental change. Because the change is so specific, securing a match with a target case is usually problematic. Hence, even though a contingent valuation application may have been focused on estimating wetland values, unless the target case involves a similar sized change in a similar wetland system, valuation inaccuracies are likely to arise. However, contingent valuation results do have the capacity to relate value estimates for a specific environmental impact to the socio-economic characteristics of the sample of people who were involved as respondents. Hence it is possible to vary the characteristics of the people whose values are of interest between the source and the target cases. Adjustments to value estimates for the target can thus be made.

Despite this, the bottom line is that for contingent valuation studies to form the basis for the wide adoption of benefit transfer, there would need to be many more studies done than there are available now, covering a much wider array of circumstances.

The use of choice modelling studies as sources for benefit transfer exercises has some specific advantages over contingent valuation. This is because the valuation estimates from choice modelling applications are not single point estimates as is the case with contingent valuation. Rather, choice modelling applications yield functional relationships between value estimates for environmental impacts and a sequence of characteristics or attributes that are used to describe those impacts. This is in addition to the capacity, similar to that of contingent valuation, to vary population characteristics between source and target cases. For example, an impact on a wetland system may be described by changes to the number of endangered species protected by the wetland, the area of the wetland and the health of the vegetation. Hence, different value estimates can be calculated for different combinations of changes to these descriptors as they occur in different target cases. The potential is for choice modelling studies to provide a much more flexible and hence useful basis for benefit transfer.

The aim of this book is to explore the potential for choice modelling applications to become widely used as source studies for use in benefit transfer exercises. It begins by giving an outline of the practical steps that constitute a benefit transfer exercise. Although superficially the benefit transfer process appears simple and straightforward, there are many traps for the novice in its application. John Rolfe provides the necessary guidance for those contemplating a benefit transfer exercise in Chapter 2. The chapter therefore provides a practical starting point for the rest of the book. Chapter 3, also written by John Rolfe, goes on to supply the necessary and complementary theoretical foundation for the applications that follow.

The theoretical flavour put in place by Rolfe is carried over into the next chapter in which John Loomis begins by comparing and contrasting the contingent valuation method with choice modelling. He argues that, given the identical theoretical base used by both techniques, the two are equally able to provide source data for benefit transfer exercises. The only difference he notes is the requirement to ask a sequence of contingent valuation questions each relating to a different change in the provision of the environmental good in question rather than a smaller number of multi-dimensional choice questions that constitutes a choice modelling application. On this basis, he goes on to use a mixture of contingent valuation and choice modelling studies to provide source data for three types of benefit transfer applications: single point estimate, value function and meta-analysis. The latter involves the combining of results from numerous studies. The context of the Loomis application is the valuation of improvements in the salmon populations in the Snake River under alternative management strategies. He notes two important conclusions. The first relates to the extent of valuation inaccuracies generated by the benefit transfer process compared with the overall scale of the benefits and costs involved in a decision. The second draws attention to the importance of diminishing marginal benefits as a concept in the benefit transfer task. He notes that most source studies to date have not been focused on the detection of differences between marginal benefit estimates at different levels of overall supply and this is a potential limitation to the use of those source studies when applied to targets where supplies are at differing levels.

The next four chapters also focus on benefit transfer in the context of river management. In Chapter 5, Morrison and Bennett report an application of choice modelling that was specifically designed to act as a source study. The context of the work was a government initiative in the Australian State of New South Wales for all rivers in the State to have a water management plan developed partly on the basis of cost-benefit analyses of alternative strategies. Benefit transfer was seen as the key to providing cost-effective value estimates for the benefits of environmental flows in rivers. Morrison and Bennett selected 'representative rivers' and conducted choice modelling applications on each of those rivers using samples of people living within the river catchments and outside. The goal was to generate a rich database of value estimates across different ecological types and beneficiary population characteristics. The results show why such a diversity of applications was necessary: differences in value estimates were found both across river types and population categories. The work demonstrates the need for a strong and detailed database of source studies if the benefit transfer is to be able to deliver accurate assessments in target cases.

Chapter 6 provides an insight into the status of choice modelling-based benefit transfer in the United Kingdom. Hanley, Wright and Alvarez-Farizo review existing studies of riverine ecology values and conclude that they are largely inadequate to form a data source for benefit transfer. The context they consider is the need for value estimates to comply with the European Union's Water Framework Directive for all waters to achieve 'good ecological status'. They go on to report the results of a new choice modelling study designed specifically to test for differences in value estimates across two different rivers. They find, similar to Morrison and Bennett in the previous chapter, that significant differences occur across differing river systems. Hence, they call for further investigations to be carried out on these value differentials in order to improve the prospects of benefit transfer when applied to decisions of such a consequence as river management in the UK.

The third river-focused chapter features another Australian case study, this time from the State of Queensland. Further tests of the viability of the benefit transfer process using choice modelling as a base are provided in the context of decisions regarding future water allocations for irrigation development in the Fitzroy River Basin. Unlike the NSW and UK river systems considered in the previous two chapters, the rivers of the Fitzroy are likely to undergo further development and allocation. Rolfe, Loch and Bennett report on a sequence of experiments designed to detect differences in estimated values for a range of environmental and social attributes of river basin developments within differing sub-catchments within the Basin and for populations resident in locations at differing distances from the rivers. The results from these tests are interpreted by the authors as supporting the conclusion reached in the earlier chapters that the benefit transfer process is 'difficult and sometimes contradictory', but they also take some encouragement for the process because the fine detail offered by choice modelling studies was found to allow accurate transfer of values in specific circumstances.

In Chapter 8, a New Zealand case study is reported. Kerr and Sharp report the results of a study commissioned by the Auckland Regional

Council as an input into its consideration of urban development proposals that have impacts on stream quality. The Council has the capacity to require land developers not only to carry out 'best-practice' in minimizing stream damage, but can also require damage mitigation in the form of offsetting stream improvements in other sites. Kerr and Sharp offer benefit transfer as one means of assisting decision makers assessing what is an acceptable level of mitigation. They conclude from the results of a number of comparability tests between source and target sites that potentially large errors can arise from the simple transference of value estimates across the variety of Auckland stream types and sub-populations.

Whitten and Bennett reach similar conclusions in Chapter 9, but this time in the context of wetland protection. The results reported are for two case study applications of choice modelling involving the estimation of values associated with the protection of wetlands on private lands in the Australian States of South Australia and New South Wales. Comparison of the results yielded by these two studies shows that the simple transference of benefit estimates across different inland wetland systems and populations of beneficiaries is not a straightforward exercise. The authors point out that the first transference issue requiring care is the question of how representative the sample of people answering the valuation questionnaire is of the population of concern. Where 'self-selection' of respondents is a problem, a correction of the value estimates derived from the survey is required before it can even be considered to be relevant to the population being surveyed. This is a step to be taken prior to the benefit transfer process and may be a difficult one where potential source studies do not report the socio-economic characteristics of the sample and its population. Whitten and Bennett also allude to the issue of diminishing marginal values raised by Loomis in Chapter 4 in that they recommend care be taken in extrapolating both the absolute and relative scales of the environmental changes involved in the source and target cases.

Social attributes are included in the choice modelling applications reported by Whitten and Bennett in Chapter 9 and by Rolfe, Loch and Bennett in Chapter 7. In the wetlands case, values were estimated for an attribute described to respondents as the number of farmers leaving a region as a result of wetlands protection measures. In the Fitzroy River Basin case detailed in Chapter 7, the attribute was 'number of people leaving the region' as a result of water resource re-allocations. This integration of resource trade-offs and social impacts is continued in the next two chapters.

In Chapter 10, van Bueren and Bennett report a study focused on establishing generic values relating to land and water resources for benefit transfer in cases of regional and national policy changes. The social attribute is described as the number of people leaving the region, while the other attributes used in the application are defined to provide generic coverage: numbers of species protected, area of land restored and length of waterways restored. This specification is designed to give maximum flexibility to the benefit transfer process. The chapter provides the results of a sequence of tests relating to the suitability of estimates for transfer — from regional to national issue level and from regional to national populations. The work also provides a set of guidelines for the use of the results in benefit transfer and suggests the use of specific adjustment 'factors' to reflect the differences observed between the alternative scales of the issues and population proximity.

In Chapters 7, 9 and 10, the social consequences of resource use policy attributes provide an additional dimension to the choice modelling exercises reported. In Chapter 11, Rolfe and Windle look at a specific social attribute: the cultural heritage of Australian Aboriginal people in the central Queensland region. In keeping with the theme of the book, the chapter reports a choice modelling application in which the prospects of transferring estimated values of Aboriginal cultural heritage are assessed. A set of hypotheses relating to differences between the cultural heritage values held by different sub-groups of the population is tested. These groups include Aboriginal people living in the region, other Australians living in the region and other Australians living in an urban area geographically remote from the sites of heritage interest. The results give the authors some confidence in recommending unadjusted value estimates transference between different sub-populations of non-Aboriginal Australians, but they find significantly higher values being held by the Aboriginal people. Again, the complexity of the benefit transfer process is exemplified.

All of the case studies set out in the book to this point focus on the transference of values resulting from changes to resource management. The final chapter takes a look at choice modelling-based benefit transfer from a different perspective. Horne and Bennett consider the prospects of benefit transfer in providing information relevant to the design of policy instruments. They explicitly recognise that the way in which resource use change is achieved forms part of the 'frame of reference' that is integral to the valuation process. The context of the study is the development of biodiversity protection policies for Finnish forests that are owned privately. Two choice modelling experiments are reported. The first sought an understanding of the strength of preferences held by the forest owners for different mechanisms through which they may receive payment for biodiversity protection on their land. The second involved the general public of Finland to find out if the way in which forest owners were paid would make a difference to their willingness to pay for forest biodiversity protection. The results of both studies provide support to the hypothesis that the terms of contracts offered to forest owners is an important part of the valuation context for both forest owners and the general public.

The conclusion that is repeated in the case study chapters of this book is that the benefit transfer process is not straightforward. The 'one-size-fits-all' approach that is often sought by policy makers, their advisers and their consultants looking for a speedy and low-cost formula for assessing options does not always generate accurate estimates of value. Adjustments to source study values for sample representation, population, ecological and scale differences as well as the policy frame have all been demonstrated as needed for accuracy. This result is heartening in terms of the validity of choice modelling results, as it shows how the technique is able to pick up preference differences. Respondents to the choice modelling applications reported did not simply answer the questions randomly. Their responses matched the varying contexts presented to them. However, the result does mean that those seeking to use benefit transfer need not only to have a strong database of source studies but will also require the capacity to develop adjustment factors of the type recommended by van Bueren and Bennett in Chapter 10 or a meta-analysis following the style of that presented by Loomis in Chapter 4.

The further implication is that the field of researching non-market valuation will require both deepening and widening if benefit transfer is to become a feature of resource and environmental policy development. The gaps that are currently evident in the scope and quality of studies suitable to act as benefit transfer 'sources' remain extensive. Furthermore, the understanding of adjustment factors or 'weights' remains incomplete. This book is therefore merely a start to what will be an ongoing evolution of the use of choice modelling in the development of the benefit transfer process.

REFERENCES

Bennett, J.W. and R.K. Blamey (2001), *The Choice Modelling Approach to Environmental Valuation*, Cheltenham UK and Northampton, MA, USA: Edward Elgar.

Portney, P. (1994), 'The contingent valuation debate: why economists should care', *Journal of Economic Perspectives*, **8** (4), 3–19.

2. A Simple Guide to Choice Modelling and Benefit Transfer

John Rolfe

1   INTRODUCTION

Benefit transfer is a pragmatic way of estimating values of potential trade-off options where there is limited time or funding available. It operates by transferring values in some way from existing valuation studies to a target study of interest. Because of its pragmatic nature, there are few definitive guidelines about how benefit transfer should be conducted, although there have been a number of studies which have identified potential flaws. Much of the benefit transfer literature has focused on the transfer of results from contingent valuation studies. The development of the choice modelling technique creates both future opportunities for benefit transfer and better understanding about where limitations might lie.

The material in this chapter is aimed at providing a relatively simple summary of the issues involved in using choice modelling and benefit transfer. The focus is aimed at the consultant and student level, where the need may be for a practical understanding or guide to implementation without developing a detailed knowledge of the technique. More detailed theoretical information on choice modelling and benefit transfer is available in the next chapter, while the case studies in the subsequent chapters illustrate many of the points summarised in this chapter.

2   THE CHOICE MODELLING TECHNIQUE

Choice modelling is a non-market valuation technique, meaning that it can be used to assess values for actions or preferences that are not revealed in market transactions. After early origins in transport and marketing fields, choice modelling (also known as choice experiments or choice-based conjoint) has been developed for applications in the environmental valuation field. The technique is versatile, and can be designed for a wide variety of purposes. These include the estimation of a variety of environmental use values, such as those associated with recreation, where it may be more flexible than a number of traditional economic assessment techniques. It can also be used to estimate values for trade-off options involving cultural and social issues, as well as for non-use environmental values, such as the benefits derived from protecting endangered species.

The technique works by surveying people to ask them what their preferred choice would be from among sets of different resource management alternatives. These are called 'choice sets'. The choice process is repeated several times, so that respondents make a series of similar, but separate choices. The choices are similar, because each choice set is made up of a fixed number of alternatives, and each alternative is described in terms of a set of outcome 'attributes'. These attributes take different values or 'levels' for each alternative. The alternatives can be thought of as different ways of dealing with some issue, so that respondents are being asked to pick which alternative among a select group is most attractive to them.

The attributes allow the alternatives to be described in a uniform manner. For example, rainforest protection options reported in Rolfe, Bennett and Louviere (2000) were described with the aid of six key attributes:

- location;
- rarity;
- effect on local people;
- potential for future visits;
- size; and
- possession of special features.

Plus an attribute to represent the cost trade-off that respondents might make, being:

- Amount of donation needed to preserve option described.

Differences between the alternatives are created by allowing the attributes to vary across several levels. The attributes can be described in a quantitative manner, in which case the levels are different numbers (e.g. 1, 10 or 100 hectares), or a qualitative manner, in which case the levels are more descriptive (e.g. small, medium, large). It is normal to include some monetary trade-off as one of the attributes in an experiment so that value estimates can subsequently be calculated.

Choice alternatives typically involve several attributes varying across two or more levels, with two or more alternatives combining to form choice sets. There is usually a very large number of potential combinations of these possibilities, and it is impractical to offer these in a single survey. A process known as experimental design is used to select a representative sample of alternatives and choice sets that can be used in a survey. If there are still too many to offer to a single respondent, the choice sets can be partitioned (blocked) into several groups and these are then used in different versions (split samples) of the survey.

An example of a choice set involving three alternatives from Rolfe, Bennett and Louviere (2000) is shown in Figure 2.1.

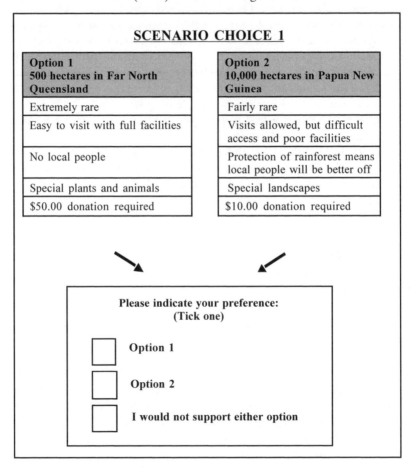

Figure 2.1 A sample choice set for rainforest protection

It is essential in a choice modelling experiment that one of the choice options remains constant between the choice sets as a way of 'grounding' the choice tasks. There are three main options for providing a constant base in each choice set. The first two involve the use of an additional profile where the levels remain constant across choice sets. The levels can reflect the current situation (a Status Quo option) or some future scenario (a Future Base option). The third option is to provide a simplified 'No Choice' category. This can be offered as several categories to capture the range of reasons why respondents may not choose one of the choice profiles.

The alternatives in a choice modelling application can be labelled or unlabelled. With unlabelled alternatives, the only differences between profiles are created by variations in the attribute levels. With labelled alternatives, an additional descriptor is added to each alternative in every choice set. The labels remain consistent across choice sets, and may be important determinants of choice behaviour. (See Table 2.1 for a summary of terms used.)

Table 2.1   Summary of choice modelling terms

Term	Description
Choice experiment	Series of choice sets, usually offered as part of a survey
Choice set	A single set of alternatives offered to respondents, where they have to indicate their preferred choice. It normally includes two or more choice profiles as well as a constant base
Choice alternative	A choice option that is described to respondents in terms of a set number of attributes and labels
Attribute	A descriptor used as part of a choice profile. Several attributes and sometimes a label are used to form profiles
Level	Describes the value that an attribute can take. Attribute values vary across levels to form differences between profiles
Experimental design	Mathematical technique used to design a representative sample of choice sets given the desired number of attributes, levels and profiles per choice set
Label	Descriptor given to a choice profile and repeated across choice sets
Constant base	An alternative that remains constant between each choice set. It can take three main forms: a 'Status Quo', 'Future Base' or 'No choice' alternative
Status quo	A constant alternative that is described like a choice profile, where the levels of each attribute depict the current situation
Future Base	A constant alternative that is described like a choice profile, where the levels of each attribute depict some future situation
No choice	A constant alternative that simply gives respondents some way of refusing the other profiles. It can be offered in several levels, e.g. 'Unsure' and 'No Choice'

Once an application has been performed and the choice data collected, the data can be analysed to explain the observed choices. The simplest models to use for this purpose are multinominal logit (MNL) models, which essentially regress the logarithm of the probability that an alternative is chosen against the levels of the attributes in the alternative. Other data, such as the attitudes and demographic characteristics of respondents, can also be included in the analysis. The statistical analysis produces a variate, similar to multiple regression, with an estimated coefficient and standard error for each variable in the analysis. An intercept, known as Alternate Specific Constants (ASCs), can be estimated for each alternative in the choice sets, with the exception of one which is omitted to act as a base in the analysis. It is normally the constant base in the choice sets which forms the base case in the statistical analysis.

A typical explanation of choice behaviour observed in a choice modelling application will take the following form:

Log of probability that a particular alternative will be chosen	=	Constant (ASC) + Beta values for attributes + Beta values for attitudinal and demographic variables

The relationship between choices made and the levels of the attributes describing the choice options and the socio-economic characteristics of the people making the choices is interpreted as an expression of the satisfaction, or utility, enjoyed by the survey respondents. Technically, this is known as an 'indirect utility function'. An example of such a function (V) for individual *i* and alternative *j* reported in Rolfe, Bennett and Louviere (2000) was reported as follows:

$$V_{ij} = 6.1722 - 0.1050(Z_{location}) + 0.00005(Z_{area}) + 0.3100(Z_{rarity})$$
$$+ 0.0732(Z_{visits}) + 0.3083(Z_{local}) + 0.1629(Z_{special\ features}) -$$
$$0.0094(Z_{price})$$

Model results are not directly comparable between choice modelling applications. This is because the model parameters are partly confounded with an error term that is unique to each statistical analysis. However, this error term is cancelled out in any ratio of model parameters. This means that any value estimates can be directly compared, as these involve some combination of attributes being divided by the coefficient for the monetary attribute.

There are two different value estimates available from a choice modelling application. The first of these estimates is the value of alternatives relative to each other. These can be any two alternatives generated from the available attributes, levels and labels, although the normal focus is to find the value of a particular alternative relative to the constant base used in the application. The explanation of choice behaviour given by the model derived from the observed choice data is used to calculate the indirect utility associated with the alternatives of interest. An economic value is assigned by dividing the utility difference between alternatives with the negative of the coefficient for the monetary attribute.

The other type of value estimate available is the marginal value associated with a change in a single attribute. These are known as part-worths, and are derived by dividing the coefficient for an attribute with the negative of the coefficient for the monetary attribute. They identify the dollar amount associated with a one unit change in the attribute in question.

As an example, the part-worth for area reported in Rolfe, Bennett and Louviere (2000) was calculated as follows:

$$
\begin{aligned}
\text{Part-worth (Area)} &= -1 \times \beta_{area} / \beta_{money} \\
&= -1 \times 0.00005/-0.009437 \\
&= 0.005298 \ (\$/ha)
\end{aligned}
$$

Both groups of values are Hicksian compensating surplus estimates, and can be directly utilised in analytical frameworks such as cost-benefit analysis.

3   THE BENEFIT TRANSFER METHOD

Choice modelling is part of a family of non-market valuation techniques that include both market-related data (revealed preferences) and non-market data (stated preferences). Choice modelling (CM) and the contingent valuation method (CVM) are stated preference techniques where people are asked to state their preferences or choices rather than reveal them through market transactions. Non-market valuation studies are relatively expensive and time-consuming to perform compared with desktop studies of markets, so there is often interest from analysts and policy makers in transferring the results from previous, similar studies rather than instigating new ones. This process is known as benefit transfer.

The concept of benefit transfer is routinely applied in the commercial world, where, for example, prices of real estate from sales data are routinely extrapolated to estimate market values for other real estate areas. The extrapolation process typically involves adjustment for the characteristics of the sales involved and the target areas specified. In some cases, a statistical process known as hedonic pricing can be used to perform the extrapolation process more rigorously.

A benefit transfer process for environmental values normally involves the transfer of values from a source site (the subject of a valuation study) to a target site. While it is standard practice with CVM and CM models to adjust values for population differences between source and target sites, it is more difficult to account for site differences. There are four main ways of performing a benefit transfer process for this purpose, as shown in Table 2.2.

Table 2.2   Types of transfer methods

Transfer method	Description	Example	Valuation technique used
Single point value transfer	A single value is transferred without adjustment from source study to target site	A rainforest protection value of $50/person is transferred from Case Study A to Site B	Outcomes of CVM often used for this purpose
Marginal point value transfer	A single value that allows for site differences is transferred	A rainforest protection value of $2/hectare/person is transferred from Case Study A to Site B. The values are adjusted for the size of the area protected	Part-worths of CM can be used for this purpose. Some CVM results can also be adjusted for this purpose, but values may not be rigorous unless multiple CVM studies are available
Benefit function transfer	A valuation function is transferred, allowing adjustment for variety of site differences	A rainforest valuation function that involves several attributes is transferred from Case Study A to Site B	Models from CM studies can be used for this purpose. Key advantage is that it allows for automatic adjustment with variations in attribute levels
Meta value analysis	Results of several studies are combined to generate a pooled model	Results from studies A, X, Y and Z are pooled to estimate a value for Site B	Can involve outcomes from both CVM and CM experiments

Some examples of the four broad types of benefit transfer are shown in Table 2.3 below, drawing on material in subsequent chapters of this publication.

Table 2.3   Examples of transfer methods

Transfer Method	Examples
Single point value transfer	Loomis (Chapter 4) transfers a single value held by the Washington State population for a change in wild salmon population in a source river (the Elwa River) to a target river (the Snake River). However, the initial value of $73/household was adjusted in three important ways by (a) adjusting values from 1994 dollars to 1996 dollars, (b) adjusting values held by a state population to those held by a regional population, and (c) identifying values only for non-angling households.
Marginal point value transfer	Hanley, Wright and Alvarez-Farizo (Chapter 6) compare the marginal values for improvements in river ecology between the River Wear in England and the River Clyde in Scotland. For example, the marginal value of an improvement in river quality in the River Wear was £12.26. They tested if it would have been accurate to transfer this marginal value to the River Clyde.
	Kerr and Sharp (Chapter 8) compare marginal values for attributes in stream health for two population groups in Auckland, New Zealand according to whether streams are in good health or are degraded. For example, the North Auckland households held marginal values of $66 for water clarity improvements in healthy streams, and $48 in degraded streams, while South Auckland households held corresponding values of $67 and $73.
Benefit function transfer	Rolfe, Loch and Bennett (Chapter 7) compare compensating surplus estimates for floodplain protection in Queensland, Australia using data from different CM experiments. The same site and population characteristics are inputted into the different benefit functions to test if they predict equivalent values.
Meta value analysis	Loomis (Chapter 4) uses the results of three CVM studies and one CM study to provide several data points about the marginal, non-use values for salmon. He then uses these data in a regression analysis to estimate a single, meta-analysis function, which relates the marginal, non-use values to the quantity of salmon being considered.
	Morrison and Bennett (Chapter 5) pool the data from a series of CM studies to estimate a single function for valuing improved river health in NSW, Australia.

Before the development of the choice modelling technique, the options for benefit transfer were simple point value transfers, or if there were enough valuation studies available, the performance of a meta-analysis. The richness of statistical outputs from a choice modelling study has allowed marginal point value transfers and benefit function transfers to be added to the pool of transfer choices. It has also allowed a better understanding of benefit transfer to develop, as well as more rigorous testing to determine when it is appropriate.

Benefit transfer is uncontroversial when:

- the sites are almost identical;
- the same population is involved;
- the extent of the change being considered is the same in both source and target cases;
- the 'frame' of the source study matches the 'frame' of the target study; and
- the initial valuation study has been performed rigorously and accurately.

However, most applications of benefit transfer involve greater differences between site and target studies, indicating that more analysis, adjustment and testing of the transfer process needs to take place. Many of the case studies reported in this book indicate that the benefit transfer process can be complex and demanding. There are many examples where differences between source and target sites are large enough to make benefit transfer problematic. This means that care needs to be taken to ensure that a benefit transfer process is not invalid.

In Table 2.4, the key stages in a benefit transfer (BT) exercise are identified.

Table 2.4   Stages in a benefit transfer exercise

#	Stage	Notes
1	Assess target situation	
2	Identify source studies available and select benefit transfer type	Transfer type largely dependent on source studies available
3	Assess site differences	(a) identify if BT possible
		(b) identify basis for BT adjustment
4	Assess population differences	(a) identify if BT possible
		(b) identify basis for BT adjustment
5	Assess scale of change in both cases	(a) identify if BT possible
		(b) identify basis for BT adjustment
6	Assess framing issues (scope, scale, instrument, payment vehicle, payment length, willingness to pay or willingness to accept format used, use versus non-use)	(a) test if source study is appropriate for BT
		(b) identify any basis for BT adjustment
7	Assess statistical modelling issues	(a) identify appropriateness of model in source study
		(b) identify any basis for BT adjustment
8	Perform benefit transfer process	

In cases where it is not appropriate to perform benefit transfer directly between a source and target study, it may be possible to use adjustment factors to make the transfer process more accurate. The adjustment process in benefit transfer can be either implicit or explicit. Implicit adjustment occurs when variations in population, site or quantity are automatically accounted in a valuation exercise. For example:

- variations in population characteristics are automatically included in any transfer of a CVM or CM benefit transfer function;
- variations in site differences are automatically included in any transfer of a CM function; and
- variations in quantity are automatically included in any marginal point value transfer.

Explicit adjustment occurs when values or function coefficients are weighted to take account of other variations between source and target studies. For example:

- values may be adjusted by Consumer Price Index factors to allow transfers into subsequent time periods (e.g. Loomis, Chapter 4);
- values may be adjusted to account for different population frames, such as between national and state populations (e.g. Loomis, Chapter 4, and van Bueren and Bennett, Chapter 10); and
- values may be adjusted to account for different scope frames (e.g. van Bueren and Bennett, Chapter 10).

4   PERFORMING BENEFIT TRANSFER FROM A CHOICE MODELLING STUDY

In this section, the key issues involved in performing a benefit transfer function are discussed, following the stages outlined in the diagram/ table above.

4.1   Assess Target Situation

This stage involves the assessment of the site characteristics, the policy change or development being considered, and the population likely to be affected. The assessment is used to identify the key issues and attributes of interest, and to provide a template for comparative assessment in the following stages. It may be helpful to assess the target situation as if a non-market valuation study was to be conducted, as this may focus the analysis. The likely magnitude of the values involved may also be considered in order to assess the prospects of an original valuation study being required.

4.2   Identify Source Studies Available

Source studies may be found in a number of ways. Several databases have been developed to assist in the sourcing of suitable case studies.

Some of the most useful are the ENVALUE site in Australia (www. epa.nsw.gov.au/envalue), and the Environmental Valuation Reference Inventory in Canada (http://www.evri.ca/).[1] The ENVALUE site has free access, while the EVRI site requires a subscription.

Not all studies are suitable for a benefit transfer process, and culling may be needed to focus on the most suitable ones. The criteria for selecting suitable source studies might include factors such as:

- similarities between source and target sites, populations and scale of changes involved;
- the type of source study available;
- the age of the source study;
- the type of statistical modelling performed in a source study; and
- the rigour of the source study (including sample size, validity tests performed and the strength of statistical relationships observed).

In some cases a single study may be targeted, while in others a number of studies may be used to provide different elements of value transfer. If several similar studies are available, then a meta-analysis may be performed. In all cases, values from source studies will need to be adjusted for the Consumer Price Index to account for the price changes during the time period between the source study and the case study of interest.

4.3   Assess Site Differences

Key characteristics of a study site might include:

- the physical characteristics;
- the type of policy or development changes being considered;
- the types of impacts being generated, including physical; environmental, social and economic impacts, and
- the size of the changes involved.

As a general rule, the focus of site assessment for comparative purposes should be on the types of impacts generated, although in some cases the types of site (e.g. rainforest) and the change mechanism involved may also be expected to be important. The key to assessing what attributes should be involved in a benefit transfer process is to identify which factors are likely to impact on peoples' preferences or satisfaction levels, i.e. compare the attributes used in the source study with those that are required in the target site.

Surveys can vary according to the types of values that are assessed. Some surveys are focused on assessing non-use values, or particular components of non-use values, while others are focused on assessing a mix of use and non-use values. Care has to be taken in a benefit transfer exercise to ensure that value components are consistent between source and target sites.

A key issue in the assessment of site differences is where marginal effects are expected because of variations in the scale or scope of the case studies. As increasing levels of an attribute are presented in a case study, marginal values are expected to fall. This means that values should not be transferred between source and target sites if there are variations in the absolute and relative scales involved. If values are to be transferred, then they need to adjusted in some way to reflect changed marginal conditions.[2]

The pattern of site differences between source and target sites can be grouped into four main categories, as shown in Table 2.5.

Table 2.5   Types of site differences

#	Extent of difference	Application	Comment
1	Little site difference exists	All transfer methods are suitable	Benefit transfer function is likely to be more accurate where sites are very similar
2	Key attributes are the same, but levels vary between sites	Single value point transfer not suitable; others are appropriate	Marginal values or benefit functions need to be adjusted for levels at target site. If levels at target site are very different to levels at source site, adjustment factors may need to be developed
3	Target site does not have all the key attributes of source site	Single value point transfer not suitable; others may be appropriate	Levels for unnecessary attributes may be set at 0 in benefit transfer function
4	Target site has extra key attributes over source site	None of the transfer methods may be fully appropriate	May be handled by a series of marginal point value transfers

The categorisation shows that where site differences can be grouped into categories 1, 2 or 3, the benefit transfer process is likely to be valid, although there are implications for the mechanism that can be used. A key caveat is that there are similar attributes involved, and the source study has been framed in an appropriate way for use in the target study (see section below). As a general rule, the greater the overlap of attributes between a source study and a target study, the more appropriate it is to use a benefit transfer function. Where there is less overlap in the attributes of the two sites, then it becomes more appropriate to use a series of point source transfers.

Where site differences can be grouped into category 4, benefit transfer between sites is more problematic. This is because of the possibility that the source and target sites are very different, making it difficult to extrapolate values between them. Where source and target sites have common attributes, the difficulty is that the additional attributes of a target site may imply different values for a particular attribute compared with those available from a source study. While it remains technically possible to perform a series of marginal point value transfers to estimate values for various components of a target site, the process may be subject to a wide variety of errors.

4.4   Assess Population Differences

Different populations may hold different preferences for the benefits involved in a case study situation. This is particularly the case where use or indirect use values are involved, and different populations have different levels of involvement with, or use of, a particular resource. Different populations may also hold different non-use values, particularly where the populations have very different characteristics and/or attitudes.

The pattern of possible population differences between source and target sites can be grouped into three main categories, as shown in Table 2.6.

Table 2.6   Types of population differences

#	Extent of difference	Application	Comment
1	None – same population for source and target sites	All transfer methods are suitable	
2	Some – Substantial overlaps between populations for source and target sites	All transfer methods are suitable	Benefit transfer function is preferred because it allows adjustment for population differences
3	Large – Different populations for source and target sites	Benefit transfer not always appropriate	Where different populations have similar preference structures, then benefit transfer still appropriate

Key issues revolve around cases where different populations are involved between source and target study sites. In cases where the populations have similar preferences, then benefit transfer may still be appropriate. For example, it might be appropriate to transfer the values held by one distant state population for a protection of a national icon to values held by another distant state population, preferably through a benefit transfer function so that adjustments can be made for differences in income levels and other factors.

In other cases it may be expected that different populations have different preference structures, in which case a benefit transfer would not be appropriate. For example, it is unlikely that the values held by one state population for a state-related issue would necessarily be held by the population of another state. In this case, proximity and responsibility factors may mean that the populations hold very different preference structures.

Where differences exist between populations, then benefit transfer functions are preferred because they allow for adjustments for population characteristics. It is possible that both CVM functions (single point value transfers) and CM benefit functions relate value estimates to core socio-economic parameters such as income, ethnicity, education, age and occupation. Where functions do include the impact of these variables, then more confidence can be attached to the transfer of values between different populations.

4.5   Assess Framing Issues

Framing issues in stated preference studies can be categorised as framing differences and framing problems. Framing differences occur when the trade-offs in stated preference studies are presented in different ways, while framing problems occur when the respondent to a survey is unduly sensitive to the context in which a particular trade-off is offered. It is anticipated that values will be sensitive to the frame in which a trade-off is offered. Framing problems refer to the situation where changing the frame appears to have no influence or excessive influence on value estimation.

There are a large number of framing issues which can affect a valuation process. These are important in a benefit transfer process because:

- framing problems in a source study can make it invalid for benefit transfer;
- differences in framing between source and target sites might invalidate benefit transfer; and
- differences in framing between source and target sites may generate requirements for benefit adjustment.

There are a number of areas where framing issues can be identified, including:

- willingness to pay versus willingness to accept formats;
- the scope and scale of the issue presented;
- the policy mechanisms involved;

- the payment vehicle used;
- the survey instrument and collection method used; and
- context factors such as wealth conditions, the political debate, and other factors.

4.5.1 WTP versus WTA

The choice between willingness to pay (WTP) and willingness to accept (WTA) formats is important because large value differences are often revealed under the two formats. It is normal for WTA formats to generate higher value estimates than WTP formats, for a variety of potential reasons that include endowment effects, uncertainty effects and strategic behaviour.

The choice of format is often determined by the type of problem being addressed and the existing structure of property rights, as well as by the choice of the constant base in the choice modelling experiment. Where the issue of interest is a potential deterioration in environmental or other assets, the adoption of a 'status quo' base implies that a WTA format is being modelled ("How much are you WTA to allow the situation to continue?"). If a 'future base' is adopted, it is easier to introduce a WTP format ("How much are you WTP to avoid the future base occurring?"). It is normally recommended that WTP formats be used in stated preference experiments, even for scenarios where the implicit or sometimes explicit property rights imply a WTA question.

Particular care needs to be taken to ensure that WTA values from a source study are not transferred to a WTP scenario in a target site, as this will have the potential effect of overestimating values. Where possible, the same choice format should be applied across both source and target sites.

4.5.2 Scope and scale of the issue presented

Values can vary according to the scope at which the issue is framed, and the scale of the issue presented to respondents. An example of a scope effect is where value estimates for a kilometre of river protection vary according to whether the good is presented in the context of a local river system, a regional area river system, or all rivers in the country. An example of a scale effect is where the value estimates for a kilometre of river protection vary according to whether 1 kilometre or 1 000 kilometres are offered to respondents.

It is expected that values will be sensitive to the ways in which choices are framed at scope and scale levels. However, potential problems can emerge if values framed in one context in a source study are transferred to a very different context in a target study. To do this, a set of adjustment 'factors' needs to be developed so that value estimates can be scaled according to the context in which they are offered.

4.5.3 The payment vehicle

There are three issues associated with benefit transfer and payment vehicles (the mechanism used to indicate the change in monetary allocation for each choice profile). The first is that assessed values may be related to the type of payment vehicle used, because of varying levels of acceptance within the community. For example, values may change depending on whether tax increases or rate increases are used as the payment vehicle. The second is that the selection of an appropriate payment vehicle is often related to the scale of the issue involved and the type of body expected to fix it (e.g. local, state or federal government). The third is that payment vehicles tend to take two main forms: a lump sum payment or an annual payment. The implication of this is that estimated values can be either total values (associated with a lump sum payment) or annual values (associated with on-going payments). If the analyst wishes to estimate annual values from a lump sum payment mechanism, or total values from an annual payment mechanism, a discount rate for converting payment amounts must be chosen.

These issues mean that care has to be taken in a benefit transfer approach where some potential differences in payment vehicles might be involved.

4.5.4 The survey instrument and collection method used

The value estimation process might also be influenced by survey design issues and collection techniques. Poor response rates in survey collection reduce the confidence with which results might be extrapolated across the population of interest. As well, there are potential problems of bias associated with stated preference surveys where appropriate design and collection techniques are not followed. Where these problems exist in source site case studies, it makes any benefit transfer process problematic.

4.5.5 Context factors

Values can be framed by the context in which they are offered, so care has to be taken that contextual factors do not vary substantially between source and target studies. An example of a context factor influencing values is where drought or other background weather conditions have a defining influence on values associated with water issues.

Two particular context issues to recognise are associated with political issues and icon status, because they mean that values tend to be embedded within a wider set of issues. For example, respondents to a stated preference survey may sometimes use the opportunity to send a political message or identify that the issue is a particular icon for them. In each case, the respondent may view the issue in question as an opportunity to set a precedent, effectively widening the set of goods to include more than those defined in the stated preference survey. This means that the context can influence how a particular issue is framed by respondents, leading to potential variations in value estimates.

4.6   Assess Statistical Modelling Issues

Although MNL models are the simplest and most common ways of analysing choice modelling data, other modelling approaches are possible. These have advantages in terms of reducing the burden in meeting restrictive assumptions in the MNL models, improving model fits, and providing richer information about heterogeneous preferences. As computing power has increased, more choice modelling studies are being analysed and reported with advanced statistical techniques.

Some of the possible approaches include:

- nested models;
- random parameters logit;
- heterogeneous models; and
- probit models.

Caution has to be taken that the context in which values are transferred between source and target sites matches the way that the results have been modelled. For example, it may be inappropriate to transfer a part-worth value estimated for a particular group under a nested model to a general population.

5   SUMMARY

The development of the choice modelling technique has enhanced the potential for more rigorous and accurate benefit transfer to occur because it makes it easier to source marginal point values and benefit transfer functions. At the same time, the choice modelling process has made benefit transfer more complex because of the larger number of variables involved and the increased awareness about where limitations to benefit transfer exist. The steps outlined in this chapter provide a summary guide to performing a benefit transfer exercise, as well as identifying when benefit transfer is appropriate.

NOTES

1. Other useful reference sites are: http://learn.lincoln.ac.nz/markval/, http://www.sscnet.ucla.edu/ssc/labs/cameron/nrs98/cvinv.htm, http://www.Ecosystemvaluation.org, and http://www.damagevaluation.com/
2. It is expected that implicit prices will display diminishing marginal utility, meaning that implicit prices should only appear to be linear within narrow ranges. If non-linear implicit prices are not available from CM source studies, then care has to be taken that the size of effect differences does not take linear estimates out of their zone of reference.

REFERENCES

Rolfe, J.C., J.W. Bennett and J.J. Louviere (2000), 'Choice modelling and its potential application to tropical rainforest preservation', *Ecological Economics*, **35**, 289–302.

3. Theoretical Issues in Using Choice Modelling Data for Benefit Transfer

John Rolfe

1 INTRODUCTION

Non-market valuation techniques can be used to estimate the value of environmental and social impacts on peoples' preferences where information is not available directly from markets. They include revealed preference methods such as the travel cost method (TCM) and stated preference techniques such as the contingent valuation method (CVM) and choice modelling (CM). The latter are capable of estimating passive (non-use) values, which may be important components of decision options involving environmental trade-offs. Choice modelling has roots in the marketing, transport and tourism fields (Carson et al. 1994), after the development of choice-based experimental methods by Louviere and Hensher (1982) and Louviere and Woodworth (1983). In the late 1990s, CM emerged in applications involving the analysis of environmental trade-offs. Early applications of the technique were reported by Adamowicz et al. (1998), Blamey et al. (2000), and Rolfe et al. (2000). More comprehensive guides to the use of the technique have been reported in Louviere et al. (2000), Bennett and Blamey (2001) and Holmes and Adamowicz (2003).

A key question that emerges from the estimation of non-market values is whether value estimates from one study can be extrapolated to other situations. This process is known as benefit transfer (BT), where information gained from a 'source' study is used in some way to predict economic values at a 'target' site (Desvousges et al. 1992). While the extrapolation and transfer of value estimates is commonplace in fields such as property valuation, there has been greater debate over the accuracy of the process when it is employed with non-market valuation techniques. Since a collection of papers on these issues appeared in *Water Resources Research* in 1992 (Brookshire and Neill 1992), the term 'benefit transfer' has become synonymous with the transfer of value estimates from non-market valuation techniques, particularly TCM and CVM.

There has been ongoing work to identify the accuracy of benefit transfer and where its limitations might lie (Boyle and Bergstrom 1992, Brookshire and Neil 1992, Loomis 1992, Downing and Ozuna 1996, Brouwer 2000, Muthke and Holm-Mueller 2004). Interest has focused on extrapolating values associated with the CVM. This is because of the conceptual issues associated with benefit transfer involving non-use values, and because of the debate surrounding the accuracy of the CVM. While the debate about what is appropriate in benefit transfer continues, the actual practice of benefit transfer has been facilitated by the development of several databases such as the Environmental Valuation Reference Inventory in Canada (http://www.evri.ca/) and the ENVALUE site in Australia (www.epa.nsw.gov.au/envalue).

The more recent development of CM means that it has not been involved in the debate to the same extent, although some development work has already occurred in relation to using CM for potential benefit transfer applications (Morrison and Bennett 2000, Rolfe and Bennett 2002, Morrison et al. 2002, van Bueren and Bennett 2004). The richness of data available from CM experiments means that different types of benefit transfer are available. In particular, it is possible to make point (single value) transfers, marginal value (part-worth) transfers or to transfer entire value functions. It is also possible that values from CM experiments have advantages over CVM in a benefit transfer process, due to a superior framing of policy contexts available in CM applications, the increased potential for value adjustment, and a better understanding of the factors and variances that drive choice processes.

To explore these issues, this chapter is structured in the following way. In the next section, an overview of the history of benefit transfer and the debates over accuracy are presented. This is followed by an overview of CM, and then a discussion about the potential use of CM results in a benefit transfer process. Final comments are provided in section 5.

2   THE DEVELOPMENT OF BENEFIT TRANSFER

As the results of non-market valuation studies became more widely available in the 1970s and 1980s, they started to be used by a variety of government agencies, consultants, economists and legal practitioners for benefit transfer purposes (Boyle and Bergstrom 1992, Parsons and Kealy 1994, Walsh et al. 1992). The need for benefit transfer has been driven by the requirement to include non-market values in assessments of policy decisions (whether formal or informal) where time, financial and skill constraints have precluded the option of collecting primary data. However, most applications of benefit transfer have not been open to scholarly review, leading to concerns that inappropriate processes have been used, and/or that predicted values may not be accurate (Boyle and Bergstrom 1992). Economists have focused on both of these issues as avenues for improving and/or validating the use of benefit transfer.

Guidelines have been suggested for benefit transfer applications involving non-use values. Boyle and Bergstrom (1992) suggest 'idealistic' technical criteria:

- the non-market commodity valued at the study site must be identical to the non-market commodity to be valued at the target site (both in the characteristics of the good and the nature and extent of the change being valued);
- the populations affected by the non-market commodity at the study site and the target site hold identical characteristics; and
- the assignment of property rights at both sites must lead to the same theoretically appropriate welfare measurement (e.g. willingness to pay versus willingness to accept).

The difficulty with these guidelines is that they do not apply to most cases of benefit transfer. Usually some variations between sites and populations exist. A further problem is that they do not identify how benefit transfer should proceed when a condition is not fully met. At a practical level, this has meant that practitioners have to make some informal judgements about the similarity of site and populations between source and target settings before they decide if benefit transfer is appropriate (Rosenberger and Loomis 2001). Another issue is that there is no strong evidence that adhering to the guidelines will automatically generate valid benefit transfer results. A number of studies have shown that benefit transfers between very similar source and target case studies may involve transfer errors (Brouwer 2000).

There has been a large number of studies (e.g. Loomis 1992) showing significant differences between estimated values at a study site and those predicted from a benefit transfer application, even when close to 'ideal' conditions are being met. For example, Downing and Ozuna (1996) report the comparison of several CVM studies involving recreational saltwater fishing at eight contiguous Texas Gulf Coast bay regions, and show that most yield statistically different welfare estimates. Brouwer (2000:140) summarises the transfer errors reported in seven studies testing the validity of environmental value transfer, and reports that the transfer errors 'can be as high as 56% in the case of unadjusted unit value transfer and 475% in the case of adjusted value transfer'.

Some of the early criticisms of benefit transfer focused on the use of the CVM, with concerns that the technique might not be robust for estimating non-market values. An implicit concern was that any inaccuracies could flow through to benefit transfer applications. These concerns were largely addressed by the NOAA Panel, which reviewed the appropriateness of the technique and made recommendations regarding its application (Arrow et al. 1993, Portney 1994). As well, there are two key factors that indicate errors in benefit transfer are not simply caused by methodological problems with CVM. First, transfer errors are also apparent with the use of other non-market valuation techniques such as the TCM (Loomis 1992, Brouwer 2000). Second, the errors do not seem to be removed by the use of carefully designed CVM studies where close to 'ideal' conditions for benefit transfer exist (Downing and Ozuna 1996, Brouwer and Spaninks 1999, Bergland et al. 2002).

Economists have developed several explanations of why benefit transfer with stated preferences appears to be inaccurate. The first is that the specification of variables in models is often limited (Brouwer 2000). Many variables are only presented in a simple format (e.g. as dummy variables) which makes it difficult to apply them in complex situations. In addition, the models that are used impose specific conditions, which may make it difficult to account for complex relationships between variables or introduce nonlinearity in benefit estimation (Downing and Ozuna 1996). The second is that the explanatory power of models used in benefit transfer is often low, meaning that benefit transfer is occurring where a significant amount of choice behaviour in the source study is unexplained (Brouwer 2000). A related argument is that variation between source and target studies may be underestimated, and more account needs to be taken of heterogeneity in preferences or other factors that differentiate values for case studies.

There have also been arguments that the standard methods of testing for benefit accuracy highlight the differences between studies rather than the similarities. The validity of benefit transfer between source and target studies can be specified in a number of ways (Bergland et al. 2002, Brouwer and Spaninks 1999). Kristofersson and Navrud (2005) argue that tests for the validity of benefit transfer tend to be conducted in the wrong way. Most tests focus on the equivalence of benefit estimates or, in some cases, the equivalence of parameter estimates in benefit functions to be transferred, with the null hypothesis that there is no difference between source and target estimates. They argue that this is flawed because some differences can normally be expected. An alternative formulation is to set the null hypothesis that environmental values differ, and then use equivalence testing. A rejection of the equivalence test would allow the analyst to conclude that values are equivalent.

There have been several different approaches taken by economists to these interlocking problems of:

- developing a theoretical basis for benefit transfer;
- making benefit transfer more accurate; and
- establishing some guidelines for appropriate benefit transfer.

Here, some of these directions are described in more detail.

2.1   Transfer of Benefit Functions

Loomis (1992), Desvousges et al. (1992) and Kirchoff et al. (1997) suggest that it is more desirable to transfer benefit functions rather than point estimates because of the more detailed information that is involved. The key argument made in favour of benefit functions relates to the potential for benefit adjustment to be made.

Adjustment allows the analyst to take account of variations in the scale of changes and population characteristics between source and target case studies. A simple transfer process is to use point transfers to transfer some rate measure such as the 'value per person', 'value per endangered species' or 'value per recreational trip' between a source study and a target site. The point estimates can then be extrapolated by the relevant quantity at the target case study to provide the estimated benefit. An implicit assumption of the point transfer process is that all other factors relating to the commodity, available substitutes and the population are identical between the source and target studies (Parsons and Kealy 1994).

Use of a benefit function allows the adjustment process to simultaneously occur across several variables. For example, transferring a CVM regression function to a target site means that the predicted estimate can be adjusted for any population differences that are represented in the regression variate. The expansion of the benefit transfer function to account for site and other differences as well as variations between populations, as made possible by the use of CM, has the potential to increase the level of adjustment in the benefit transfer process, thus tailoring it better to a target case study.

Associated with the focus on the transfer of benefit functions has been interest in expanding the use of explanatory variables to improve the accuracy of the transfer process. Brouwer and Spaninks (1999) report the addition of attitudinal and behavioural variables as a mechanism to better predict the heterogeneity in choice decisions. While the inclusion of more variables can be expected to increase the predictive power of models, a major limitation in benefit transfer is that data on attitudinal and behavioural variables are rarely available for target sites. An additional issue is the problem of spurious relationships emerging when attitudes are used to predict stated behaviour (Rolfe and Bennett 1996).

Colombo et al. (2005) use choice experiments to estimate the benefits of the off-site impacts of soil erosion in two different watersheds in south-eastern Spain. They improved the accuracy of benefit transfer by allowing for preference heterogeneity within the choice models. This was achieved by using a random parameters logit model and by including socio-economic characteristics. The results demonstrate that by allowing choice behaviour to vary with changes in respondent characteristics, the accuracy of benefit transfer can be improved.

2.2   Use of Adjustment Factors for Preference Calibration

Implicit adjustment occurs when the benefit transfer process allows for variations between sites and populations to be automatically considered. Explicit adjustment occurs when the coefficients in a benefit transfer function are weighted in some way to take account of framing or other factors. For example, van Bueren and Bennett (2004) suggest that some adjustment of part-worths may be needed to reconcile differences in values when the frame of analysis is at a regional level compared with a national level.

Smith et al. (1999) suggest that rather than carrying out single point value or benefit function transfers, the available information should be used to identify the parameters of an overall preference function. That information can then be used to calibrate preference parameters from an individual source study. The approach provides a theoretical basis for combining data from different types of studies, as well as from a number of studies. An important feature of the approach is the emphasis on an overall preference function and the implication that different valuation exercises may draw on this function but, because of methodological and other factors, generate different results. As a result, some adjustment may be required to particular point or benefit function estimates to ensure consistency with other results.

Adamowicz et al. (1994) demonstrate the potential for preference calibration with CM by comparing the results of a choice experiment with revealed preference data for recreation choices. The same respondents making recreation trips were also asked to participate in a stated preference experiment. The results indicated that the preferences underlying both models were similar, and that it was possible to combine the results in a joint model. This indicates that the addition of the revealed preference data can be used to adjust the results of the stated preference model, with potential for more accurate benefit transfer.

To some extent, the preference calibration approach has been pursued under two other different approaches to benefit transfer. The logic of combining the results from several studies to generate more efficient predictions is captured in the use of meta-analysis, while the use of adjustment factors is implicit in the development of Bayesian approaches.

2.3   Meta-analysis

Meta-analysis for use in benefit transfer involves the summarizing of results for several existing source studies in a regression function, and the subsequent use of this function to predict value estimates for a target site (Walsh et al. 1992, Rosenberger and Loomis 2000, Florax et al. 2002, Shrestha and Loomis 2003, Bateman and Jones 2003). The essential benefits of this approach are that it can combine the results of several studies, thus utilizing more source information, and it can minimise potential errors generated by a single, inaccurate study. Meta-analysis normally involves each source function being used to generate value estimates for the target issue of interest (Brouwer 2000). These value estimates are then included in a regression function together with relevant variables, and the resulting variate is used to generate an estimate of the target issue value. Another form of the meta-analysis approach that is more rarely employed is to combine the data from several source studies in a single statistical model. This can then be used to predict values for the target case. As the number of non-market valuation studies increases, more opportunities will emerge to apply meta-analysis.

The use of meta-analysis emphasizes a number of methodological or framing issues that distinguish different studies (Engel 2002). These include the context in which trade-offs have been offered, the type of surplus measure being estimated, the survey instrument, the collection technique, the functional form assumed for the variate, and the distribution of the random error term. These factors are consistent within a single study, and are often not considered when benefit transfer is undertaken from a single source study. One benefit of using meta-analysis is that it emphasizes the potential role of these additional framing issues. However, a disadvantage is that the limited number of source studies available as inputs means that meta-analysis is often conducted with studies that vary widely in terms of their site, population and framing characteristics, making it difficult to achieve robust results (Engel 2002).

2.4   Bayesian Approaches

The Bayesian approach to benefit transfer was suggested by Atkinson et al. (1992). This approach involves the establishment of a set of prior beliefs about the parameters of interest, by drawing on existing data and/or experience and beliefs from a range of stakeholders. This prior can then be modified as new data (e.g. additional source studies) are incorporated so that predictions for value estimates take account of new information. Modified priors are normally referred to as 'posterior' beliefs. Both priors and posteriors are usually presented in the form of distribution functions (Brunsdon and Willis 2002).

The use of a Bayesian approach means that information from a variety of sources can be potentially included in the formation of a prior, and that it is relatively simple to update the results of previous studies with additional data. The most common type of approach is to combine information from available source studies with a small pilot study at the target site of interest. The results of the pilot study can be used to update and modify the benefit function.

Brunsdon and Willis (2002) identify four advantages from using a Bayesian approach. The first is that it is possible to examine a new study in relation to the results of several previous studies. The second advantage is that it is the updated posterior distribution that is used to generate predictions, so that estimates of value effectively contain a summary of all relevant information. The third advantage is that the probability distributions generated contain more information than the classic confidence interval approach. A fourth is that Bayesian approaches are a broad framework and allow a great deal of flexibility in the way that analysis is performed. A key disadvantage is that they are difficult to apply with standard statistical packages, and this limits their application (Brunsdon and Willis 2002). Another disadvantage is that the use of a small pilot study can involve substantial costs and time delays.

2.5   Guidelines for Performing Benefit Transfers

A paradox has emerged with the use of benefit transfer. While the academic evidence for the accuracy of the process remains weak, increasing demands for value predictions, together with an expanding number of source studies and better databases, means that the use of benefit transfer is becoming more commonplace. In response to this, different pragmatic approaches have been suggested as alternatives to the 'idealistic' guidelines for benefit transfer suggested by Boyle and Bergstrom (1992).

Brouwer (2000) emphasizes the potential involvement of stakeholders in determining the validity of value estimates and in aggregating the values as a way of ensuring that benefit transfers are acceptable. However, this process may be open to rent-seeking behaviour. Rosenberger and Loomis (2001) focus on the pragmatic approach that practitioners have to undertake in deciding whether the environmental resources, the changes being considered and the populations involved are similar enough for benefit transfer to proceed.

A number of researchers (e.g. Desvousges et al. 1992, Morrison et al. 2002, Rosenberger and Loomis 2003) have identified the necessary steps involved in benefit transfer. A summary is as follows:

Step 1   Define the policy context, with a focus on the characteristics of the target site, the policy change being considered, and the type of units that would be involved.

Step 2   Locate and gather original research (source) studies through a literature review.

Step 3   Screen the original research studies for relevance and methodological appropriateness.

Step 4   Gather summary data for the target site that is relevant to the independent or explanatory variables that are included in the source studies.

Step 5   Predict the target site benefit estimate by multiplying the summary statistics reflecting the target site by the regression coefficients in the transfer relationship or function. This results in a tailored estimate for the target site.

Step 6   Check the predicted values meet some internal and/or external validity criteria.

To determine the potential strengths of CM in relation to benefit transfer, it is first necessary to outline CM in some detail. This is the focus of the next section.

3   THE CHOICE MODELLING TECHNIQUE

The CM technique requires respondents in a survey format to choose a single preferred option from a set of a number of resource use options (Bennett and Blamey 2001). The options presented to respondents use a common set of underlying attributes that vary across a set number of levels. In some cases the options are labelled to differentiate further the choices to respondents. The variation in the levels of attributes, together with any labels used, differentiates the options to respondents. By offering the combinations of attributes and levels in a systematic way through the use of an experimental design (Louviere et al. 2000, Holmes and Adamowicz 2003), the key influences on choice can be identified.

A choice experiment follows a number of design and methodological stages (Louviere et al. 2000, Bennett and Blamey 2001, Holmes and Adamowicz 2003). These can be described as follows:

1. Characterise the decision problem, taking into account the information needs of analysts and decision makers as well as identifying the key elements of economic value relevant to the population of interest.
2. Identify and describe the attributes and levels, the payment vehicle to be offered, as well as the scenario frame in which trade-offs are to be made. Focus groups are an important stage in developing these elements.
3. Develop an experimental design. This needs to be tailored according to the types of relationships between variables that are anticipated or need to be tested.
4. Design the questionnaire. This typically involves a series of framing questions to make respondents aware of trade-offs and opportunity costs and to introduce them to the style of choices being made, information to describe the trade-offs involved and describe potential solutions to the problem of interest, reminders of substitutes and budget constraints, the choice sets, debriefing questions, and a section collecting socio-economic data about respondents.
5. Conduct a survey and collect the data. Types of collection techniques include personal interviews, drop-off and collect, mail surveys, telephone interviews and electronic formats.
6. Analyse the data. Models are normally checked for statistical power, and the results assessed for internal validity and congruence with other studies.
7. Interpret the results for policy analysis and decision support. This typically involves an application of consumer surplus estimates or part-worths to the target issue of interest.

Logistic regression techniques are normally employed to analyse the choice data. The resulting statistical model predicts choice behaviour as a function of the attributes and labels that identify the different choice sets, as well as the characteristics of respondents. As information about choice is the basic requirement for generating data about compensating marginal adjustments in attributes, choice-based models are preferred for theoretical validity. As well, the use of a constant base in the application of the CM technique ensures that responses to the various profiles are evaluated against a set standard and are thus comparable. This use of the set base (often a 'status quo' option), together with an opportunity cost attribute in monetary terms, allows estimates of conditional and absolute value to be made. These estimates can be used as Hicksian welfare measures (McConnell 1995, Flores 2003).

The random utility approach underlying the CM technique provides the theoretical basis for integrating choice behaviour with economic valuation. In a Random Utility Model (RUM) the probability of an individual choosing a good is assumed to be dependent on the utility of that good relative to the utility of alternative goods. That is, an individual *i* will choose alternative *j* in preference to alternative *h* only if the utility of *j* exceeds that of *h*:

$$P_{ij} = \text{Prob}(U_{ij} > U_{ih}) \qquad \text{for all h in Choice set C, } j \neq h \qquad (3.1)$$

To an outside observer, the utility of an alternative can be divided into a systematic (explainable) component and an error (unexplainable) component. The following equation formalises the basic relationship where V_{ij} represents the measurable component of utility and eij captures the effect of unobserved and omitted influences on choice.[1]

$$U_{ij} = V_{ij} + e_{ij} \qquad (3.2)$$

The systematic component of choice can be disaggregated further, as in the following example where utility is held to be a function of the characteristics of the relevant good (represented by Z_{ij}) and the characteristics of the individual (represented by S_i), together with the error term.

$$U_{ij} = V(Z_{ij}, S_i) + e_{ij} \qquad (3.3)$$

Choices made between alternatives will be a function of the probability that the utility associated with a particular option (j) is higher than for alternatives, as in (3.3).

$$P_{ij} = \text{Prob}(V_{ij} + e_{ij} > V_{ih} + e_{ih}) \quad \text{for all h in Choice set C, } j \neq h \qquad (3.4)$$

This can be restated in the following form:

$$P_{ij} = \text{Prob}[(\beta_k Z_{ij} + \beta_k S_i) - (\beta_k Z_{ih} + \beta_k S_i) > e_{ih} - e_{ij}] \quad \text{for all h in Choice set C, } j \neq h \quad (3.5)$$

where β^k is a vector of utility coefficients associated with a vector of attribute and personal characteristics explanatory variables (Louviere 2001).

The parameters for the relationship can be introduced by assuming that the relationship between utility and characteristics follows a linear in the parameters and variables function, and by making specific assumptions about the distribution of the error terms. If the error terms are assumed to follow a normal distribution, then the appropriate statistical model for analysing choice is a binary probit model. If the error terms are assumed to be distributed according to a double log (Gumbel) distribution, then the choice probabilities have a convenient closed-form solution known as the multinominal logit model (MNL) (McFadden 1974). The MNL model is generally preferred because it is computationally easier to use (Stern 1997), and takes the general form:

$$P_{ij} = \exp(\lambda V_{ij})/\Sigma \exp(\lambda V_{ih}) \qquad \text{for all h in Choice set C, } j \neq h \qquad (3.6)$$

where λ represents a scale parameter which is commonly normalised to 1 for any particular data set. The scale parameter is inversely proportional to the variance of the error term, as in the following where μ^2 is equal to the variance of the error term:

$$\lambda = \pi^2/6\mu^2 \qquad (3.7)$$

The scale parameter cannot be identified in a specific model because the error terms are confounded with the vector of utility parameters where β_k (the vector of utility parameters) can be more accurately represented as $\lambda\beta_k$ (Swait and Louviere 1993). Each parameter coefficient is associated with the scale parameter, and hence with the variance of error components. For the estimation of values, this deficiency is irrelevant, because the scale parameter effects are cancelled out as a result of the calculation of the ratios of different attribute coefficients in the value estimation process. However, the existence of the scale parameter directly affects the estimation of model parameters, and hence the accuracy of parameter estimates. For models where the variance of the error term approaches infinity, the value of the scale parameter approaches zero as a consequence of being inversely proportional. This causes the MNL model to predict equal choice probabilities for all alternatives. In contrast, in models where the variance of the error term is low, the scale parameter is asymptotic to the value one, leading to a deterministic formulation of the MNL model according to the underlying systematic utility (Swait and Louviere 1993).

Hence, results of different models are not directly comparable, as differences in variance affect the magnitude of model parameters. However, it is possible to estimate the ratio of scale parameters between different data sets, and hence, test the equality of parameter estimates (Swait and Louviere 1993).

The MNL model generates results for a conditional indirect utility function of the form:

$$V_{ij} = \lambda(\beta + \beta_1 Z_1 + \beta_2 Z_2 + ... \beta_n Z_n + \beta_a S_1 + \beta_b S_2 + ... \beta_m S_j) \qquad (3.8)$$

where β is the constant term, β_1 to β_n is the vector of coefficients attached to the vector of attributes (Z), and β_a to β_m is the vector of coefficients attached to the vector of socio-economic variables (S), that together influence utility. The constant term β can be partitioned into alternate specific constants (ASCs) that are unique for each of the alternatives that are considered in the choice sets. These ASCs capture the influence on choice of unobserved attributes relative to specific alternatives, but also include residual modelling effects.

The observed function V_{ij} is a conditional indirect utility function because it is derived from observed behaviour where budget or other constraints are imposed. The derivation of the function thus occurs indirectly rather than directly (Green 1976). Furthermore, the function is conditional because of the constraints that are imposed in terms of the choice trade-offs that are offered to respondents.

The parameters of a MNL model can be used to estimate Hicksian welfare measures. Compensating surplus (CS) can be defined as the change in income that will leave an individual indifferent between the current situation and some defined alternative, given an implied right to the current situation (Flores 2003). It is equivalent to the individual's willingness to pay (WTP) for some improvement in environmental quality, and can be defined as the amount of CS that satisfies the relationship:

$$V_i(p,q^0,y,s) + e = V_i(p,q^1,y\text{-CS},s) + e \qquad (3.9)$$

where p is the vector of marketed goods, q is the vector of environmental goods, y is income, and s is the vector of individual characteristics. The utility of two situations involving an environmental improvement (q^0 to q^1) is held to remain constant because of a corresponding change in income. This change can be represented by the change in income or willingness to pay (WTP) that individuals express for an improvement in environmental conditions. For a loss in environmental conditions, the necessary change in income to hold utility constant is positive, implying some willingness to accept (WTA) mechanism. Because utility remains constant, the welfare measure is compensating rather than equivalent. When the situation to be assessed is a change in quantity, the appropriate Hicksian measure is a surplus, while if the value of a change in price needs to be assessed, then the appropriate Hicksian measure is a variation (Flores 2003).

Estimation of CS from the parameters of a MNL function can be achieved in the following way. The MNL function gives the probability that a particular alternative will be selected relative to others. Inclusion of a monetary attribute into the function allows a model of choice to be developed where decreases in the WTP trade-off increase the probability of selection (McConnell 1995). Integrating this probability function gives results equivalent to finding the area under a demand curve.[2]

Welfare change estimates can be generated from MNL models through the use of the following formula:

$$CS = -1/\alpha[\ln\Sigma\exp V_{i0} - \ln\Sigma\exp V_{i1}] \qquad (3.10)$$

where CS is the compensating surplus welfare measure, α is the marginal utility of income (generally represented by the coefficient for the monetary opportunity cost attribute in an experiment), and V_{i0} and V_{i1} represent indirect utility functions before and after the change under consideration. In situations where the choice set includes a single before and after option, the welfare measure described in equation 3.10 reduces to:

$$CS = -1/\alpha[\ln(\exp V_{i0}) - \ln(\exp V_{i1})] = -1/\alpha[V_{i0} - V_{i1}] \qquad (3.11)$$

In some cases the 'before' and 'after' options may differ only because of changes in a single attribute. For attributes representing non-continuous data, the CS will be represented by the difference between the attribute coefficients for the relevant levels, divided by the monetary attribute coefficient, as prescribed by equation 3.11. For continuous data, though, the marginal value of a change within a single attribute can be represented as a ratio of coefficients, where equation 3.11 reduces further to:

$$W = -1 x \beta_{attribute}/\beta_{money} \qquad (3.12)$$

This part-worth formula effectively provides the marginal rate of substitution between income change and the attribute in question.

It is possible to generate different models in choice experiments by relaxing assumptions about the heterogeneity of preferences or the standard ratio of probabilities between any two alternatives. Each of these possibilities is considered in turn.

The assumption that preferences are held consistently across all respondents can be relaxed to generate three different types of models (Holmes and Adamowicz 2003). The first is achieved by including interactions involving respondent characteristics within models. The second involves latent class models, where the population of respondents is partitioned into segments, so that the probability function estimated reflects the likelihood that respondents from a particular segment (latent class) will choose an alternative. The third type of model is the random parameter or mixed logit approach, where the respondent characteristics are included in models as a random parameter following a distribution rather than as a fixed variable (Lusk and Schroeder 2004).

The other broad way of generating different types of models is to vary the assumptions relating to the distribution of error terms (Louviere et al. 2000, Holmes and Adamowicz 2003, Lusk and Schroeder 2004). The assumptions implicit in the use of the MNL model impose a restriction known as the Independence from Irrelevant Alternatives (IIA) condition. This states that the probability of a particular alternative being selected is independent of the other alternatives, and has an underlying condition that the error terms are independently and identically distributed (IID). To avoid these strict IIA/IID conditions, other forms of logit models have been developed, including nested logit and heteroskedastic extreme value (HEV) models. A further option is to use a multinomial probit model.

Nested logit allows the distribution of error terms to vary across groups (nests) of choices, essentially allowing the random error component to vary according to which group of choices respondents might select. For example, choices for conservation options may share similar error distributions, but may be very different to the error distribution for the 'no support' option. A nested model allows a decision pathway to be modelled, where respondents make an initial choice between 'support/no support' and, if they choose the 'support' branch, then a subsequent choice about which option is more attractive. An inclusive value parameter identifies the level of correlation that exists between the nested choices, and links the model together.

The HEV model allows error variances to differ across alternatives, rather than across groups of alternatives as with the nested logit models. With HEV models, the error terms are assumed to be independent, but not identically distributed for each alternative. A scale parameter is estimated for each alternative (with the parameter for one alternative set to one) so that the relativities of the error terms can be identified. This model formulation is suitable for combining data sets because it is possible to control for differences at the individual alternative level (Lusk and Schroeder 2004).

A multinomial probit model is similar to a HEV model in that it allows error variances to differ across alternatives, but is different in that the distribution of error terms is assumed to be normally distributed. This means that a multinomial probit should be more general than logit models, but this comes at a cost of computational needs. Probit models have other advantages over logit models in the analysis of some CM data because the underlying treatment of explanatory variables as categorical rather than continuous is appropriate in some case studies.

As computing power increases, multinomial probit models are becoming more popular.

A key advantage of CM is that its rich statistical output allows insights into whether additional factors apart from the description of the scenarios and the socio-economic characteristics of respondents affect value estimates. These include factors such as the way that trade-offs are framed to respondents, the existence of substitute and complementary goods, and the choice processes that might be employed. For convenience, these additional influences can be thought of as framing effects. Framing problems occur when the respondent to a survey is unduly sensitive to the context in which a particular trade-off is offered (Rolfe, Bennett and Louviere 2002). Where framing problems occur, the use of CM data in a benefit transfer process is problematic, because it may be very difficult to replicate the frame of a valuation experiment between source and target sites.

CM appears to offer several advantages over other non-market valuation techniques for framing purposes (Rolfe et al. 2002). The first, and perhaps most significant advantage, is that it allows the simultaneous presentation of a pool of alternative and substitute goods. This explicitly requires respondents to consider complementary and substitution effects in the choice process. As well, problems of bias can be minimised because the amenity of interest can be 'hidden' within the pool of available goods used in a CM experiment.

A second major advantage of CM is that it provides a more realistic way for respondents to trade off opportunity costs than CVM allows. This occurs in two important ways: (1) the WTP attribute is only one of several attributes that defines profiles, and hence is de-emphasised in importance relative to its central role in the CVM; and (2) CM allows the introduction of a variety of opportunity costs, not just some WTP mechanism.

A third framing benefit involves the ability to analyse and compare CM experiments. This allows the analyst to test whether differences in framing the choices to respondents cause variations in the parameters of the resulting choice models. For convenience, differences in framing can be categorised into slight variations in the description of essentially the same good, and larger variations that change the structure of the choices involved (Boyle 1989). Both of these possible differences can be tested by examining the internal validity of models and differences in choice model parameters.

4   BENEFIT TRANSFER OF CHOICE MODELLING FUNCTIONS

The issues involved in the benefit transfer of choice modelling functions can be represented in the following way, using the arguments of Rosenberger and Loomis (2003). The underlying premise of benefit transfer is that the estimated values for a source site (VS) can be represented as a function of the site characteristics (ZS) and population characteristics (SS):

$$V_S = f(Z_S, S_S) \tag{3.13}$$

The transfer of a benefit function can be defined as:

$$V_{S|T} = f(Z_{S|T}, S_{S|T}) \tag{3.14}$$

where $V_{S|T}$ represents the estimated value at the target site using the functional relationship f for the source site S, $Z_{S|T}$ represents the site characteristics adjusted to the target site, and $S_{S|T}$ represents the population characteristics adjusted to the target population. This can be done within CM by adjusting the indirect utility functions for site and population differences between source and target sites. This is shown below where the site characteristics (Z_{Tn}) and population characteristics (S_{Ti}) of the target case study can be used as inputs in the benefit transfer equation:

$$V_{Tij} = \lambda(\beta + \beta_1 Z_{T1} + \beta_2 Z_{T2} + \dots \beta_n Z_{Tn} + \beta_a S_{T1} + \beta_b S_{T2} + \dots \beta_m S_{Ti}) \tag{3.15}$$

When only marginal values are being transferred, the underlying assumption is that the value per some quantitative unit is the same between source and target sites. This can be defined as:

$$V_T / Z_{iT} = V_S / Z_{iS} \tag{3.16}$$

where Z_i represents the quantitative variable of interest. In CM, there are normally several quantitative variables used to describe a source site, so the marginal value transfer function can be more accurately represented as being conditional on Z_i being drawn from a wider set. This is likely to provide some framing advantages which are described further below.

Bergland et al. (2002) show that there are two main approaches to testing benefit transfers. The first is to test for equality of value estimates, as in the following:

$$V_T = V_{S|T} \tag{3.17}$$

where V_T represents the value of the policy change at the target site and $V_{S|T}$ represents the value of the policy change at the source study adjusted for the target site. Tests of value equivalence can be used both with estimates of compensating surpluses (equation 3.10) and estimates of part-worths (equation 3.12).

The second approach outlined by Bergland et al. (2002) to testing benefit transfers is to test for equality of benefit function parameters. The test can be represented as:

$$\beta_T = \beta_S \qquad (3.18)$$

where β_T and β_S represent the vector of parameters for the relevant target and source study models.

Even in cases where there are no site or population differences between source and target case studies, some differences between models and value estimates may emerge. There are a number of reasons for this. One reason is that the distribution of error terms may vary between case studies. This can largely be overcome by focusing on value estimates (where the error term cancels out), although some residual modelling effects may still be present in the ASC. Another reason is that there may be random variations in the selection of respondents, which in turn influences choice models, although this may be addressed by selecting for larger sample sizes.

The key area where differences may emerge between CM applications lies in framing effects. This can include the way that a choice experiment is structured, the way that the trade-offs are framed to respondents, both explicitly and implicitly, and the way that the choice data are modelled. Where differences exist between survey applications, there is potential for model coefficients and value estimates to be significantly different.

The potential variation between CM models for source and target sites can be illustrated in the following way. Suppose that within a region it is possible to select a number of similar sites and population groups to estimate value functions for a particular resource use change of interest. Each CM study of a particular population and site reveals a specific model which is unique because of the population and site factors and the way that issues are framed to survey respondents. This means that predictions for an individual's WTP within the broader region could be drawn from a family of potential CM functions, which can be defined as follows:

$$V_{ij} = f \left(\text{Set} \left[\text{CM}_{(Z, S, F)} \right] \right) \qquad (3.19)$$

where Z represents site characteristics, S represents population characteristics, and F represents the frame used, which includes the function form and distribution of error terms adopted. Under this formulation, it is clear that even with equivalent sites and populations, variations between models can arise if there are differences in the way that the issues are framed or modelled.

This situation is illustrated in Table 3.1, where the potential indirect utility functions that can be identified for three population groups and three sites of interest is further identified by framing factors. While utility functions may vary according to the site and population group involved, they may also vary for a specific site and population group because of framing effects, including modelling issues.

Table 3.1   Identification of utility functions across sites and population groups

	Variety of population groups		
		Population group 1	Population group 2	Population group 3
Variety of sites available	Site 1	$V(Z_1 S_1, F_{a-z})$	$V(Z_1 S_2 F_{a-z})$	$V(Z_1 S_3 F_a z)$
	Site 2	$V(Z_2 S_1 F_{a-z})$	$V(Z_2 S_2 F_{a-z})$	$V(Z2S3Fa-z)$
	Site 3	$V(Z_3 S_1 F_{a-z})$	$V(Z_3 S_2 F_{a-z})$	$V(Z_3 S_3 F_{a-z})$

V = indirect utility, Z_n = Site characteristics, S_n = population characteristics, and F_z = frame used.

The key assumption of a benefit transfer exercise is that an indirect utility function estimated for one population group and site can be accurately transferred to another situation. For example, a benefit transfer exercise from Table 3.1 might involve the indirect utility function in the first cell ($V(Z_1 S_1, F_{a-z})$) being used to estimate the indirect utility for site 3 and population group 3. A standard test of the benefit transfer exercise would be whether a source utility function adjusted to account for specific site and population characteristics in the target case is equivalent to a utility function that has been estimated directly for the target site:

Null hypothesis: $V(Z_1 S_1, F_a)$ for $Z_3 S_3 = V(Z_3 S_3, F_a)$ for $Z_3 S_3$

There are four key areas to focus on in efforts to achieve appropriate benefit transfer with choice modelling data. These relate to dealing with site differences, framing issues, the role of the ASC and population differences.

In some cases the attributes used to describe a source study site may not be fully appropriate for the target study site. This can occur when there are missing attributes for the target study, or the range of attribute levels used in the source study are not appropriate for the target case. This means that the value function may only account for a proportion of the value associated with the target case. In some cases, there is a possibility that the coefficient for a site attribute can be 'adjusted' to reflect a different context, although there needs to be some basis for the use of adjustment factors. In other cases, the way that the site attributes are modelled can be important for benefit transfer. This can occur when more accurate functional relationships, such as those involving interactions between attributes, can be estimated.

Differences in framing can affect the way that respondents in a CM experiment view the trade-offs, and hence affect estimates of value. Most problems can be expected when the results of separate CM experiments for source and target studies are being compared, and differences in the way that the trade-offs are presented flow through to variations in value estimates. Where the results of one experiment are being transferred to a target site, the underlying assumption is that the structure of underlying trade-offs is consistent.

If there are variations in framing, then there may be some potential for adjustment factors to be used to correct for framing effects. This might occur, for example, when values for addressing an environmental issue in a national context are transferred to a local context case study. The smaller scope and proximity to the issue involved would suggest that higher values might be held by the local population. However, some methodological basis for the use of adjustment factors would need to be established.

The role of the ASC can be problematic in benefit transfer applications. One purpose of the ASC is to capture the impact of unobserved attributes on choice. This is particularly important when values for labelled options are being transferred, because the ASC incorporates information about how labels are preferred to each other. The ASC also incorporates residual modelling effects, so that for poorer fitting models the ASC can play a more dominant role in value estimation. This can cause problems in the benefit transfer process, so that it may be more appropriate to transfer marginal values from weaker models than full benefit functions. Other ways of dealing with problems of dominant ASC values is to vary the assumptions relating to the distribution of error terms and to estimate more accurate models of choice.

Population differences between source and target sites can cause minor difficulties in a benefit transfer process. In some cases, the demographic variables collected for a source study are inappropriate for a target population. In other cases, the way that population characteristics are included in models does not match the choice processes undertaken by the source population, and these errors are magnified in a transfer process. The development of more accurate models that allow the heterogeneity of preferences to be incorporated into models can alleviate these issues.

This analysis helps to provide some guidance about when benefit transfer might be accurate for indirect utility functions estimated with the CM technique. The transfer of value functions should be accurate when the following four conditions are met:

1. The key attributes used to describe the source study site are relevant and comprehensive for the target study site;
2. The key variables used to describe the source study population are relevant and comprehensive for the target study population;
3. The frame of the issue being addressed is similar in both the source and target studies; and
4. The impact of unobserved attributes and model characteristics are consistent between sites.

Some of the benefits of using the CM technique for benefit transfer can be identified by comparing these conditions with the idealistic conditions set by Boyle and Bergstrom (1992). A key advantage of using benefit functions for transfer is that variations between sites and populations are possible so long as the attributes and variables used in the source study are relevant and comprehensive for the target study (Morrison et al. 2002, Rosenberger and Loomis 2003). This means that it is theoretically possible to apply benefit transfer to a wider group of valuation problems. Adoption of the CM technique for benefit transfer means that it is possible to relax the strict conditions about site and population equivalence set by Boyle and Bergstrom (1992). Instead of equivalence, the necessary condition for benefit transfer is that the function describing the site and population characteristics can be mapped from the source study to the policy setting.

There may also be modelling benefits available from the use of CM data. This can occur when varying the assumptions about the distribution of error terms or the level of heterogeneity in models reduces the level of unexplained behaviour in models. Subsequent use of the models for benefit transfer purposes is likely to generate more accurate results.

There are also major framing advantages available from the use of the CM data compared with data from other non-market valuation techniques. It is possible that the identification of framing differences can explain why valuation experiments across similar sites and populations generate different results. There is also potential for adjustment factors to be used to account for framing differences. Another key advantage is that values drawn from CM exercises tend to be framed against a variety of substitutes and opportunity costs. This means that there is more likelihood of transferring values from a CM exercise without major concerns about the double counting issues of Hoehn and Randall (1989), because the values have been assessed in the context of each other.

5 SUMMARY

In a theoretical context, the key benefit of using the CM technique is that it is appropriate to use benefit transfer where site and population differences exist. This allows a major relaxation of the idealistic criteria set by Boyle and Bergstrom (1992). There are also benefits in that potential differences between source and target studies may be related to variations in framing between the studies.

There are also a number of practical advantages with the use of CM for benefit transfer compared with other non-market valuation techniques. These relate to the ease with which site and population differences can be adjusted in a function transfer process, the options for using either marginal value transfers or functional value transfers, and the future potential for adjustment factors to be used to account for framing differences. There is also the potential for the range of modelling variations to improve the depiction of choice processes. This in turn should help to improve the accuracy of transfer to target studies.

Despite these potential advantages, the number of case studies dealing with CM and benefit transfer is limited, and many studies do not show value convergence even when benefit transfer conditions appear close to ideal. This indicates that further work is needed to demonstrate potential applications of benefit transfer, to identify ways of improving the process, and to understand what causes value differences in some circumstances.

ACKNOWLEDGEMENTS

Earlier versions of this chapter have benefited from the helpful comments of Jeff Bennett and Jill Windle.

NOTES

1. More formally, a stochastic error term is associated with the utility of choice to represent the effect of random response shocks, while another error term is associated with the influence of unobserved characteristics. The latter error term is unique to each individual respondent and may be reduced by introducing heterogeneity into choice models. Alberini, Kanninen and Carson (1997) demonstrate this in relation to CVM. In this analysis, the two error components are confounded.
2. For other derivations of welfare measures from discrete choice models, see Hanemann (1984).

REFERENCES

Adamowicz, W., P. Boxall, M. Williams and J. Louviere (1998), 'Stated preference approaches for measuring passive use values: choice experiments and contingent valuation', *American Journal of Agricultural Economics*, **80**, 64–75.

Adamowicz, W., J. Louviere and M. Williams (1994), 'Combining revealed and stated preference methods for valuing environmental amenities', *Journal of Environmental Economics and Management*, **26**, 271–92.

Alberini, A., B. Kanninen and R. Carson (1997), 'Dichotomous choice contingent valuation data', *Land Economics*, **73** (3), 309–24.

Arrow, K., R. Solow, P. Portney, E. Leaner, R. Radner and H. Schuman (1993), 'Report of the NOAA panel on contingent valuation', *Federal Register,* **58**, 4601–14.

Atkinson, S., T. Crocker and J. Shogren (1992), 'Bayesian exchangeability, benefit transfer and research efficiency', *Water Resources Research*, **28** (3), 715–22.

Bateman, I. and A. Jones (2003), 'Contrasting conventional with multi-level modelling approaches to meta-analysis: expectation consistency in U.K. woodland recreational values', *Land Economics*, **79**, 235–58.

Bennett, J. and R. Blamey (2001), *The Choice Modelling Approach to Environmental Valuation*, Cheltenham, UK and Northampton, MA, USA: Edward Elgar.

Bergland, O., K. Magnussen and S. Navrud (2002), 'Benefit transfer: testing for accuracy and reliability', in R. Florax, P. Nijkamp and K. Willis (eds), *Comparative Environmental Economic Assessment*, Cheltenham, UK and Northampton, MA, USA: Edward Elgar, pp. 117–32.

Blamey, R., J. Bennett, J. Louviere, M. Morrison and J. Rolfe (2000), 'The use of policy labels in environmental choice modelling studies', *Ecological Economics*, **32**, 269–86.

Boyle, K. (1989), 'Commodity Specification and the Framing of Contingent-Valuation Questions', *Land Economics*, **65** (1), 57–63.

Boyle, K. and J. Bergstrom (1992), 'Benefit transfer studies: myths, pragmatism and idealism', *Water Resources Research*, **28** (3), 657–63.

Brookshire, D. and H. Neill (1992), 'Benefit transfers: conceptual and empirical issues', *Water Resources Research*, **28** (3), 651–55.

Brouwer, R. (2000), 'Environmental value transfer: state of the art and future prospects', *Ecological Economics*, **32**, 137–52.

Brouwer, R. and F. Spaninks (1999), 'The validity of environmental benefits transfer: further empirical testing', *Environmental and Resource Economics*, **14**, 95–117.

Brunsdon, C. and K. Willis (2002), 'Meta-analysis: a Bayesian approach', in P. Nijkamp, K. Willis and R. Florax (eds), *Comparative Environmental Economic Assessment*, Cheltenham, UK and Northampton, MA, USA: Edward Elgar, pp. 208–31.

Carson, R., J. Louviere, D. Anderson, P. Arabie, D. Bunch, D. Hensher, R. Johson, S. Kuhfeld, D. Steinberg, J. Swait, H. Timmermans and J. Wiley (1994), 'Experimental analysis of choice', *Marketing Letters,* **5** (4), 351–68.

Colombo, S., N. Hanley and J. Calatrava-Requena (2005), *Testing Choice Experiments for Benefit Transfer with Preference Heterogeneity*, Working Paper, Stirling: University of Stirling.

Desvousges, W., M. Naughton and G. Parsons (1992), 'Benefit transfer: conceptual problems in estimating water quality benefits using existing studies', *Water Resources Research*, **28** (3), 675–83.

Downing, M. and T. Ozuna (1996), 'Testing the reliability of the benefit transfer function', *Journal of Environmental Economics and Management*, **30**, 316–22.

Engel, S. (2002), 'Benefit functions transfer versus meta-analysis as policy-making tools: a comparison', in P. Nijkamp, K. Willis and R. Florax (eds), *Comparative Environmental Economic Assessment*, Cheltenham, UK and Northampton, MA, USA: Edward Elgar, pp. 133–53.

Florax, R., P. Nijkamp and K. Willis (eds) (2002), *Comparative Environmental Economic Assessment*, Cheltenham, UK and Northampton, MA, USA: Edward Elgar.

Flores, N. (2003), 'Conceptual framework for non-market valuation'. in P. Champ, K. Boyle and T. Brown (eds), *A Primer on Nonmarket Valuation*, Netherlands: Kluwer Academic Publishers.

Green, H. (1976), *Consumer Theory*, London: Macmillan.

Hanemann, W. (1984), *Applied Welfare Analysis with Quantitative Response Models*, Working Paper No. 241, Berkeley: University of California.

Hoehn, J. and A. Randall (1989), 'Too many proposals pass the benefit cost test', *American Economic Review*, **79** (3), 544–51.

Holmes, T. and V. Adamowicz (2003), 'Attribute-based methods', in P. Champ, K. Boyle and T. Brown (eds), *A Primer on Nonmarket Valuation,* Netherlands: Kluwer Academic Publishers.

Kirchoff, S., B. Colby and J. LaFrance (1997), 'Evaluating the performance of benefit transfer: an empirical inquiry', *Journal of Environmental Economics and Management*, **33**, 75–93.

Kristofersson, D. and S. Navrud (2005), 'Validity tests of benefit transfer – are we performing the wrong tests?', *Environmental and Resource Economics*, **30**, 279–86.

Loomis, J. (1992), 'The evolution of a more rigorous approach to benefit transfer: benefit function transfer', *Water Resources Research*, **28** (3), 701–5.

Louviere, J. (2001), 'Choice experiments: an overview of the concepts and issues', in J. Bennett and R. Blamey (eds), *The Choice Modelling Approach to Environmental Valuation*, Cheltenham, UK and Northampton, MA, USA: Edward Elgar, pp. 13–36.

Louviere, J. and D. Hensher (1982), 'On the design and analysis of simulated choice or allocation experiments in travel choice modelling', *Transportation Research Record*, **890**, 11–17.

Louviere, J., D. Hensher and J. Swait (2000), *Stated Choice Models – Analysis and Application*, Cambridge, UK: Cambridge University Press.

Louviere, J., and G. Woodworth (1983), 'Design and analysis of simulated consumer choice or allocation experiments: an approach based on aggregate data', *Journal of Marketing Research*, **20**, 350–67.

Lusk, J., and T. Schroeder (2004), 'Are choice experiments incentive compatible? A test with quality differentiated beef steaks', *American Journal of Agricultural Economics*, **86** (2), 467–82.

McConnell, K. (1995), 'Consumer surplus from discrete choice models', *Journal of Environmental Economics and Management*, **29**, 263–70.

McFadden, D. (1974), 'Conditional logit analysis of qualitative choice behaviour', in P. Zarembka (ed), *Frontiers in Econometrics*, New York: Academic Press, pp. 105–42.

Morrison, M. and J. Bennett (2000), 'Choice modelling, non-use values and benefit transfer', *Economic Analysis and Policy*, **30** (1), 13–32.

Morrison, M., J. Bennett, R. Blamey and J. Louviere (2002), 'Choice modelling and tests of benefit transfer', *American Journal of Agricultural Economics*, **84** (1), 161–70.

Muthke, T. and K. Holm-Mueller (2004), 'National and international benefit transfer testing with a rigorous test procedure', *Environmental and Resource Economics*, **29**, 323–36.

Parsons, G. and M. Kealy (1994), 'Benefit transfer in a random utility model of recreation', *Water Resources Research*, **30** (8), 2477–84.

Portney, P. (1994), 'The contingent valuation debate: why economists should care', *Journal of Economic Perspectives*, **8** (4), 3–17.

Rolfe, J. and J. Bennett (1996), 'A comment on Blamey, Common and Quiggan's citizen value hypothesis', *Australian Journal of Agricultural Economics*, **40** (2), 129–34.

Rolfe, J. and J. Bennett (2002), 'Assessing rainforest conservation demands', *Economic Analysis and Policy*, **32** (2), 51–67.

Rolfe, J., J. Bennett and J. Louviere (2000), 'Choice modelling and its potential application to tropical rainforest preservation', *Ecological Economics*, **35**, 289–302.

Rolfe, J., J. Bennett and J. Louviere (2002), 'Stated values and reminders of substitute goods: testing for framing effects with choice modelling', *Australian Journal of Agricultural and Resource Economics*, **46** (1), 1–20.

Rosenberger, R. and J. Loomis (2000), 'Using meta-analysis for benefit transfer: in sample convergent validity tests of an outdoor recreation database', *Water Resources Research*, **36** (4), 1097–107.

Rosenberger, R. and J. Loomis (2001), *Benefit Transfer of Outdoor Recreation Use Values: A Technical Document Supporting the Forest Service Strategic Plan (2000 Revision)*, General technical report, U.S. Department of Agriculture, Forest Service, Rocky Mountain Research Station.

Rosenberger, R. and J. Loomis (2003), 'Benefit transfer', in P. Champ, K. Boyle and T. Brown (eds), *A Primer on Nonmarket Valuation*, Netherlands: Kluwer Academic Publishers, pp. 445–82.

Shrestha, R. and J. Loomis (2003), 'Meta-analytic benefit transfer of outdoor recreation values: testing out-of-sample convergence validity', *Environmental and Resource Economics*, **25**, 79–100.

Smith, V., G. Van Houtven and S. Pattanayak (1999), *Benefit Transfer as Preference Calibration*, Discussion Paper 99–36, Washington, DC: Resources for the Future.

Stern, S. (1997), 'Simulation-based estimation', *Journal of Economic Literature*, **35**, 2006–39.

Swait, J. and J. Louviere (1993), 'The role of the scale parameter in the estimation and comparison of multinomial logit models', *Journal of Marketing Research*, **30**, 305–14.

van Bueren, M. and J. Bennett (2004), 'Towards the development of a transferable set of value estimates for environmental attributes', *Australian Journal of Agricultural and Resource Economics*, **48**, 1–32.

Walsh, R., D. Johnson and J. McKean (1992), 'Benefit transfer of outdoor recreation demand studies', *Water Resources Research*, **28** (3), 707–13.

4. Stated Preference Benefit Transfer Approaches for Estimating Passive Use Value of Wild Salmon

John Loomis

1 SIMILARITY OF CHOICE MODELLING AND CONTINGENT VALUATION METHODS FOR BENEFIT TRANSFER

As is well known, both the contingent valuation method (CVM) and choice modelling (CM) are stated preference methods in that they ask individuals what they would do in a particular circumstance. Each method started from a different disciplinary tradition: CVM from natural resource economics and CM from marketing. More recently, the two methods are looking more and more indistinguishable. This is especially true of applications of choice methods for economic valuation as compared to marketing purposes. Specifically, while choice methods used to focus more on conjoint analysis using ratings or rankings, they are often now done using a discrete choice (select one alternative). Contingent valuation questioning format has also evolved from open-ended questions (what is the most you would pay), to a discrete choice format (would you pay $X, yes or no). Underlying the discrete choice CVM and CM is random utility theory (McFadden 1974; Hanemann 1984). The random utility theory relied upon by both CVM and CM partitions the utility an individual receives from some choice into deterministic (i.e. observable) and random (non-observable) components. Not only do discrete choice CVM and CM share the same utility-theoretic foundation, but they share very similar empirical methods as well. Specifically, both approaches usually rely on some form of a logistic regression model to estimate the parameters from which benefit estimates are calculated.

In some respects, a series of dichotomous choice CVM questions asked to elicit willingness to pay (WTP) for various levels of a particular natural resource look very similar to the question format in CM. In Hoehn and Loomis (1993) a series of dichotomous choice CVM questions were asked that allowed valuation of two different levels of wetlands protection, two different levels of waterfowl contamination control and an increase in the level of salmon protection. In the CM world, these would be three attributes, two with two levels and one with one level. In the CVM example, pooling these responses and including dummy variables for the levels of the attributes allows the researcher to calculate part-worths or marginal values for these attributes, similar to CM.

Loomis and duVair (1993) asked each respondent a series of dichotomous choice CVM questions about greater and greater reductions in risk. This allowed estimates of a WTP function with risk level as a variable. In this case, there was one attribute for which marginal values could be calculated. Cameron's (1988) reparameterisation of the logistic regression coefficients into marginal values or part-worths makes transparent that a series of dichotomous choice questions yields a WTP function quite comparable to that of CM. Just as in CM, in Cameron's reparameterisation the marginal values are calculated by dividing the attribute coefficient by the coefficient on cost. Specifically if the logistic regression is:

$$\log (Y/1\text{-}Y) = Bo - B1(\$Bid) + B2(A1) + B3(A2) + ...Bn(An) \qquad (4.1)$$

then the WTP equation is:

$$WTP = (Bo/B1) + [B2/B1](A1) + [B3/B1](A2) + ...[Bn/B1](An) \qquad (4.2)$$

Thus the part-worths or marginal WTP for one more unit of A1 is B2/B1 just like one would arrive at using CM. Thus, if CVM is done using a series of questions with different quality levels, it can produce marginal values of attributes that can be used in benefit transfer such as those from CM. It is only when CVM is used to value one programme, that CVM becomes much more limited in its benefit transfer capability than CM.

With this demonstration of the similarity of the two methods in mind, we now turn to an example of using benefit transfer from CVM and CM for valuing passive use benefits of salmon in the Pacific Northwest. In this case study we are attempting to estimate a marginal value per salmon from the existing literature and apply it in a real-world policy analysis on the Snake River in Washington. Some of the pitfalls of conducting such a benefit transfer are illustrated.

2   SETTING OF THE CASE STUDY AND NEED FOR THE PASSIVE USE VALUE ANALYSIS

Wild salmon populations are declining throughout the states of Idaho, Oregon and Washington, an area collectively known as the Pacific Northwest. This problem is particularly acute on the Columbia River and its largest tributary, the Snake River. This large river stretches from Idaho to Washington and had historically provided habitat for many different types of salmon. However, a series of four large hydroelectric dams built along the last 140 miles of the Snake River just up from its confluence with the Columbia River essentially blocked off much of the Snake River in Idaho from migrating salmon. The four dams created 140 miles of nearly continuous slack reservoir water which makes downstream migration of young salmon very slow, delaying their migration to the ocean. While the dams have fish ladders, they are only partially effective at moving adult salmon upstream.

The cumulative influence of these dams resulted in the Snake River sockeye salmon being listed as endangered in 1991. Within a few years the chinook salmon and steelhead were listed as threatened under the Endangered Species Act (ESA). The National Marine Fisheries Service and US Army Corps of Engineers (the COE is the agency which operates the dams) are required by ESA to develop a plan to recover the species using any reasonable and prudent alternatives. Under the existing baseline situation (A1), the average annual return of wild salmon is 67 116 fish. One alternative (A4) is to remove the four large hydroelectric dams and restore a free-flowing river that would allow natural salmon migration. Another alternative (A2) is to maximise artificial transport of juvenile salmon around the dams through barging and trucking. Finally, another alternative (A3) is to make a series of minor system operating improvements at the dam to minimise young salmon intake in the turbines.

While all of these alternatives have costs in the millions of dollars, dam removal (A4) had annualised direct costs and opportunity costs of forgone hydropower of over $300 million. Unlike the few past dam removal efforts that focused on small or very old dams that had often outlived their usefulness, the four Lower Snake River dams are very large hydropower producers, and facilitated barge transportation from Washington into Idaho. In addition the dams are relatively new, being just 20–30 years old at the time when the analysis of dam removal was being studied. Yet dam removal was estimated by biologists to result in more than a 50 per cent increase in wild salmon and steelhead populations. However, being biologically the best does not necessarily translate into having positive net economic benefits, given the several hundred million dollar costs. The US Water Resources Council (1983) project evaluation guidelines require the Corps of Engineers to evaluate the net economic benefits of each alternative before selecting the preferred alternative.

3   IMPORTANCE OF PASSIVE USE VALUES IN ECONOMIC ANALYSIS OF ENDANGERED SPECIES

Dam removal would eliminate 140 miles of reservoir recreation and replace it with 140 miles of river recreation. Eventual recovery of the species and removal from the Endangered Species List will allow for improved salmon and steelhead fishing. But the economic justification for recovery of a threatened and endangered species probably does not hinge on future recreation use values which get heavily discounted at most interest rates. Rather, the economic justification probably hinges on the option, existence and bequest values that the general public has for wild salmon in the Snake River.

Avoiding extinction of endangered species is recognised as a source of existence or passive use values (Meyer 1974; Randall and Stoll 1983; Stoll and Johnson 1984). Existence values are defined as the benefit received from simply knowing the resource exists, even if no use is made of it. Free-flowing rivers were one of the first examples of such resources with existence values (Krutilla and Fisher 1975). Essentially, people who never plan to visit, raft, or fish these rivers may still pay something to have a free-flowing river. Wild stocks of Snake River sockeye and chinook salmon clearly fit into this picture. As noted by Olsen et al. (1991) in his existence value of salmon study, 'Existence value as the value an individual (or society) places on the knowledge that a resource exists in a certain state is theoretically sound and can be measured for assessment within the resource decision making arena'. Passive use values are also public goods, in that these benefits can be simultaneously enjoyed by millions of people all across the region and the country (Loomis 1996a).

Government agencies are increasingly including passive use values when evaluating actions that affect fisheries. Passive use values are often important, because often the vast majority of the species affected by a project are non-game/non-sport species, or the population levels of the game species are so low that fishing is no longer allowed. However, due to limited time and budget, agencies often quantify passive use value through benefit transfer. For example, the US Environmental Protection Agency (2002) suggests that benefit transfer can be used to value threatened and endangered species when evaluating cooling water intake structures. The USDA Economic Research Service's economic analysis of salmon recovery efforts on the Snake River included estimates of passive use values drawn from the existing literature (Aillery et al. 1996). Nonetheless, passive use values have not been formally part of the COE's economic analysis. This may be due, in part, to the benefit-cost procedures which must be followed by the COE being originally written more than 20 years ago (US Water Resources Council 1979), before measurement of passive use values had become common. These benefit-cost procedures are silent on measurement of passive use values, although they do allow for measurement of other categories of benefits as long as the procedures are documented and WTP is used. Passive use values are estimated using a method recommended by the US Water Resources Council for valuing recreation, but its use to measure passive use values has been controversial (Diamond and Hausman 1994; McFadden 1994). Nonetheless, using CVM to measure passive use values has been given a limited endorsement by a Blue-Ribbon panel chaired by two Nobel Laureate economists (Arrow et al. 1993).

In the Snake River case, the interagency Drawdown Economic Workgroup (DREW) guiding the COE economic analysis asked that passive use values be included in the benefit and cost summary in the economic analysis section of the Final Environmental Impact Statement. Therefore, passive use values were calculated to be included in that part of the overall economic analysis. DREW had originally requested an original passive use value survey, and such a survey was pre-tested. However, due to political pressure, the COE decided that passive use values for the Lower Snake River would be approximated, based on existing passive use value estimates using a benefit transfer approach rather than a new survey as was originally proposed.

Before reviewing the specific studies on the economic value of salmon and free-flowing rivers, it is important to define benefit transfer. There are several closely related definitions of benefit transfer. A commonly referred-to definition is provided by Boyle and Bergstrom (1992, p. 657): 'benefit transfer is defined as the transfer of existing estimates of nonmarket values to a new study [site] which is different from the study for which the values were originally estimated.'

4 EXISTING EMPIRICAL MEASUREMENTS OF PASSIVE USE VALUES FOR SALMON

A review of two large computerised economic databases (American Economic Association's EconLit and Environment Canada's recently developed Environmental Values Reference Inventory or EVRI) yielded four published studies, only three of which presented original passive use values for salmon. These three are:

1. Olsen, Richards and Scott's 1991 article published in *Rivers* on existence values for doubling the size of Columbia River Basin salmon and steelhead runs;
2. Loomis's 1996 article in *Water Resources Research* on the economic benefits of increased salmon from removing the dams on the Elwha River in Washington state; and
3. Hanemann, Loomis and Kanninen's 1991 article published in *American Journal of Agricultural Economics* on the benefits of increasing chinook salmon populations in the San Joaquin River in California.

An unpublished, stated CM discrete choice survey of Washington residents undertaken by Layton, Brown and Plummer (1999) was made available by the authors for this benefit transfer as well. To provide the reader with the salient details for the benefit transfer application, we summarise the studies below.

The Olsen et al. (1991) study involved a telephone interview of Pacific Northwest households, using an open-ended WTP question format. Their means of payment (i.e. payment vehicle) was an increase in the household electric bill. The change in salmon was a doubling from 2.5 million to 5 million salmon, for a net change of 2.5 million salmon. The response rate on the phone interviews was quite good at 72 per cent. The original study existence value is $26.52 per household amounting to $32.52 in 1996 dollars.

The Loomis (1996a) Elwha study used a mail questionnaire and a dichotomous choice WTP question format. An increase in federal taxes was the payment vehicle. The mail survey had a response rate of 68 per cent for Washington residents and 55 per cent for the rest of US residents. Respondents were shown a bar chart in the survey indicating the increase in salmon population due to dam removal was approximately 300 000 fish. The Washington residents' value was $73 per household in 1994 dollars or $76.48 in 1996 dollars.

The Hanemann et al. (1991) study involved a combination phone contact, mail survey booklet and then phone interview of respondents using the survey booklet. A dichotomous choice WTP question was used, with taxes as the means of payment. The resource was an increase from 100 chinook salmon to 15 000 chinook salmon for a net increase of 14 900 in the San Joaquin River in California. The combination phone-mail-phone survey had a 51 per cent response rate. The value per household was $181 in 1989 dollars or $222 in 1996 dollars.

The Layton et al. (1999) study was a CM survey that asked Washington residents to rate four different scenarios which involved five different stocks of fish species. These species included the species of relevance for the Snake River (Eastern Washington and Columbia River migratory fish) as well as freshwater species and Western Washington/Puget Sound freshwater, migratory and saltwater fish. This study was specifically designed to allow valuation of a wide variety of fish improvement scenarios in the state of Washington, similar to its application here to the Lower Snake River. Half the respondents received a survey that set a non-declining future fish population as the baseline future, and half received a baseline future that involved further declines if nothing is done. As expected, the stable or non-declining baseline results in lower values per fish than the declining baseline, confirming the existence of diminishing marginal value of incremental gains in fish. Layton et al. (1999) found that their estimated values per household were consistent with past passive use value studies of Loomis (1996a) and Olsen et al. (1991) using the non-declining future baseline. The use of the non-declining baseline is consistent with the interagency assumption of non-declining future salmon numbers, although other biologists using past trend data suggest continued future declines (Weber 1999).

The survey by Layton et al. (1999) was conducted by mail and had a response rate of 68 per cent, which is quite good. The survey design included a budget reminder exercise which involved households having to determine how their household spending would change with a reduction in monthly income that was equal to the dollar amounts the households were asked to pay for the four different fish programmes. Layton et al. (1999) analysed their data using a censored rank order logit model.

From the results of their statistical analysis, a value per household for a one million increase in Eastern Washington/Columbia River migratory fish (e.g. salmon and steelhead) was computed by the authors. This represents a 50 per cent increase in fish population, comparable to the percentage changes being evaluated in the COE Environmental Impact Statement (EIS) for the Lower Snake River. The resulting value is $119 per household annually for each additional one million salmon and steelhead.

5   BENEFIT TRANSFER APPROACHES AND ESTIMATES

Three approaches are used to transfer benefits from this existing literature to estimate the change in passive use value for salmon populations in the Lower Snake River: (a) point estimate transfer of a value per salmon per household from the most similar study is applied to the gain in salmon in the Lower Snake River; (b) value function transfer using the marginal value per fish from the stated CM study is applied to the gain in salmon in the Lower Snake River; (c) a mini-meta analysis regression function is estimated using the values per salmon, and this new value function is applied to the gain in salmon in the Lower Snake River.

While none of these approaches is perfect (which is why a Lower Snake River specific passive use value study was originally planned), each provides an indication of the likely range of the passive use values for increasing salmon populations. All of these approaches do a reasonable job of meeting the criteria for benefit transfer presented by Boyle and Bergstrom (1992). In particular, all of the original empirical studies used in the three approaches valued the same resource of interest in the Lower Snake River, namely, salmon. Three out of the four original empirical studies measure this value of salmon in the same state as the Lower Snake River, i.e. Washington. All the original studies, and all three of our benefit transfer approaches use the same valuation measure, i.e. WTP.

It should be noted that to the extent these existing studies do not perfectly match the policy setting on the Lower Snake River, the direction of error is in the conservative direction. That is, most of the source studies did not provide specific reference in their surveys to whether the salmon were listed as threatened or endangered species. The salmon in the Lower Snake River are listed as threatened and endangered. Had the surveys in the source studies been of threatened and endangered stocks, and had this been pointed out to survey respondents, the resulting values per fish would have likely been higher. Thus, the existing value per salmon estimates are likely conservative measures of WTP to increase threatened and endangered stocks in the Lower Snake River. Second, most of the existing studies valued a larger increase than is being evaluated at the Lower Snake River. Given diminishing marginal existence values found in these studies and confirmed in other literature (Rollins and Lyke 1998), the larger the increase in fish proposed in a survey, the smaller the marginal value per fish. Thus, taking a marginal value per fish from a study that valued a large increment and applying it to a smaller increment on the Lower Snake River will underestimate the value of that smaller increment.

5.1 Value per Fish Estimate Transfer from the Elwha River CVM Study

Point estimate transfer is the simplest approach to calculate the passive use values for wild salmon in the Lower Snake River. The transfer can be performed by matching the change in wild salmon populations in the Lower Snake River alternatives A1 to A4 to an existing study which valued a similar sized change in salmon, the Loomis (1996a) Elwha River study. The Washington residents' value was $73 per household in 1994 dollars or $76.48 in 1996 dollars for an increase in 300 000 salmon. However, to apply this to the rest of the Pacific Northwest so as to calculate total passive use value, two further adjustments need to be made to this point estimate transfer.

To adapt this Washington household value to what households in the rest of the Pacific Northwest and California would pay, it is possible to make a downward adjustment based on a past survey (Loomis 1996a), which compared Washington residents' WTP for salmon on the Elwha River to what households in the rest of the US would pay for the same increase in salmon on the Elwha River. Specifically, Washington household WTP was $73 annually while the rest of US households would pay $68 annually (Loomis 1996a, p. 445). Dividing the $68 by $73 yields a downward adjustment ratio of 0.93, meaning households outside of Washington would pay 93 per cent of what a Washington household would pay. This 0.93 is an average adjustment and actually overstates the downward adjustment since the rest of US households included those in the eastern US where the ratio was 0.75. See Loomis (1996b) for a graph of the distance-WTP function for salmon.

The second adjustment is to multiply the value per household by the number of non-angler (i.e. non-user) households in California, Idaho, Oregon, Washington, and western Montana (our expanded definition of the Pacific Northwest for this study). Given the public good nature of restoring salmon in the Snake River, the total passive use value in the study area is the sum of passive use values held by non-user households in these states. This Pacific Northwest market area is quite conservative as it assumes that users and households in the rest of the United States receive no passive use values from restoring Snake River salmon, an unlikely situation.

Applying the 0.93 adjustment factor to the Washington value of $76.48 yields a value to the rest of Pacific Northwest residents of $71.12 in 1996 dollars. To calculate the total passive use value in the Pacific Northwest, we multiplied per household values by the respective non-user populations. We utilised non-user households, defined as non-fishing households from the US Fish and Wildlife Service's National

Survey of Hunting, Fishing and Wildlife Associated Recreation. In Washington, the number of non-fishing households was 1.4 million while it was 11.1 million for the rest of the Pacific Northwest. Therefore, passive use value for an additional 300 000 salmon was $110.3 million for Washington non-anglers, while for the rest of the Pacific Northwest it was $789.5 million, for a total of $899.7 million. Dividing the $899.7 million by the 300 000 additional salmon posited in the Elwha River survey, yields a value of $2,999 per salmon.

Applying this value per salmon to the increase in number of salmon with dam removal (alternative A4 minus A1) yields an annualised gain in passive use value of about $48.8 million per year over the 50-year project analysis time period. This is a reasonable and conservative benefit transfer. It is conservative because the Lower Snake River salmon are threatened and endangered while the salmon returning to the Elwha were not listed species at the time the survey was written. Thus, while the definition of the public good is not exactly equivalent between Elwha River and the Lower Snake River, the direction of the error is to underestimate the passive use values for the Lower Snake River's threatened and endangered salmon. This is a reasonable benefit transfer because the proposed action to increase salmon is dam removal in both the original Elwha River case study and the Snake River policy case. Finally, the change in number of salmon with the Elwha (around 300 000) is the closest match of the change in salmon likely to result from dam removal on the Lower Snake River (around 37 000). While the change in salmon on the Elwha River is about eight times that expected on the Lower Snake River, this further reinforces the conservative nature of the passive use value per fish calculated from the Elwha due to diminishing marginal existence values.

5.2   Transfer of Layton, Brown and Plummer Columbia River Choice Modelling Estimates

Because Layton et al. (1999) used a CM approach that yields a marginal value per salmon, it is possible to apply their point estimate directly. From the results of their statistical analysis, a value per household for a one million increase in Eastern Washington/Columbia river migratory fish (e.g. salmon and steelhead) was computed by the authors. This represents a 50 per cent increase in fish population, comparable to the relative change from A1 to A4. The resulting value is $119 per household annually for each additional one million salmon and steelhead. This is a larger absolute increment in fish than A1 to A4, and will result in a very conservative estimate of the passive use values per fish. The same adjustment described above in the Elwha River study was used to adjust the Washington household values to estimate the rest of the Pacific Northwest values. For the Layton et al. (1999) study, marginal value per salmon was $1,400 per salmon for the entire Pacific Northwest and California non-user households. If one uses the declining future baseline salmon population, and the additional associated gain of 250 000 salmon, the value per salmon is $10,172 for the entire Pacific Northwest and California non-user households.

The Layton et al. (1999) study illustrates the strength of CM for benefit transfer as compared to the Elwha CVM study. In the Layton et al. (1999) study, households were explicitly valuing the number of salmon as a separate and distinct attribute. In the Elwha study, the number of salmon was an attribute but it was part of the overall dam removal and river restoration programme. In some sense, calculating the marginal value per salmon from the Elwha CVM could overstate the WTP per salmon, as it attributes the entire programme value to salmon. To the extent that the other attributes, such as a free-flowing river, have value separate from the salmon, the Elwha CVM derived fish values may overstate their true part-worths. As noted in the introduction, this is not an inherent limitation of CVM, but rather it is a feature of having just one CVM scenario or programme being valued in the CVM survey. If several CVM scenarios with different numbers of salmon were being valued, then a separate part-worth for salmon from the CVM could be accurately estimated.

In the Snake River case study, the value per fish calculated from the Layton et al. (1999) study is then applied to the number of wild salmon and steelhead that would return with each EIS alternative to estimate the passive use values associated with each alternative. Using Layton et al.'s (1999) first scenario of an assumed stable future salmon population baseline, the annualised gain from A1 to A4 is $22.8 million over the 50-year time period of analysis.

5.3   Meta-analysis Regression Approach

Rather than relying on point estimate transfers which imply a constant marginal value per fish, one could utilise meta analysis to improve the benefit transfer in two dimensions by: (a) use of more than one study, and (b) allow the marginal value per salmon to vary with the absolute increase in the number of salmon that each EIS alternative produces. The meta approach involves the statistical estimation of a WTP function for salmon using incremental passive use values per salmon calculated from the four studies of West Coast residents' WTP for increasing salmon populations discussed above. We obtained one estimate of value from the Olsen et al. (1991), Hanemann et al. (1991) and Loomis (1996a) studies, and two from Layton et al. (1999) due to use of declining versus non-declining baseline salmon populations.

In order to arrive at commensurate passive use values per salmon from the different studies, several steps were necessary. The first was to calculate a marginal value per salmon from each study. This is straightforward with CM, as this value is simply the attribute value. For the available CVM studies only one programme was valued. For each programme, the WTP was divided by the change in the number of salmon from baseline (the no payment status quo) to the number of salmon if the programme is implemented. Then, study values were updated for inflation. This value per salmon per household was aggregated upwards to account for the pure public good nature of passive use values in the Pacific Northwest. That is, multiplying the value per household, per fish by the number of households valuing that increment. The geographic area being used for all the economic analyses was residents of California, Idaho, Oregon, Washington and western Montana. Performing these steps for the Olsen et al. (1991) study yields a marginal value per salmon of $153 for the 2.5 million salmon increase (in 1996 dollars). For the Hanemann et al. (1991) study, the marginal value per salmon in the Pacific Northwest and California was $175,256 for the 14 900 salmon increase. As previously stated, the Loomis Elwha River study had a value of $2,999 for a 300 000 salmon increase.

A double log model fits the data best. The regression equation is:

Natural Log of Marginal Passive Use Values /Salmon in 4 state region
$$= 24.953 - 1.315426 \text{ (Natural Log \# of Salmon)}$$
T-statistics: (12.21)   (-8.214)   (4.3)

The regression has an explanatory power of 95.7 per cent and the number of salmon is significant at the one per cent level, even given the limited degrees of freedom (dof=4). The negative sign on the natural log of salmon indicates that marginal value per salmon decreases as the salmon population increases. This is as would be expected with a declining marginal benefit curve. This equation is then applied to the number of salmon in each EIS alternative in each time period to calculate the benefit estimates shown in Table 4.1.

Table 4.1   Change in annual passive use value of Pacific Northwest non-user households for salmon by EIS alternative (in millions)

Alternative	Avg annual wild return during 50 yrs	Adapting Layton et al. CM	Meta regression	Adapting Elwha River CVM
Baseline (A1)	67 116	-	-	-
Improved Transport (A2)	67 286	$0.25	$4.02	$5.39
System Improvements (A3)	66 288	-$0.66	-$31.08	-$1.41
Dam Removal (A4)	104 000	$22.80	$301.50	$48.80

6   APPLICATION OF BENEFIT TRANSFER APPROACHES TO LOWER SNAKE RIVER ALTERNATIVES

Using the point estimates from the Elwha River study, the Washington CM and the meta-analysis function, the change in annual total passive use values with different levels of wild salmon and wild steelhead recovery is calculated. Data on population size of wild chinook salmon and wild steelhead associated with each alternative over the time period of analysis were obtained from PATH analyses provided by Shannon Davis (Radtke, Davis and Johnson 1999). Application of this function to wild salmon and steelhead populations in alternative A1 is treated as the baseline or future without. The change in annual passive use values is then calculated for each of the three alternatives for an increase in wild salmon and steelhead populations.

Dam removal and restoration of natural river conditions (Alternative A4), is estimated by biologists to yield a 55 per cent higher run of wild salmon and wild steelhead, and produces a $301 million average annual increase in passive use values using the meta-regression equation. Given the reduction in wild salmon and steelhead run sizes of A3 from the baseline (A1), there is a reduction in passive use values for A3 of $31 million annually. These changes in aggregate passive use values are conservative estimates as they assume no passive use value for households in the rest of the US outside of the study area, despite evidence from past surveys that such households do receive passive use values from salmon recovery and dam removal in the Pacific Northwest (Loomis 1996a,b). The results of these calculations are displayed in Table 4.1 for all three benefit transfer approaches.

7   COMPARISON OF PASSIVE USE VALUES TO PROJECT COSTS

Excluding passive use values, the Corps of Engineers (COE 2002) indicated that there were negative net benefits to dam removal of $266.7 million annually. The costs of dam removal were dominated by forgone hydropower production, which was not completely offset by the gains in river recreation, including fishing. The fact that commercial and recreational fishing values for a threatened species are likely to be a small part of the initial benefits of salmon restoration is not surprising. It will take many years to rebuild the depleted salmon stocks to the levels where they can be removed from the Endangered Species List. It will be several decades before initial catch levels will produce significant economic benefits. Given the effect of discounting, these meagre use values cannot overcome the upfront cost of dam removal and forgone hydropower.

However, it seems somewhat paradoxical to economically evaluate recovery of threatened and endangered species solely on their use value. The importance of passive use values in this case is simply too great to overlook. Yet, passive use values are not always the trump card. Only the meta-analysis benefit transfer estimate of $301 million annually is large enough to change the outcome of the benefit-cost analysis. Using the Elwha River point estimate or Layton et al. (1999) CM benefit transfer estimates, the dam removal still has negative net benefits.

However, given the large variance in estimated benefits from using benefit transfer and the very high stakes in the policy decision, an original passive use value study would probably be justified. With literally millions of dollars at stake every year, and billions in present value, even a $250,000 passive use value study that could determine whether it is economically efficient or not to remove the dams would pay its investment back in less than a month. Unfortunately, benefit transfer was used in this real policy case not because of lack of money or time, but lack of political will. The ability of just one senator from one of the four states to block the passive use value study due to the mere possibility that it might show dam removal was economically feasible (an outcome this senator was publicly against), indicates the symbolic as well as empirical importance of passive use values.

8   CONCLUSION

It is clear that passive use or existence value is a relevant value for decision-making involving threatened and endangered salmon at risk in the Lower Snake River. The challenge in this study was to approximate these values based on the existing literature. Four studies, three of which valued salmon in the Pacific Northwest, were applied in three different ways to estimate the passive use values of increases in salmon populations in the Lower Snake River. The incremental passive use values for the increase in anadromous fish due to the dam breaching ranges from a high of $301 million for households in the Pacific Northwest and California to a low of $23 million with a middle estimate of $49 million.

From a methodological perspective, this chapter has illustrated how CVM and CM approaches can be used for benefits transfer. In the meta-regression benefit transfer approach, the marginal values per salmon estimates from CVM and CM studies were utilised to estimate a WTP function.

This chapter also discussed the situations where CVM and CM can yield conceptually similar marginal values, and when this is not the case. Specifically, if a series of CVM willingness-to-pay questions are asked for programmes that have differing levels of attributes, then marginal values for these attributes can be calculated. The calculation is similar to CM where the attribute coefficient is divided by the cost coefficient to yield a marginal value. However, when CVM is used to value just one programme, calculation of a marginal value per unit for one of the attributes may overstate its marginal value as the entire value of the programme change may be reflected in that attribute value.

Improvements in CM and CVM for increasing the accuracy of benefit transfer include allowing for declining marginal values per unit of attributes as the level of the attributes increases. Currently most CM and CVM studies provide constant marginal values per unit, which is equivalent to assuming a horizontal marginal benefit curve. This may be locally correct, but for large changes such as those in the Lower Snake River dam removal, the application of a constant marginal value may overstate the total benefits of an increase in the resource. Layton (2001) has demonstrated two refinements in empirical estimation of discrete choice models to allow for diminishing marginal value per unit of attribute. This can also be accomplished in CVM using quadratic terms in the WTP equation. These are important refinements to enhance the use of CM and CVM in future benefit transfers.

REFERENCES

Aillery, M., P. Bertels, J. Cooper, M. Moore, S. Vogel and M. Weinberg (1996), *Salmon Recovery in the Pacific Northwest: Agricultural and Other Economic Effects*, Report No 727, Washington DC: USDA Economic Research Service.

Arrow, K., R. Solow, P. Portney, E. Leamer, R. Radner and H. Schuman (1993), 'Report of the NOAA panel on contingent valuation', *Federal Register* **58** (10), 4602–14.

Boyle, K. and J. Bergstrom (1992), 'Benefit transfer studies: myth, pragmatism and idealism', *Water Resources Research*, **28** (3), 657–63.

Cameron, T. (1988), 'A new paradigm for valuing non-market goods using referendum data: maximum likelihood estimation by censored logistic regression', *Journal of Environmental Economics and Management*, **15** (3), 355–79.

Corps of Engineers (2002), *Final Lower Snake River Juvenile Salmon Migration Feasibility Report and Environmental Impact Statement on the Lower Snake River*, Walla Walla, WA: Walla Walla District.

Diamond, P. and J. Hausman (1994), 'Contingent valuation: is some number better than no number?' *Journal of Economic Perspectives*, **8**, 45–64.

Hanemann, M. (1984), 'Welfare evaluations in contingent valuation experiments with discrete responses', *American Journal of Agricultural Economics*, **66**, 332–41.

Hanemann, M., J. Loomis and B. Kanninen (1991), 'Statistical efficiency of double bounded dichotomous choice contingent valuation', *American Journal of Agricultural Economics*, **73** (4), 1255–63.

Hoehn, J. and J. Loomis (1993), 'Substitution effects in the valuation of multiple environmental programs', *Journal of Environmental Economics and Management*, **25** (1), 56–75.

Krutilla, J. and A. Fisher (1975), *The Economics of Natural Environments*, Resources for the Future, Washington DC: Johns Hopkins University Press.

Layton, D. (2001) 'Alternative approaches for modelling concave willingness to pay functions in conjoint valuation', *American Journal of Agricultural Economics*, **83** (5), 1314–20.

Layton, D., G. Brown and M. Plummer (1999), *Valuing Multiple Programs to Improve Fish Populations*, Dept of Environmental Science and Policy, Davis, CA: University of California.

Loomis, J. (1996a), 'Measuring the economic benefits of removing dams and restoring the Elwha River: results of a contingent valuation survey', *Water Resources Research*, **32** (2), 441–7.

Loomis, J. (1996b), 'How large is the extent of the market for public goods: evidence from a nationwide contingent valuation survey', *Applied Economics* **28**, 779–82.

Loomis, J. and P. duVair (1993), 'Evaluating the effect of alternative risk communication devices on willingness to pay: results from a dichotomous choice contingent valuation experiment', *Land Economics*, **69** (3), 287–98.

McFadden, D. (1974), 'Conditional Logit Analysis of Qualitative Choice Behaviour', in P. Zarembka (ed.), *Frontiers of Econometrics*, New York: Academic Press, pp. 105–42.

McFadden, D. (1994), 'Contingent valuation and social choice', *American Journal of Agricultural Economics* **76** (4), 689–708.

Meyer, P. (1974), *Recreation and Preservation Values Associated With Salmon of the Frasier River*, PAC/IN-74-1, Vancouver, Canada: Environment Canada.

Olsen, D., J. Richards and R. D. Scott (1991), 'Existence and sport values for doubling the size of Columbia River Basin salmon and steelhead runs', *Rivers* **2** (1), 44–56.

Radtke, H., S. Davis and R. Johnson (1999), *Anadromous Fish Economic Analysis. Lower Snake River Juvenile Salmon Migration Feasibility Study* EIS, Corvallis, OR: Oregon State University.

Randall, A. and J. Stoll (1983), 'Existence and Sport Values in a Total Valuation Framework', in R. Rowe and L. Chestnut, *Managing Air Quality and Scenic Resources at National Parks and Wilderness Areas*, Boulder, CO: Westview Press, pp. 265–74.

Rollins, K. and A. Lyke (1998), 'The case for diminishing marginal existence values', *Journal of Environmental Economics and Management*, **36** (3), 324–44.

Stoll, J. and L.A. Johnson (1984), 'Concepts of Value, Nonmarket Valuation and the Case of the Whooping Crane', in *Transactions of the 49th North American Wildlife and Natural Resources Conference*, Washington DC.: Wildlife Management Institute, pp. 383–93.

US Environmental Protection Agency (2002), *Case Study Analysis for the Proposed Section 316(b) Phase II Existing Facilities Rule*, EPA-821-R-02-002. Washington DC: Office of Water (4303).

US Water Resources Council (1979), 'Procedures for Evaluation of National Economic Development (NED): Benefits and Costs of Water Resources Planning (Level C) Final Rule', *Federal Register*, **44** (242), 72892–977.

US Water Resources Council (1983), *Economic and Environmental Principles and Guidelines for Water and Related Land Resources Implementation Studies*. 10 March, Washington DC: US Government Printing Office.

Weber, E. (1999), Stock Stability. Email from Earl Weber CRITFC Biologist to Phil Meyer, 28 June, 1999.

5. Valuing New South Wales Rivers for Use in Benefit Transfer[1]

Mark Morrison and Jeff Bennett

1   INTRODUCTION

Benefit transfer refers to the extrapolation of non-market value estimates generated at a 'source' site to a second 'target' site. Benefit transfer is particularly popular with policy makers and consultants providing advice to policy makers, because value estimates so derived are relatively cheap and easy to obtain. However, there is a tension between these advantages and the greater potential inaccuracy that results from using benefit transfer rather than generating original estimates. One possible strategy for dealing with this implicit trade-off is to recognise that some decisions require less accurate value estimates (Brookshire and Neill 1992). For these sorts of analyses, the use of benefit transfer may be acceptable. For instance, threshold value analysis (e.g. Bennett 1999) may require value estimates that are sufficiently robust to indicate an order of magnitude difference between benefits and costs. An alternative response is to consider the development of methods to improve the accuracy of benefit transfer, so that it can be used more widely.

Benefit transfer can be undertaken with varying levels of sophistication. At its most basic level, analysts attempt to use 'mean household' or 'unit day' value estimates. For instance, a value might be established for a day of recreation and this estimate combined with estimates of the number of recreators at various sites to estimate the recreation value of each site. This approach was widely used by the US Corps of Engineers to value recreation sites in the USA (Loomis 1992). The advantage of this approach is that it is straightforward for analysts to use and intuitive

The material presented in this chapter is substantially based on the publication by Morrison, M. and Bennett, J. 2004 'Valuing New South Wales rivers for use in benefit transfer', *Australian Journal of Agricultural and Resource Economics*, 48(4), pp. 591 - 611. Permission to publish this chapter has been kindly granted by Blackwells Publishing.

to most stakeholders. However, its limitation is that there may be differences in the preferences of the populations at each of the sites as well in the biophysical characteristics of the sites, both of which may affect value estimates.

Because of these limitations, various researchers have advocated the transfer of demand functions when using benefit transfer (e.g. Desvousges, Naughton and Parsons 1992). Initially, these transfers involved the use of value functions derived from the travel cost and contingent valuation methods. Analysts altered the mean values for the socio-demographic variables within the value function so that they reflected the characteristics of the relevant population (e.g. Loomis 1992). Later studies also included variations in site characteristics when conducting benefit transfer (Morrison et al. 2002). These studies made use of multi-attribute stated preference techniques, such as discrete choice modelling. They allowed the analyst to adjust for different changes in environmental quality across sites. That is, if a small change in environmental quality is occurring at the 'target' site, then a corresponding small value estimate can be extrapolated, rather than simply extrapolating the value for the environmental change that occurred at the 'source' site.

While the use of value functions is likely to improve the rigour of benefit transfer, the benefit transfer process may still yield inaccuracies. Differences in sites are not likely to be completely captured by adjusting the 'change' in environmental quality across sites. This is because sites differ in several respects including: (1) the base level of environmental quality, (2) the range of improvements that might occur, and (3) the community's perceptions of the importance of the site and of improvements at the site. In addition, differences in populations may not be completely accounted for by the standard socio-demographic variables included in demand functions (e.g. income, age, education, gender, work status). Differences in values may be more closely related to factors such as whether a population is urban or rural, or lives in proximity or is remote to the site of interest. The development of methodologies to account for these sorts of factors may lead to more accurate benefit transfer estimates, and a greater range of acceptable applications for benefit transfer.

This chapter has three main objectives. The first is to present the results from a series of choice modelling applications designed to value improved health of rivers across New South Wales. Because of the large number of rivers in the State and a budget constraint, it was only feasible to value a subset of these rivers. Five catchments were selected for valuation (Gwydir River, Murrumbidgee River, Clarence River, Bega River and Georges River), because they were seen to be representative of catchments within New South Wales. To value the remaining rivers in the State, it was planned to make use of benefit transfer. However, as discussed above, benefit transfer may be subject to additional error if the base level of environmental quality, the range of improvements or the preferences of the population are different. Therefore, the second objective of this paper is to present the results of a pooled model that can be used to remedy some of these deficiencies. We believe this to be an innovation in the use of benefit transfer. The third objective is to discuss the process of aggregation and how the value estimates can be used in practice.

Discrete choice modelling is the technique used in this study to derive value estimates of improved river health. Choice modelling is a multi-attribute technique in which estimates of the value of changes in the attributes of a good are derived (Bennett and Blamey 2001; Louviere, Hensher and Swait 2000).

The chapter proceeds in the following way. In Section 2, the case study used for this paper is reviewed, in Section 3 the questionnaire design is described, and in Section 4 survey logistics are discussed. In Section 5, the choice models estimated for the five catchments are presented and in Section 6 the results for the pooled model are presented. In Section 7, the results for a model designed to value improved river health across the State are reported, and in Section 8 the issue of aggregation is considered. Finally, in Section 9, implications of the results are discussed.

2   CASE STUDIES

Within New South Wales, reform of the water allocation process is being undertaken to achieve a more appropriate balance between consumptive and environmental uses. As part of the reform process, the State Government established Water Management Committees (WMCs) to provide advice regarding the allocation of water resources. To fulfill their goals, the WMCs required information relating to the biophysical consequences of alternative water-sharing arrangements. For instance, predictions of the impacts on the number of fish species present in a river and the quantities of irrigated crops harvested given increased allocations of water to agriculture were relevant. However, biophysical predictions alone are no indication of the relative values of alternative water-sharing regimes. To consider the impact on the community of changes in fish species numbers and tonnes of crops harvested, the values held by the community for these changes also had to be established.

To provide these value estimates, five rivers from within different geographical regions of NSW were selected for valuation. These 'representative' rivers were selected after consultation with ecologists and river managers, because they were representative of the main types of rivers within NSW. The rivers were the Bega River, the Clarence River, the Murrumbidgee River, the Gwydir River and the Georges River.

The current conditions of the rivers and their catchments are summarised in Table 5.1. The Georges River is the only urban catchment, and both the Georges River and Bega River are relatively small in size compared with the other three rivers. Three of the rivers are coastal (Georges, Clarence and Bega) and the other two (Murrumbidgee and Gwydir) are inland rivers. In terms of irrigated agriculture, the Murrumbidgee and Gwydir Rivers provide the greatest value. For the environmental attributes, the Bega and Clarence Rivers have the highest percentages of healthy riverside vegetation and wetlands. For recreational uses, none of the rivers are particularly well-suited for fishing, with all rivers having more than 50 per cent of sites monitored being of inadequate quality for this recreational use (more than 50 per cent of the time). For swimming, only the Georges and Bega Rivers had more than 50 per cent of sites being good enough for swimming (more than 50 per cent of the time). All rivers, apart from the Clarence and Bega, have lost more than 50 per cent of their native fish species.

3   QUESTIONNAIRE DESIGN

Discrete choice modelling (CM) was employed to estimate the value of improvements in river health in NSW. In environmental choice modelling questionnaires, there are several well-defined elements. These include: (1) a description of the environmental issue, (2) a description of possible solutions to the problems faced, (3) a description of the payment scenario, including the payment vehicle and (4) choice sets. These elements are now described to provide contextual information for the value estimates that have been generated.

3.1   The Environmental Issue

For each of the rivers, the issue of declining river health was initially described. Within the questionnaire, the information was described as shown in Box 5.1 (for the Bega River). Respondents were told that there had been falls in the main environmental attributes of concern, and what has led to these declines. The actual decline in the four environmental attributes used to describe the condition of the rivers was specified in detail in the fold-out cover of the questionnaire, as shown in Table 5.1.

Table 5.1   Past and current characteristics of the five rivers

	Bega	Clarence	Georges	Gwydir	Murrumbidgee
Location	Southern, coastal	Northern, coastal	Central, coastal	Northern, inland	Southern, inland
Urban/rural	Rural	Rural	Urban	Rural	Rural
Population in catchment	5 000	55 000	800 000	30 000	400 000
Area of catchment	2 000 km^2	23 000 km^2	960 km^2	26 000 km^2	84 000 km^2
Length of river	50 km	390 km	96 km	330 km	1 690 km
Value of irrigated agricultural production	$55 million	$78 million	N/A	$240 million	$410 million
Attribute 1: Current % healthy vegetation and wetlands	30%	40%	20%	10%	10%
Attribute 2: % sites not good enough for:					
(1) fishing	(1) 75%	(1) 100%	(1) 87%	(1) 67%	(1) 62%
(2) swimming*	(2) 25%	(2) 79%	(2) 33%	(2) 86%	(2) 95%
Attribute 3: Native fish species:					
(1) past level	(1) 25 species	(1) 35 species	(1) 25 species	(1) 25 species	(1) 25 species
(2) current level	(2) 15 species	(2) 22 species	(2) 12 species	(2) 10 species	(2) 8 species
Attribute 4: Waterbirds and other fauna:					
(1) past level	(1) 88 species	(1) 95 species	(1) 102 species	(1) 79 species	(1) 85 species
(2) current level	(2) 48 species	(2) 67 species	(2) 65 species	(2) 45 species	(2) 60 species

Note: * more than 50 per cent of the time.

Box 5.1: Description of the Environmental Issues Facing the Bega River

Scientists agree that the quality of many parts of the Bega River and its tributaries has declined over time. There have been falls in:

- the number of native fish species
- the amount of healthy riverside vegetation and wetlands
- the number of water bird and other fauna species
- recreation opportunities such as fishing and swimming

☛ *Please read carefully the information in the fold-out cover. It gives some details about these changes.*

Various factors have contributed to this,

- use of water for irrigation has reduced the amount of water in the river
- treated water from sewage treatment flowing into the river
- polluted run-off from urban areas, especially during wet weather (Run-off is water that runs off the land into streams and rivers.)
- land clearing which has increased erosion and the depositing of sediment in the river
- erosion of river banks because of stock grazing and walking down to the river to drink
- farmland run-off containing fertilizers and pesticide
- non-native fish species and weeds (such as willow trees)

3.2   Description of Possible Solutions

After describing the environmental problem, several alternative ways of improving river health were described. These alternatives included: improving water use efficiency, construction work to reduce erosion, fencing to protect riverside vegetation, and control of feral species. In addition to a verbal description, a photo of each of these alternatives was included in the questionnaire.

3.3   Payment Scenario

Payment scenarios are important in all stated preference applications as they specify the method and timing of payment, both of which have been demonstrated to affect value estimates (Stevens et al. 1994; Morrison et al. 2000). In the questionnaires for this project, as shown in Box 5.2, respondents were told that adopting the alternative river management strategies would be expensive and that it would be necessary to collect a one-off levy on water rates.

Box 5.2: The Payment Scenario
How this could affect you?

These projects would improve the quality of the Bega River but they would be expensive.

One possibility for funding this scheme is for the State Government to collect a one-off levy on water rates for all households in the Bega River catchment during the year 2001. If your household does not pay water rates, an alternative way of collecting the levy would be arranged. This money would be used for projects like the ones described above.

The size of the levy and the environmental improvements achieved would depend on which projects were chosen.

3.4 Choice Sets

An example of a choice set from the Bega River Case Study is shown in Figure 5.1.

Question 7: Carefully consider each of the following three options for the Bega River. Suppose Options A, D and E were the ONLY ones available, which one would you choose?

	Levy on water rates (one-off) $	Recreational uses	Healthy riverside vegetation and wetlands	Native fish	Waterbirds and other fauna
Option A (Current situation)	no extra cost	✓ Picnics ✓ Boating ✗ Fishing ✗ Swimming	Along 30% of river	15 native species present	48 species present
Option D	$50	✓ Picnics ✓ Boating ✓ Fishing ✓ Swimming	Along 80% of river	21 native species present	59 species present
Option E	$50	✓ Picnics ✓ Boating ✗ Fishing ✗ Swimming	Along 80% of river	25 native species present	88 species present

Which of these options would you choose?

☐ I would choose Option A

☐ I would choose Option D

☐ I would choose Option E

☐ Not sure

Figure 5.1   Example of a choice set from the Bega River questionnaire

In each questionnaire, respondents answered five of these questions. The experimental design, which was an orthogonal design selected from Hahn and Shapiro (1966), had a total of 25 alternatives. Therefore there were five versions of the questionnaire for each catchment.

The attributes in the choice sets were selected after a literature review, a survey of experts and through the use of four focus groups (Bennett et al. 2000). In the expert survey, 23 industry experts were asked to list (a) up to ten indicators of river health, and (b) the five most important indicators. In the focus groups, slightly different procedures were used. In the first two focus groups, participants were asked to indicate what attributes of river health they would like to know about if they were to evaluate whether a project improving river health should proceed. In the second set of two focus groups, respondents were shown a list of the attributes identified by the survey of ecologists and river managers and asked to add any other attributes that they considered to be important.

Five main attributes were identified using this methodology. These were flow, fish, vegetation, water quality and water dependent fauna. For the choice modelling questionnaire, flow was excluded as an attribute because increases in flow were believed to be one of the main causes of change in the remaining attributes. There were also concerns that water quality would be seen to be a causally prior attribute to the other attributes (Blamey et al. 2002). Therefore, water quality was instead given the descriptor 'recreational use'. Thus the attributes employed in the CM application were recreational use, healthy riverside vegetation and wetlands, native fish species, and waterbirds and other fauna species. Three of these variables are normally associated with existence values (healthy riverside vegetation and wetlands, native fish species and waterbirds and other fauna species), although in some cases they can be use values. However, the remaining variable (recreational use) is clearly a use value. An additional attribute – a tax on water rates – was used as a payment vehicle.

Another important aspect of designing a choice modelling questionnaire is the selection of levels for attributes. Levels refer to the quantities or qualitative descriptors for each attribute. Identifying appropriate levels is arguably more difficult than selecting attributes, because there are often many ways to describe the same attribute. In the initial focus group, participants had difficulty in suggesting suitable descriptors for the attributes. Therefore in the remaining focus groups, participants were shown a list of descriptors based on findings from the literature review and the survey of experts, and asked to indicate which descriptors they most preferred. This information was used as a basis for selecting the levels used in the questionnaires.

The levels for these attributes were catchment specific (apart from water rates and recreational uses), but an example is shown in Table 5.2 for the Bega River. The range for the attribute levels was chosen so that it would be as wide as possible, while still maintaining plausibility. Based on the recommendations of Pearmain et al. (1991), unequal increments were used to select attribute levels.

Table 5.2   Attribute levels for the Bega River case study

Attribute	Symbol	Current	Level 1	Level 2	Level 3
Water rates	$	No extra cost	$50	$100	$200
Recreational uses (across entire river)		Picnics Boating	Picnics Boating Fishing	Picnics Boating Fishing Swimming	
Healthy vegetation and wetlands		Along 30% of river	Along 40% of river	Along 60% of river	Along 80% of river
Native fish		15 native species present	18 native species present	21 native species present	25 native species present
Waterbirds and other fauna		48 species present	59 species present	72 species present	88 species present

4   SURVEY LOGISTICS

Surveys were conducted in each of the five catchments (Bega, Clarence, Georges, Gwydir and Murrumbidgee catchments). However, it is possible that people that reside outside of these five catchments will also value improved river health. Indeed, several previous studies have identified distance decay functions (e.g. Sutherland and Walsh 1985; Pate and Loomis 1997) implying that respondents who do not reside within a catchment may nevertheless value improved catchment quality. For instance, people in Sydney may be willing to pay for improved water quality in the Murrumbidgee River, located 500 kilometres away. Therefore there is a rationale for obtaining 'out-of-catchment' samples in addition to those collected 'within-catchment'. Unfortunately, resource constraints and funding requirements meant that out-of-catchment samples could only be collected for two of the rivers: the Gwydir and Murrumbidgee. These two catchments were selected because both were inland catchments. Testing in this study would therefore indicate whether out-of-catchment values were equivalent for two relatively similar rivers. Testing in future studies could then be used to extend this testing and determine whether out-of-catchment values from more different rivers were also equivalent. Thus seven samples were collected: five within-catchment (Bega, Clarence, Georges, Gwydir and Murrumbidgee catchments) and two out-of-catchments (Gwydir and Murrumbidgee).

To implement this sampling plan, seven samples of 900 respondents were drawn from 'Australia on Disk', a listing of people based on the White Pages telephone directory. For the five 'local' or within-catchment samples, respondents were selected at random on the basis of postcodes relating to the corresponding river catchments. For two of the catchments (Gwydir and Murrumbidgee) a further 900 respondents were drawn from outside of these catchments within the State of NSW.

A four-stage surveying process was employed. First, an introductory letter advising those drawn in the sample that they would shortly be receiving a questionnaire was dispatched. Those receiving the letter were given the option of withdrawal. As well as heightening the significance of the survey, this preliminary letter was designed to filter out names and/or addresses from the sample that were redundant – such as people who had moved, were incapable of answering or who were deceased. The second stage of the survey involved the mailing of the questionnaire with an accompanying letter and a reply-paid envelope. The number of successfully delivered surveys ranged from 703 to 763 across the seven surveys. A reminder card comprised the third stage and a re-mail of the questionnaire to those yet to respond completed the process. The overall response rate for the seven surveys was 39.6 per cent, ranging from 30.4 per cent to 45.9 per cent. These response rates compare favourably with other mail surveys of this genre (Mitchell and Carson 1989).

The socio-demographics of the survey samples are shown in Table 5.3. In general, respondents to the questionnaire self-selected to be older, better educated, and more affluent than the population they represent. Respondents were also more likely to be male.[2]

Table 5.3   Socio-demographics of the survey samples

	Clarence	Bega	Georges	M'bidgee within	M'bidgee outside	Gwydir within	Gwydir outside
Average Age (yrs)	55.9	52.6	51.1	50.5	52.9	51. 5	52.4
Sex (% female)	41%	41%	30%	45%	39%	34%	36%
Children	87%	83%	89%	84%	85%	85%	80%
Education*	3.9	4.3	4.1	4.1	4.3	4.1	4.3
Income	$32,256	$38,899	$46,069	$50,548	$50,251	$43,517	$47,989

Note: * 1 – never went to school, 6 – tertiary degree.

5   MODELLING RESULTS

The most common model used for analysing discrete choice data where there are multiple alternatives that can be chosen is the conditional logit model. With the conditional logit model, the probability of choosing an alternative is a function of the utility of the alternative relative to the utility of all alternatives. The error distribution of the conditional logit model is independently and identically distributed (IID) Gumbell, which leads to the independence from irrelevant alternatives (IIA) property. This implies that the probability of choosing one alternative over another is independent of the presence/absence of any other alternatives. In practice, violations of this property occur for many reasons, including the existence of heterogeneous preferences. Therefore it is becoming more common to use altenative models that either do not require this property or have less restrictive assumptions. In this paper, each of the data sets has been analysed using a nested logit model, as violations of the IIA property were identified using the test recommended by Hausman and McFadden (1984). In the nested logit model, unobserved components of utility are assumed to be shared between certain alternatives; hence the errors of the alternatives within branches are correlated and not independent. Thus, this model is used to avoid problems associated with violations of the IIA property.

When using nested logit models, a 'tree-structure' needs to be pre-specified. Tree structures reflect the existence of homogeneous sets of alternatives that have correlated errors. They can have multiple levels. All of the homogeneous alternatives are in the branches at the bottom of the structure. These alternatives are then grouped at the next level using the limbs of the tree. Following Kling and Thompson (1996), the nested logit model can be specified as follows. The probability of a particular alternative being chosen (P_{jm}) is equal to the probability that the limb that the alternative is in is chosen ($P(m)$) multiplied by the probability that the alternative is chosen from within the limb $P(j|m)$. That is:

$$P_{jm} = P(j|m).P(m) \tag{5.1}$$

where:

$$P(j \mid m) = \frac{\exp(V_{jm} \mid \alpha_m)}{\exp(I_m)} \tag{5.2}$$

$$P(m) = \frac{\exp(\alpha_m I_m)}{\sum_{k=1}^{M} \exp(\alpha_k I_k)} \tag{5.3}$$

$$I_m = \log \left[\sum_{i=1}^{J_m} \exp(V_{im} / \alpha_m) \right] \tag{5.4}$$

In the above equations, I_m is the inclusive value and is the sum of the utility of all of the alternatives. The model works by estimating the probability that an alternative is chosen within a limb, $P(j|m)$, and estimating the probability that a limb is chosen $(P(m))$.

The coefficients estimated using the nested logit model are used to derive estimates of the value of an environmental improvement. The focus of this paper is on the estimation of implicit prices. These are point estimates of the value of a unit change in an attribute. They are useful for management decisions where information is required about the value of marginal changes in environmental quality, such as the value of an extra waterbird species preserved. They are also useful for identifying the relative importance that people place on different attributes. Implicit prices are calculated as follows, if utility is a linear function of all attributes:

$$IP = \beta_A/\beta_M \qquad (5.5)$$

where IP is the implicit price, β_A represents the coefficient of a non-monetary attribute, and β_M represents the coefficient for the monetary attribute.

The variables used in the nested logit models (and in the pooled model presented in Section 6), and their expected signs, are presented in Table 5.4.

Table 5.4   Variables used in the nested and conditional logit models

Variable	Definition	Expected sign
ASC1, 2	Alternative Specific Constants	?
RATE	Increase in water rates	−
VEGET	% healthy native riverside vegetation	+
FISHSPEC	Number of native species present	+
FISHING	Suitable for fishing	+
SWIMMING	Suitable for swimming	+
FAUNA	Number of waterbirds and other fauna present	+
PROGRE	Pro-green environmental orientation	−
PRODEV	Pro-development environmental orientation	+
AGE	Age (years)	+
INCOME	Income ($)	−
INCDUM	Dummy variable that takes on a value of one if a respondent did not report their income	?
COASTAL	Whether a catchment is inland or coastal (1 – coastal, 0 – inland,)	?
NORTH	Whether a catchment is in the north or south of NSW (1 – north, 0 – south)	?
LOCAL	Whether a respondent resides within a catchment (1 – resides inside catchment, 0 – resides outside of catchment)	+

Note that for the socio-demographic variables, the expected signs are opposite to what would normally be expected as these variables have been interacted with the constant representing the 'continue the current situation' option. So, for example, you would expect the income variable to have a negative sign, because people with higher income would be expected to be less likely to choose to continue the current situation.

The nested logit models are presented in Table 5.5. The models were structured so that respondents are assumed to make two choices: (1) whether to improve river health or to continue the current situation and (2) if improving river health is chosen, a choice between two options that improve river health. The choice at the first or upper level choice is assumed to be a function of the respondents' socio-demographic characteristics (AGE, INCOME), environmental attitude (PROGRE, PRODEV), the attributes of the alternatives (RATE, VEGET, etc.) and a constant (ASC1). The choice at the second or lower level is assumed to be a function only of the attributes of the alternatives and the second constant (ASC2). These models were estimated using LIMDEP 7.0. The choice set attributes are significant and correctly signed in all models except for FISHSPEC (Clarence, Georges) and FAUNA (Georges and Gwydir outside-catchment sample). INCOME is significant in five models, AGE is significant in five models, and PROGRE is significant in all seven models, providing evidence of theoretical validity. The explanatory power of the models is relatively high, with the adjusted rho-squared ranging from 0.21 to 0.41 (values greater than 0.2 indicate a robust model).

Implicit prices derived from these nested logit models are presented in Table 5.6. The implicit prices were calculated using the formula presented in equation (5.5). For instance, the value for VEGET in the Bega catchment is 0.035/0.015 = 2.33. It is these estimates that can be used for valuing improved river health in each of the five catchments. These estimates may also be used to value river health in other similar catchments via benefit transfer. Tests of differences between the implicit price estimates in different catchments are reported in Morrison and Bennett (2004).

Table 5.5   Nested logit models

Variables	Bega	Clarence	Georges	Murrumbidgee inside catchment	Murrumbidgee outside catchment	Gwydir-inside catchment	Gwydir-outside catchment
ASC1	0.22*	0.17	0.22	0.20*	0.15	0.24*	0.12
RATE	-0.15E-1**	-0.18E-1**	-0.16E-1**	-0.14E-1**	-0.13E-1**	-0.15E-1**	-0.13E-1**
VEGET	0.35E-1**	0.37E-1**	0.24E-1**	0.21E-1**	0.28E-1**	0.23E-1**	0.26E-1**
FISHSPEC	0.11**	-0.82E-3	0.28	0.39E-1**	0.53**	0.33**	0.46E-1**
SWIM1	0.77**	0.65**	0.58**	0.54**	0.57**	0.80**	0.39**
FISHING	0.39**	0.42**	0.35**	0.39**	0.19**	0.38**	0.20**
FAUNA	0.13E-1*	0.34E-1*	0.92E-3	0.25E-1**	0.23E-1*	0.27E-1**	0.72E-2
ASC2	-2.16**	-1.14	0.86	-1.53**	-1.04	-1.89**	-1.38**
PROGRE	-0.39**	-0.27**	-0.29**	-0.15*	-0.68**	-0.26**	-0.44**
PRODEV	0.64**	0.82**	-0.51E-1	0.30	0.42*	0.22	0.22
AGE	0.26E-1**	0.17E-1**	0.11E-1*	0.24E-1**	0.63E-2	0.23E-1**	0.47E-2
INCOME	-0.42E-5	-0.16E-4**	-0.22E-4**	-0.15E-4**	-0.21E-4**	-0.42E-5	-0.15E-4**
INCDUM	1.11**	0.38*	-0.62*	-0.12	-0.34	0.97**	-1.45**
IV	0.42**	0.39**	0.39**	0.45**	0.30**	0.27**	0.43**
Summary Statistics							
Log-likelihood	-1075.54	-1049.94	-728.62	-875.39	-758.47	-896.27	-708.16
Rho-squared adj	0.27	0.21	0.21	0.29	0.41	0.22	0.38
N	3 855	3 774	2 481	3 201	3 120	3 081	2 760

Note: **significant at 1% level, *significant at 5% level.

84

Table 5.6   Implicit prices

	VEGET (per % of river covered with healthy native vegetation)	FISHSPEC (per species)	SWIMABLE (across river)	FISHABLE (across river)	FAUNA (per species)
Within-Catchment Estimates					
Bega	$2.33	$7.23	$100.98	$51.33	$0.88
Clarence	$2.07	-$0.05*	$72.77	$46.63	$1.92
Georges	$1.51	$1.77*	$73.88	$45.26	$0.59*
Gwydir	$1.46	$2.12	$104.07	$48.94	$1.76
Murrumbidgee	$1.46	$2.77	$75.24	$54.16	$1.73
Outside-Catchment Estimates					
Gwydir	$1.98	$3.51	$59.98	$29.93	$0.55*
Murrumbidgee	$2.15	$4.05	$86.46	$28.75	$1.79

Note: * insignificant coefficients in model.

6   A POOLED MODEL FOR BENEFIT TRANSFER

A limitation of the results described in the previous section is that outside-of-catchment estimates were not derived for the Bega or Clarence rivers. Therefore, benefit transfer is likely to be subject to error when outside-of-catchment estimates are transferred to substantially different river catchments. Another limitation is that for several attributes (fish species in the Clarence and fauna species in the Gwydir Rivers) it was not possible to derive statistically significant value estimates.

A pooled benefit transfer model (Table 5.7) was estimated to remedy these limitations. By pooling the data, it may be possible to identify systematic differences in value estimates due to catchment or sampling differences. This is especially important for identifying how value estimates differ when sampling is conducted outside of a catchment, instead of within a catchment, given that outside-of-catchment sampling was only conducted for two catchments. Secondly, the pooled model can be used to estimate values for attributes where they are found to be insignificant in individual models. By increasing the sample size, insignificance due to low statistical power will potentially be minimised.

The data from six samples were included in this model. The Georges River sample was excluded from the pooled model, as it is an urban catchment and hence is unlike the other rural catchments for which benefit transfer estimates are sought.

Three dummy variables were interacted with each of the four environmental attributes to identify catchment-specific values. These are whether (1) the catchment is inland or coastal (COASTAL), (2) the catchment is in the north or south of the state (NORTH), and (3) the sample of respondents is located within or outside of the catchment (LOCAL). Only those variables that were significant were included in the model.

The model specification has been kept simple because of the large number of variables in the model. A multinomial logit model has been used because of problems encountered with convergence of a pooled nested logit model; however this change in model specification should not significantly affect implicit prices which is the primary objective of this research (Hausman and Ruud 1987).

Table 5.7   Pooled model

Variables	Coefficients	P-values
ASC1	0.574	0.000
ASC2	0.510	0.001
ASC * PROGRE	0.379	0.000
ASC * PRODEV	-0.422	0.000
ASC * NORTH	-0.240	0.002
ASC * LOCAL	-0.790	0.000
ASC * COASTAL	-0.534	0.001
RATE	-0.854E-02	0.000
RATE * INCOME	0.514E-07	0.000
RATE * INCOME DUMMY	-0.331E-02	0.000
RATE * AGE	-0.783E-04	0.000
VEGETATION	0.216E-01	0.000
VEGETATION * LOCAL	-0.742E-02	0.000
VEGETATION * COASTAL	0.807E-02	0.001
FISHABLE	0.171	0.000
FISHABLE * LOCAL	0.144	0.009
SWIMMABLE	0.391	0.000
SWIMMABLE * LOCAL	0.892E-01	0.112
FISH SPECIES	0.368E-01	0.000
FISH * COASTAL	0.343E-01	0.015
FISH * NORTH * COASTAL	-0.482E-01	0.000
FAUNA SPECIES	0.986E-02	0.000
Summary statistics		
Log-likelihood	-5786.911	
Adjusted rho-squared	0.198	
N	6 575	

The coefficients for the variables in the model have expected signs, and importantly, almost all reported interactions are significant at the 1 per cent level, allowing estimation of values for catchments where attributes were insignificant in the models estimated using individual data sets. The model has an acceptable level of explanatory power, with an adjusted rho squared of 0.198.

The implicit prices estimated using the pooled model are presented in Table 5.8. When calculating implicit prices, income and age were set at the mean value across the samples. The results from this model indicate that:

- use values are higher in the within-catchment samples;
- non-use values for vegetation are higher in coastal catchments, and lower for respondents living within a catchment;
- non-use values for fish species are higher for respondents living in a coastal catchment, but lower for respondents living in northern coastal catchments;
- non-use values for fauna species are not systematically affected by catchment characteristics (inland/coastal or north/south);
- respondents to the inland, southern and out-of-catchment samples were more likely to choose an option to improve river health;
- respondent's environmental orientiation (i.e. pro-green or pro-development) influenced their likelihood of choosing an option to improve river health; and
- willingness to pay is a function of socio-demographic characteristics (income and age).

Table 5.8   Attribute value estimates generated using the pooled model

Catchment/Sample	Vegetation	Fish species	Fauna species*	Boatable to fishable	Fishable to swimmable
Southern, coastal, within-catchment	$1.96	$6.27	$0.87	$55.55	$29.00
Southern, coastal, outside-catchment	$2.61	$6.27	$0.87	$30.10	$38.74
Northern, coastal, within-catchment	$1.96	$2.02	$0.87	$55.55	$29.00
Northern, coastal, outside-catchment	$2.61	$2.02	$0.87	$30.10	$38.74
Southern, inland, within-catchment	$1.25	$3.25	$0.87	$55.55	$29.00
Southern, inland, outside-catchment	$1.90	$3.25	$0.87	$30.10	$38.74
Northern, inland, within-catchment	$1.25	$3.25	$0.87	$55.55	$29.00
Northern, inland, outside-catchment	$1.90	$3.25	$0.87	$30.10	$38.74

Note: * The estimates of value for the fauna attribute are the same across all catchments/samples. This indicates that the pooled model did not detect any significant impact of catchment or respondent location on the value held for additional species of fauna.

The attribute values generated by the benefit transfer model can be compared with those generated for the single catchments presented in Table 5.6. For instance, the value of the vegetation attribute for the Clarence River estimated through the benefit transfer model is $1.96 compared to the direct estimate of $2.07. This represents a prediction error of only 3 per cent. Other attribute value predictions are not so accurate. Estimate errors are presented in Tables 5.9 and 5.10.

Table 5.9   Benefit transfer model estimate errors (%)ᵃ: within catchment samples

	Vegetation	Fish	Fauna	Fishable	Swimmable
Southern coastal/Bega	-19	-19	-6	+4	-69
Northern coastal/Clarence	-3	b	-115	+14	+16
Southern inland/Murrumbidgee	-16	+21	-83	+4	+30
Northern inland/Gwydir	-19	+27	-171	+8	-108

Note:
ᵃ   A positive sign on the error indicates that the benefit transfer model overestimates the direct estimate.
ᵇ   Insignificant attribute value estimate at the 5 per cent level.

Table 5.10   Benefit transfer model estimate errors (%)ᵃ: outside catchment samples

	Vegetation	Fish	Fauna	Fishable	Swimmable
Southern inland/Murrumbidgee	-14	-17	-107	-1	-57
Northern inland/Gwydir	-6	-6	b	+3	+22

Note:
ᵃ   A positive sign on the error indicates that the benefit transfer model overestimates the direct estimate.
ᵇ   Insignificant attribute value estimate at the 5 per cent level.

The inconsistency of the benefit transfer model's ability to predict the value estimates generated directly from the choice modelling data means that it should only be used where the direct data are unavailable or inappropriate. This is the case for the values held by outside-catchment people for the attributes of southern and northern coastal rivers and the fauna attribute of inland northern rivers and for the within-catchment values for the fish attribute in northern coastal rivers. In addition, the fauna attribute value estimate for the urban rivers would need to be generated from the benefit transfer model.

7   STATE-WIDE ESTIMATES OF THE VALUE OF ENVIRONMENTAL ATTRIBUTES OF NSW RIVERS

At the same time as the individual catchment surveys were being undertaken, a separate survey of NSW residents' values for the environmental attributes of rivers across the whole State was carried out. The aim of the additional survey was to identify the likely extent of framing effects in the outside-catchment value estimates when multiple rivers are being considered for environmental improvement measures. Because the State-wide sample was drawn from across the whole State, the appropriate comparison to be made is between the outside-catchment surveys and the State-wide survey.

The questionnaire used for the State-wide survey was of the same form as that used for the individual catchment surveys apart from two notable features. First, the description of the situation respondents were asked to consider was broadened from one river to all the rivers of the State. Second, the payment vehicle was modified from being a one-off levy on water rates as used in the individual catchment questionnaire to a levy over three years. This change in payment vehicle was necessary to reflect the extent of the additional budgetary pressure the scale of the proposed changes would impose on respondents. A survey protocol identical to the one used for the individual catchments was employed.

The details of the survey response rate and the socio-demographic features of the sample are set out in Tables 5.11 and 5.12 respectively.

Table 5.11 Response rate: State-wide survey

	State-wide sample
Useable responses	239
Successfully delivered	717
Response rate	33.3%

Table 5.12: Socio-demographics of sample: State-wide survey

	State-wide sample
Age (yrs)	52.9
Sex (% female)	39%
Children	81%
Education*	4.3
Income	$51,662

Note: *1 – never went to school, 6 – tertiary degree.

The data collected in the State-wide survey were analysed using a nested logit model following the same process as was used for the individual catchments' data. The model is reported in Table 5.13, and the implicit prices generated using the model in Table 5.14.

Table 5.13   State-wide model of respondents' choices

Variables	Coefficients	P-values
ASC1	0.175	0.091
RATE	-0.017	0.000
VEGET	0.025	0.000
FISHSPEC	0.046	0.001
SWIM1	0.388	0.000
FISHING	0.130	0.087
FAUNA	0.014	0.086
ASC2	-1.591	0.019
PROGRE	-0.321	0.000
PRODEV	0.751	0.000
AGE	0.002	0.726
INCOME	0.000	0.016
INCDUM	0.178	0.490
IV	0.372	0.000
Summary statistics		
Log-likelihood	-815.183	
Adjusted rho-squared	0.258	
N	950	

Table 5.14   Attribute value estimates: State-wide model

Attribute	Value per annum over three years ($)	Present value at 7 per cent discount rate ($)
Vegetation	1.51	4.23
Fish	2.74	7.70
Fauna	0.84	2.37
FISHABLE (across river)	15.69	44.05
SWIMMABLE (across river)	31.04	87.17

Comparisons between the State-wide survey results and the outside-catchment surveys for the individual catchment results are difficult to make because of a number of confounding factors. The difference in the scope of the individual catchments and the whole of the State's rivers is sufficiently large to make direct comparisons unreliable. Comparisons are also confounded because the vast majority of NSW residents live in the catchment of a river, and so in answering the State-wide survey, may have included some element of a within-catchment value as well as outside-catchment values. A further confounding difference between the individual and State-wide surveys was the difference in payment vehicle time horizon – from a one-off to three yearly payments.

Given these difficulties, direct comparisons should not be made. The usefulness of the State-wide results is two-fold. First, they provide an indication of the value held by NSW residents for environmental improvements in the State's rivers. This is important from a policy perspective in terms of the assessment of budgetary priorities for the government. Second, the value estimates provide a boundary for the use of outside-catchment value estimates when framing effects are expected.

8 AGGREGATION AND BENEFIT TRANSFER

The attribute value estimates provided by the individual catchment CM applications and the benefit transfer models can be used in the process of calculating estimates of the total value that society gains from improvements in the environmental conditions of rivers across the State. However, to generate such estimates of aggregate value, a process of extrapolation must be applied.

First, it should be noted that the attribute values estimated in this project do not require aggregation over time. They were estimated as one-off payments made by households and, as such, represent respondents' 'present values' of the stream of value they will enjoy from the attributes through time.

The 'within' catchment value estimates can be extrapolated to the catchment population with reference to the number of households, given that the value estimates were generated on a per respondent household basis. As a conservative measure, the extrapolation could be based on the response rates achieved in each of the individual surveys. For example, in the Bega survey a response rate of 41 per cent was achieved, so if the value estimates from the Bega survey were transferred, they would only be extrapolated for 41 per cent of the population.

The practice of extrapolating the value estimates to the proportion of the population that responded to the survey is consistent with Boyle and Bishop (1987) who assumed that non-respondents have a willingness to pay equal to zero. Their rationale for this assumption is that by not answering the survey, respondents have implicitly indicated their willingness to pay. The problem with this approach is that the reasons people have for not responding are varied and not necessarily indicative of a zero value for the good in question. For instance, some respondents may be unwell or away at the time of the survey. Or they may simply be too busy to take the required time to complete the questionnaire. It is difficult, therefore, to gauge what proportion of non-respondents have positive values without a comprehensive ex-post survey of non-respondents. An alternative to the Boyle and Bishop approach is to use the method suggested by Morrison (2000). In a study that involved the estimation of values derived from environmental improvements to wetlands, Morrison found that, potentially, about one-third of non-respondents have value estimates similar to respondents. For the current analysis, this would imply that the appropriate proportion of the population across which extrapolation could be made is 41 per cent plus one-third of the 59 per cent non-respondents: that is, 61 per cent. Clearly, this is a less conservative approach to the estimation of aggregate values.

Consider now an example of the aggregation process. Suppose that a river management option under consideration in a catchment on the south coast would increase the vegetation attribute by 5 per cent, ensure the reintroduction of two fish species and improve the water quality across 15 per cent of the length of the river from boatable to fishable. If the catchment had a household population of 4 000, then the appropriate calculation (based on the value estimates set out in Tables 5.6 and 5.8) is:

Within-catchment aggregate value estimate
$$= 4\,000 \times 0.61\,[5 \times 2.32 + 2 \times 7.37 + 0.15 \times 53.16]$$
$$= \$83,726$$

Given a NSW population of approximately 1.8 million households, the appropriate aggregation calculation for outside-catchment values is:

Outside-catchment aggregate value estimate
$$= 1.8 \text{ mill} \times 0.61\,[5 \times 2.61 + 2 \times 6.27 + 0.15 \times 30.10]$$
$$= \$37.68 \text{ million}$$

The total value to all the people of NSW of the improved river environment provided by the proposed management option is therefore in the order of $38 million. It is important to note that the aggregate value reported above is rounded to the nearest $10,000. This is done to avoid impressions of spurious accuracy. This process can be used for rivers that are located within the regions represented by the five rivers specifically considered in this chapter.

The relative magnitudes of the 'within' and 'outside' catchment aggregate value estimates provides a graphic illustration of the importance of the values enjoyed by people who live at a distance from the river. It also underlines the importance of ensuring that potential framing effects caused by the simultaneous assessment of multiple rivers are taken into account when estimating outside-catchment values.

The aggregation process outlined in this section is subject to a limitation involving the aggregation of individual attribute values. Theoretically, these values are estimates of what respondents are willing to pay to see them increase by one unit, given that no other changes occur simultaneously. Hence, to use them in the context of changes across a number of attributes theoretically can cause inaccuracy.

The more appropriate way to estimate the benefits of changes that involve multiple attributes is to use a more complete model of respondent choice behaviour. This involves the calculation of the benefits that people receive from the environmental condition of rivers both before and after the change in water management that is being proposed. Technically, this value is called the Compensating Surplus of the proposed change. The following equation is used to perform these calculations:

$$CS = - 1/\beta_M * (V_0 - \alpha_m V_1) \tag{5.6}$$

where β_M is the coefficient for the monetary attribute and is interpreted as the marginal utility of income, V_0 represents the utility of the initial state, and V_1 represents the utility of the subsequent state, and αm is the coefficient of the inclusive value.

Value estimates for environmental improvements defined by the mid-range levels used in the construction of the alternative options in the choice sets are provided in Table 5.15. A clear trend emerges from the comparison. In all cases, the aggregate values estimated using the attribute approach are greater than their compensating surplus counterparts. In most cases the extent of the difference is significant.

Table 5.15 Value estimates for multiple attribute changes (within-catchment samples)

Proposed Change	Aggregation Technique	Bega ($)	Clarence ($)	Georges ($)	Gwydir ($)	M'bidgee ($)
To mid range levels from the choice sets	Aggregate Attributes	189.10	122.37	125.97	152.64	145.59
	Compensating Surplus	66.82	9.71	51.60	142.83	95.60

The difference between the estimates provided by the two approaches is explained by the fundamental differences that underpin their calculation. The aggregate attribute approach ignores the overall picture that encompasses the proposed change. For instance, the impact of factors other than the specifics of a single attribute change are omitted from the calculation. In contrast, the compensating surplus calculation incorporates the impacts of the numerous factors that influence respondents' values. One factor that is incorporated in the compensating surplus calculation, but omitted from the aggregate attribute approach, is the propensity for respondents to reject change for reasons that go beyond the extent of the attribute change that is offered. For instance, respondents may simply reject change because they are inherently conservative. Such motivations are clearly important when large-scale changes are involved (such as those which are depicted in Table 5.15). However, where the proposed changes are marginal, such motives are likely to be irrelevant. The danger of using the compensating surplus measure in such cases is to grossly underestimate the value of the proposed change. Similarly, the danger of using the aggregate attribute approach for more substantial changes (as in Table 5.15) is one of overestimation. It is therefore recommended that:

• for proposed changes which involve multiple attributes varying by less than 25 per cent, the aggregate attribute value should be used; and,
• for multiple attribute changes where larger variation is expected, the compensating surplus value should be used.

Because most river improvement projects will involve only marginal changes (less than 25 per cent increases in attributes), the aggregate attribute approach is likely to be most frequently employed.

9   SUMMARY AND IMPLICATIONS

In this chapter, the methodology used for estimating implicit prices for river health in five catchments across NSW has been described. Implicit prices were estimated using choice modelling for four environment attributes: recreational uses, fish species, healthy vegetation and wetlands, and waterbirds and other fauna. These attributes encompass both use and non-use values. Each of these values was found to exist for the majority of catchments. There was also evidence of theoretical validity, as shown by the existence of significant socio-demographic variables such as income and environmental attitude. This is supportive of the use of choice modelling for the purpose of valuing improved river health.

The results from a pooled model were also presented. This represents one of the first attempts of which we are aware to estimate a model where value estimates are a function of (1) within-catchment site characteristics, (2) catchment characteristics and (3) the location of respondents. The results of the model indicate that existence values tend to vary systematically across catchments, but that values associated with recreation are relatively constant. In addition, whether a respondent is located within or outside of a catchment was found to systematically affect value estimates. We recommend the further use of pooled models in large-scale benefit transfer exercises where it is not possible to sample all relevant sites and populations within a research design.

The results from a choice modelling application where values are estimated for improving the health of all rivers across the State were also presented. The results from this application demonstrated that respondents are generally willing to pay more for the health of additional rivers to be improved, but not substantially more. To some extent this may be because of budget constraints. Nonetheless, it does demonstrate the importance of ensuring that framing effects that are likely to occur when more than one river is being assessed are taken into account when estimating out-of-catchment values.

Finally, issues associated with aggregation have been discussed. One of the goals of discussing aggregation was to demonstrate how aggregation is done in the context of benefit transfer. However, an effort has also been made to show how assumptions made at the aggregation stage have a substantial impact on the value estimates that are used in cost-benefit analyses. In particular, aggregate estimates can be sensitive to the proportion of the population for which value estimates are extrapolated, and whether implicit prices are summed, or compensating surplus estimates are generated.

NOTES

1. An earlier version of this paper was presented at the Second World Congress of Environmental and Resource Economists, Monterey, June 2002.
2. The self-selection bias evident in the sample is problematic only if the values estimated from the sample are extrapolated beyond the proportion of the population that responded to the questionnaire (see Morrison 2000).

REFERENCES

Bennett, J. (1999), 'A threshold value analysis of proposed forestry reserves', *Australian Forestry*, **61** (4), 1–8.

Bennett, J. and R. Blamey (2001), *The Choice Modelling Approach to Non-Market Valuation*, Cheltenham UK and Northampton, MA, USA: Edward Elgar.

Bennett, J., M. Morrison and R. Harvey (2000), 'A River Somewhere – Valuing the Environmental Attributes of Rivers', paper presented at the ISEE 2000 Conference, ANU Canberra , 5–8 July.

Blamey, R., J. Bennett, J. Louviere, M. Morrison and J. Rolfe (2002), 'Attribute causality in environmental choice modelling', *Environmental and Resource Economics*, **23**, 167–86.

Boyle, Kevin J. and Richard C. Bishop (1987), 'Valuing Wildlife in Benefit Cost Analyses: A Case Study Involving Endangered Species', *Water Resource Research*, **23** (5), 943–950.

Brookshire, D.S. and H.R. Neill (1992), 'Benefit transfers: conceptual and empirical issues, *Water Resources Research*, **28** (3), 651–55.

Desvousges, W.H., M.C. Naughton and G.R. Parsons (1992), 'Benefit transfer: conceptual problems in estimating water quality benefits using existing studies', *Water Resources Research*, **28** (3), 675–83.

Hahn, G.J. and S.S. Shapiro (1966), *A Catalogue and Computer Program for the Design and Analysis of Symmetric and Asymmetric Fractional Factorial Experiments*. Report No 66-0-165, New York: General Electric Research and Development Centre.

Hausman, J. and D. McFadden (1984), 'Specification tests for the multinomial logit model, *Econometrica*, **52**, 1219–40.

Hausman, J.A. and P. Ruud (1987), 'Specifying and testing econometric models for rank-ordered data', *Journal of Econometrics*, **34**, 83–104.

Kling, C.L. and C.J. Thomson (1996), 'The implications of model specification for welfare estimation in nested logit models', *American Journal of Agricultural Economics,* **78**, 103–14.

Loomis, J.B. (1992), 'The evolution of a more rigorous approach to benefit transfer: benefit function transfer', *Water Resources Research*, **28** (3), 701–5.

Louviere, J.J., D.A. Hensher and J.D. Swait (2000), *Stated Choice Methods – Analysis and Application,* Cambridge: Cambridge University Press.

Mitchell, R.C. and R.T. Carson (1989), *Using Surveys to Value Public Goods: The Contingent Valuation Method*, Washington DC: Resources for the Future.

Morrison, M. (2000), 'Aggregation biases in stated preference studies', *Australian Economic Papers*, **39** (2), 215–30.

Morrison, M.D. and J.W. Bennett (2004), 'Valuing New South Wales rivers for use in benefit transfer', *Australian Journal of Agricultural and Resource Economics*, **48** (4), 591–611.

Morrison, M.D., R.K. Blamey and J.W. Bennett (2000), 'Minimising payment vehicle bias in contingent valuation studies', *Environmental and Resource Economics*, **16** (4), 407–22.

Morrison, M.D., J.W. Bennett, R.K. Blamey and J.J. Louviere (2002), 'Choice modelling and tests of benefit transfer', *American Journal of Agricultural Economics*, **84** (1), 161–70.

Pate, J. and J. Loomis (1997), 'The effect of distance on willingness to pay values: a case study of wetlands and salmon in California', *Ecological Economics*, **20** (3), 199–207.

Pearmain, D., J. Swanson, E. Kroes and M. Bradley (1991), *Stated Preference Techniques: A Guide to Practice*, Surrey and Netherlands: Steer Davies Gleave and Hague Consulting Group.

Stevens, T.H., T.A. Moore and R.J. Glass (1994), 'Interpretation and temporal stability of CV bids for wildlife experience: a panel study', *Land Economics*, **70** (3), 355–63.

Sutherland, R.J. and R. Walsh (1985), 'Effect of distance on the preservation value of water quality', *Land Economics*, **61**, 281–91.

6. Testing for Benefit Transfer Over Water Quality Benefits

Nick Hanley, Robert E. Wright and Begona Alvarez-Farizo

1   INTRODUCTION

The Water Framework Directive (2000/60) is a major regulatory reform of water resource management within the European Union, which will bring about major changes in the regulation and management of Europe's water resources. Major changes include:

- a requirement for the preparation of integrated catchment management plans, with remits extending over point and non-point pollution, water abstraction and land use;
- the introduction of an EU-wide target of 'good ecological status' for all surface water and groundwater, except where exemptions for 'heavily-modified' water bodies are granted;
- the introduction of full social cost pricing for water use; and
- the incorporation of estimates of economic costs and benefits in catchment management plans.

How exactly regulators will interpret 'good ecological status' is at present not finalised. However, it is clear that it represents a wider set of parameters than the chemical and biological measures of water quality that have previously dominated EU water quality regulation, such as Biological Oxygen Demand or ammonia (NH_3) levels. In this chapter, we use three indicators of ecological status which ordinary people see as important, but which are also consistent with regulators' expectations

Some of the material presented in this chapter has been reprinted from the *Journal of Environmental Management*, 78(2), Nick Hanley, Robert E. Wright and Begona Alvarez-Faruzo, "Estimating the economic value of improvements in river ecology using choice experiments: An application to the water framework directive", pp. 183 – 193, Copyright (2006), with permission from Elsevier.

about the scientific interpretation of this concept. We take ecological status to be determined by three broad factors: healthy wildlife and plant populations; absence of litter/debris in the river; and river banks in good condition with only natural levels of erosion. Recent assessments for UK waterbodies indicate that a significant fraction of rivers, lochs (lakes), estuaries and coastal waters will require improvements if they are to meet 'good ecological status' (WRc 1999; Scottish Executive 2002).

One main focus in this chapter is therefore on the values people place on improvements in these three indicators, and thus on the non-market economic benefits of moves towards good ecological status. Whilst benefit estimates do exist for implementation of the Water Framework Directive (WFD), these are at present highly incomplete (WRc 1999; Scottish Executive 2002). However, we are also interested in the practicalities of environmental management using environmental valuation. Valuation exercises are expensive and time-consuming, and regulators are very unlikely to have the time or money to commission original valuation studies for every catchment. Benefit transfer, the process of taking estimates from one context and adjusting and then applying them to another, is therefore likely to be important. Accordingly, we conduct a benefit transfer test across two similar rivers, to see what errors are likely to be experienced if benefits transfer procedures are used as part of implementing the WFD.

In what follows, Section 2 briefly describes the choice experiment method of environmental valuation and outlines some current issues in benefit transfer. Section 3 describes the case study rivers and survey design. Section 4 presents results, whilst Section 5 concludes.

2   METHODOLOGICAL APPROACH

2.1   Choice Experiments

The methodology we use to estimate the value of improvements in river ecology is choice experiments. Choice experiments (CE) are becoming a popular means of environmental valuation (Hanley, Mourato and Wright 2001; Bennett and Blamey 2001). CE are one example of the stated preference approach to environmental valuation, since they involve eliciting responses from individuals in constructed, hypothetical markets, rather than the study of actual behaviour. The CE technique is based on random utility theory and the characteristics theory of value: environmental goods are valued in terms of their attributes by applying probabilistic models to choices between different bundles of attributes.

By making one of these attributes a price or cost term, marginal utility estimates can be converted into willingness-to-pay (WTP) estimates for changes in attribute levels, and welfare estimates obtained for combinations of attribute changes.

2.2 Previous Studies of River Ecology Changes Using Choice Experiments

Several authors have previously used CE to estimate the value of improvements in river quality. Adamowicz, Louviere and Williams (1994) study people involved in water-based recreation in Alberta. They recruited a sample of 1 232 members of the general public, from which a 45 per cent response rate was achieved. The attributes used were landscape terrain, fish size, catch rate, water quality, facilities (e.g. campsite), distance from home and fish species present. The authors found significant effects on utility from changes in fish size, catch rate, water quality and distance from home.

Burton, Marsh and Patterson (2000) studied public preferences for catchment management plans in the Moore Catchment, Australia. This area is subject to problems of salinity, eutrophication and flooding, which are all linked to farming activities. Two populations were surveyed, one in the city of Perth and one in rural towns. The attributes used were area of farmland affected by salinity, area of farmland planted with trees, ecological impacts on off-farm wetlands, risk of major flood, change in farm income, and annual contribution to management plan. The main findings were that the importance people placed on the cost attribute depended on their attitudes to environmental responsibility. High adverse impacts on wetlands, and losses (but not gains) in farm incomes also had significant impacts on utility.

Heberling, Fisher and Shortle (2000) study the benefits of reducing pollution from acid mine drainage in western and central Pennsylvania. Focus groups helped identify the attributes used in the questionnaire. These were water quality, miles restored, travel time from home to site, easy access points, and household costs. Water quality was measured according to what uses could be made of the stream, and took the levels 'drinkable', 'fishable' and 'swimmable'. The water quality variables were statistically significant determinants of choice in the majority of models, with costs always being significant.

A closely-related technique to CE is contingent ranking. Georgiou et al. (2000) used contingent ranking to estimate the benefits of water quality improvements in the River Tame in Birmingham. Three levels of improvement were included, namely small, medium and large. In the ranking exercise, people were asked to rank three combinations of four attributes. These were:

- type of fishing (trout/salmon and good game; some game fish species return; a few game fish species return; fish stocks extinct);
- plants and wildlife (otters survive; increase in number and types of insects and greater numbers of birds; more plants and waterfowl; very limited wildlife);
- boating and swimming (both, boating only, swimming only, neither); and
- cost (extra council taxes: £2.50/month, £1.25/month, £0.42/month, zero).

Responses were used to estimate WTP for marginal reductions in Biological Oxygen Demand and total ammonia.

Studies using other stated preference techniques to estimate values of ecological changes in river quality may also be found in the literature, notably contingent valuation studies of improvements in low-flow conditions (Hanley, Schlapfer and Spurgeon, 2003; Garrod and Willis, 1996). However, we do not review them here.

A conclusion from this brief review of existing literature is that no study exists which uses CE (or contingent ranking) to estimate the value of improvements in the concept of ecological status as embodied within the Water Framework Directive. Our study is a first step in this policy-relevant direction. Before detailing our study design, however, it is important to review another aspect of environmental valuation relevant to the Directive: namely benefit transfer.

2.3   Benefit Transfer

Valuation studies are extensive and time-consuming. For this reason, the policy community has become increasingly interested in benefit transfer techniques (Bateman et al. 2002). Benefit transfer (BT) is a method for taking value estimates from original studies, and adjusting them for use in some new context. The two main approaches to BT are:

- The transfer of adjusted mean values. Mean WTP estimates taken from the original study or studies are adjusted to account for differences in the environmental characteristics of the new site context, and/or for differences in the socio-economic characteristics of the affected population at the new site.
- The transfer of benefit functions. Benefit functions are regression equations which explain variations in WTP and/or preferences across individuals according to variations in socio-economic factors and, in some cases, environmental characteristics. A benefit function can be used to produce estimates of WTP.

In both cases, meta analysis (that is, the quantitative analysis of a collection of past studies) can be used to inform the BT process.

Much academic work has taken place in the past ten years, testing alternative BT methods, and assessing their accuracy. The academic jury is still 'out' on the validity of BT. Studies by Bergland et al. (1995) and by Barton (2001) largely reject the validity of benefit transfer, both in terms of the transfer of adjusted mean values and the transfer of benefit functions. Brouwer (2000) surveys seven recent benefit transfer studies and finds that the average transfer error is around 20–40 per cent for means and as high as 225 per cent for benefit function transfers, whilst Ready et al. (2001) find a transfer error of around 40 per cent in a multi-country study on the health benefits of reduced air pollution. Shrestha and Loomis (2001) find an average transfer error of 28 per cent in a meta analysis model of 131 US recreation studies. As Barton points out, though, even fairly small transfer errors (11–26 per cent in his case) can be rejected using the statistical tests favoured by economists. However, this has not stopped the development of large BT software packages, such as the EVRI package, developed by Environment Canada, for use in policy analysis.

One on-going debate is whether more complex BT approaches necessarily do better than simple ones. Barton (2001) finds a simple adjusted means transfer gets closer to original site values than the transfer of benefit functions. The opposite finding, however, is reported in Desvouges et al. (1998). Finding acceptable benefit transfer methods is essential to the wider use of environmental valuation in policy. However, the standards of accuracy required in academic work may exceed those viewed as tolerable by policy-makers, especially in prioritising or filtering alternative investments in water quality.

3   STUDY DESIGN

3.1   Physical Context

We located our choice experiment in the context of improvements to the ecology of the River Wear, in County Durham, England and the River Clyde, in Central Scotland. These were chosen as broadly representative of the kind of waterbodies in the UK where moderate improvements in water quality are likely to be needed in order to meet 'good ecological status'. The River Wear catchment extends from Burnhope Moor in the Pennines to the North Sea. Population is concentrated in the eastern half of the area, which includes Durham and Sunderland. Throughout much of the 20th century the lower sections of the river were heavily polluted by industry and mining, but have now recovered and support a migratory fishery. The focus for this study is that part of the River Wear which flows through the city of Durham, and which is graded as C Grade on the Environment Agency's General Quality Assessment scheme (interpreted as 'fair' quality). Existing problems include litter, algal growth and acidity problems due to mine drainage. Problems also exist with loss of bankside vegetation, increased erosion and a decline in habitat and associated fish and wildlife populations. Within the Wear are many structures built in and across river channels. These have important impacts on the way the river functions, altering flows and gravel movements and hindering migration of fish upstream. In terms of recreational uses, the River Wear is important as a coarse and game fishery and also as a centre for other water-based recreation (formal and informal). The river also plays an important role in recreation and tourism.

The River Clyde is approximately 121 km long. During its journey from its source in the Beattock Hills to its tidal estuarine limits in Glasgow, its quality varies greatly. Discussion with regulators (the Scottish Environmental Protection Agency) led to the selection of the Clyde from Lanark to Cambuslang Bridge as the area for study. This mainly urbanised stretch has recreational and tourist attractions, and encompasses areas of great beauty such as the Falls of Clyde, but also has some of the most problematic stretches of the Clyde in terms of water quality. Most of this section was graded 'B' using the Scottish river classification system, which is equivalent to the 'C' grade for the Wear under the General Quality Assessment classification system (i.e. fair quality, but in need of improvement to reach 'good ecological status').

3.2   Steps in Choice Experiment Design

Focus groups were drawn from local residents living around the two rivers in both case study areas in order to (a) gauge local attitudes to the rivers and to its problems (b) investigate current uses of the two rivers and (c) identify the attributes by which the river could best be characterised. We also gauged reaction to the idea of the need to pay for improvements in river ecology. As a result of group discussion, backed up by discussion with officers from both the Environment Agency (the regulator in England) and the Scottish Environmental Protection Agency, three river quality attributes were chosen for the CE. These were in-stream ecology, aesthetics/appearance, and bankside conditions, and are shown in detail in Table 6.1. Each attribute was set at one of two levels. The 'fair' level was described in such a way as to be consistent with current conditions on the Rivers Wear and Clyde. The 'good' level was consistent with regulators' expectations as to what will likely constitute good ecological quality status under the Water Framework Directive.

Table 6.1   Environmental attributes and levels used in the choice experiment

	'Good' Level	**'Fair' Level**
Ecology	• Salmon, trout and coarse fish (e.g. pike) • A wide range of water plants, insects and birds	• Only coarse fish (e.g. pike) • A poor range of water plants, insects and birds
Aesthetics / Appearance	• No sewage or litter	• Some sewage or litter
River Banks	• Banks with plenty of trees and plants • Only natural erosion	• Banks with few trees and plants • Evidence of accelerated erosion

A cost or price attribute was established as higher water rates payments by households to the local sewerage operator, Northumbria Water, for the River Wear sample and to the local authority (Lanarkshire Council) for the River Clyde sample.[1] Focus groups generally accepted the idea that improvements had to be paid for, and water rates were viewed as a realistic payment mechanism. The price vector used in the design was (£2, £5, £11, £15, £240), and was chosen based on previous contingent valuation studies of river improvements in the UK.

Attributes and levels were then assigned into choice sets using a fractional factorial design. Due to the simple nature of the design, blocking was not necessary. Each respondent answered eight choice questions. Each question consisted of a three-way choice: option A and option B, which gave an improvement in at least one attribute for a positive cost, and the zero-cost, zero-improvement status quo. Each choice card showed the attribute levels pictorially; a preceding section of the questionnaire explained the importance of each attribute to overall ecological quality.[2] Options A and B can be thought of as representing the outcomes of alternative catchment management plans for each river, with their associated costs.

Sampling was undertaken with a randomised quota-sampling approach, using in-house surveys by trained market research personnel in the autumn of 2001. We collected 210 responses for each river.

4   RESULTS

4.1   Logit Models and WTP Estimates for the Rivers Clyde and Wear

Responses from choice experiments are analysed using logit or probit models. We make use of a simple multinomial logit approach in this chapter. According to this framework, the indirect utility function for each respondent i (Ui) can be decomposed into two parts: a deterministic element (V), which is typically specified as a linear index of the attributes (X) of the j different alternatives in the choice set, and a stochastic element (e), which represents unobservable influences on individual choice:

$$U_{ij} = V_{ij}(X_{ij}) + e_{ij} \tag{6.1}$$

The probability that any particular respondent prefers option g in the choice set to any alternative option h, can be expressed as the probability that the utility associated with option g exceeds that associated with all other options:

$$P[(U_{ig} > U_{ih}) \, \forall \, h \neq g] = P[(V_{ig} - V_{ih}) > (e_{ih} - e_{ig})] \tag{6.2}$$

In order to derive an explicit expression for this probability, it is necessary to know the distribution of the error terms (e_{ij}). A typical assumption is that they are independently and identically distributed with an extreme-value (Weibull) distribution:

$$P(e_{ij} \leq t) = F(t) = \exp(-\exp(-t)) \tag{6.3}$$

The above distribution of the error term implies that the probability of any particular alternative g being chosen as the most preferred can be expressed in terms of the logistic distribution (McFadden, 1974) stated in equation (6.4). This specification is known as the conditional or multinomial logit model:

$$P(U_{ig} > U_{ih}, \forall h \neq g) = \frac{\exp(\mu V_{ig})}{\sum_{j} \exp(\mu V_{ij})} \tag{6.4}$$

where μ is a scale parameter, inversely proportional to the standard deviation of the error distribution. This model can be estimated by conventional maximum likelihood procedures using software such as LIMDEP.

Estimating (6.4) for both the River Wear and River Clyde samples, we obtain the results shown in Table 6.2. Columns (2) and (3) show the simplest version of these models, where only river quality attributes and Alternative-Specific Constants are used as regressors. These constants can be thought of as representing all other determinants of utility for each option not captured by the attributes. As may be seen, the three environmental quality attributes are strongly significant determinants of choices for both rivers. People can be seen to prefer the 'improved' level of attribute, since in all cases the coefficient has a positive sign. For the River Wear, the price of improvements is also strongly significant, and negative, as one would expect: people prefer lower-cost environmental improvements, other things being equal. For the Clyde, price is again negatively signed, but is not statistically significant. This is a little problematic since WTP measures are inferred from this price coefficient. We thus re-ran the model including a price-income interaction term. This is not significant for the Wear, but is significant for the Clyde, and price is now also significant (see columns 4 and 5 of Table 6.2).

Table 6.2 Multi-nomial logit model results

Attribute	Attribute only models		Models including an income-price interaction	
	R. Wear	R. Clyde	R. Wear	R. Clyde
River ecology	0.302	0.256	0.302	0.253
	[5.8]	[5.1]	[5.8]	[5.1]
Aesthetics	0.302	0.178	0.302	0.179
	[5.2]	[3.5]	[5.2]	[3.5]
Bankside condition	0.314	0.288	0.314	0.287
	[8.1]	[7.7]	[8.1]	[7.6]
Price	-0.0493	-0.0101	-0.0442	-0.0316
	[6.7]	[1.5]	[4.6]	[3.8]
Price * Income	-	-	-0.204×10^{-6}	0.156×10^{-5}
			[0.8]	[4.4]
ASCa	1.082	0.401	1.082	0.409
	[10.7]	[4.5]	[10.7]	[4.5]
ASCb	0.862	0.173	0.862	0.177
	[7.4]	[1.6]	[7.4]	[1.6]
N	177	197	177	197

Note: ASCa and ASCb are alternative specific constants associated with choice A and choice B respectively (the omitted case is choosing neither). Sample sizes are full sample (210) minus observations with missing income. Values in square brackets are t-statistics.

WTP estimates for a marginal change in any attribute can be obtained by dividing the estimated coefficient on that attribute by the coefficient on price, having adjusted for how the data is coded (here, using effect coding). For example, for a change in river ecology from 'fair' to 'good' for the River Wear data, WTP is equal to (-2 (0.302/0.0493)). Table 6.2 gives results for both samples, using calculations which allow for the effect coding used to set the data up prior to estimation. Since the price coefficient is statistically insignificant in model 3 for the Clyde (Table 6.2), we computed the implicit prices shown for the Clyde in Table 6.3 using the price-income interaction version of the model (model 5), setting income equal to the sample mean of £13,868 per household.

Table 6.3   WTP estimates for improvements in water quality in each river, £ per household

	River Wear	River Clyde [a,b]
River ecology: from fair to good	12.16	50.68
	(8.34 to 16.18)	
Aesthetics: from fair to good	12.24	35.92
	(7.81 to 16.67)	
Banksides: from fair to good	12.74	57.54
	(8.82 to 16.66)	

Notes:
   [a] Using the price-income interaction version of the model.
   [b] 95% confidence intervals not given for Clyde sample since parameter estimate is not significant at 95%, so confidence intervals span zero. Variances for implicit prices for R. Wear sample computed using the Delta method.

As may be seen, values are much higher for the River Clyde sample than for the River Wear sample. This is despite the fact that mean household income is lower in the Clyde sample than in the Wear sample. Another feature of the results is that, for the River Wear, each attribute is valued very similarly in terms of implied WTP for an improvement. This suggests either that people view these river attributes as being close substitutes for each other in terms of how they value the Wear, or that they are equally good indicators of some overall, underlying idea of 'river quality'. Note that, for the Clyde, WTP for improvements in aesthetics (fewer shopping trolleys in the river, less visible sewage pollution) is much lower than WTP for improvements in river ecology or bankside condition.

4.2   Benefit Transfer Tests

Two benefit transfer tests are to compare benefit functions, and to compare (adjusted) mean WTP values. In CE the former is equivalent to testing for differences in parameters. This can be achieved by testing the null hypothesis:

$H_0 : \beta(A) = \beta(B)$

Or more formally

$H_0 : \beta(A) - \beta(B) = 0$

where $\beta(A)$ and $\beta(B)$ are the vectors of parameter estimates for sample A and sample B respectively. The appropriate test statistic in a choice experiment framework is a likelihood ratio test analogous to the so-called 'Chow test for structural breaks' (see Chow, 1960): $\chi^2 (test) = -2 [L(A+B) - L(A) + L(B)]$, where $L(A+B)$ is the likelihood value for the model estimated across both samples, and $L(A)$ and $L(B)$ are the likelihood values for models estimated separately for samples A and B, respectively. This test statistic is distributed χ^2 with the degrees of freedom equal to the number of parameters in the model (including constants). We construct this test for the Wear and Clyde samples, and find that H_0 is strongly rejected (calculated $\chi2 = 47.1$). We may therefore conclude that the choice models – which are representative of underlying indirect utility functions – are significantly different from each other for the two samples. This implies that preferences differ between the two samples for the same improvements on two different rivers.

The above test statistics are concerned with the parameters of the model as a group. One can also test for differences in individual parameter values:

$H_0 : \beta j(A) = \beta j(B)$

Or more formally

$H_0 : \beta j(A) - \beta j(B) = 0$

where 'j' refers to some individual parameter (e.g. price). This hypothesis can be tested using the standard 'Wald test for linear restrictions' (see Greene, 1993, Chapter 7). Although this test does not use all information available in the samples, it does have considerable intuitive appeal since it is testing whether the confidence interval of the point estimate of sample A overlaps the point estimate of sample B (and vice versa). Based on this test, which is distributed F, we can also reject the hypothesis that the parameter estimates for each of the attributes (i.e. river ecology, aesthetics and banksides) are the same between the two samples (test statistics not reported). It is more important to note that this test can also be used to test for differences in implicit prices (WTP) across the two samples, since implicit prices are simply a linear combination of two parameters: WTP = $\beta j(1/\beta p)$. The results of this testing are given in Table 6.4. The Wald tests suggest that we can also comprehensively reject the null hypothesis that WTP values are equivalent across the two samples: people living around the River Clyde value identical improvements in river ecology, aesthetics and banksides very differently from people living around the River Wear.

Table 6.4   Comparison of WTP estimates for the two samples

	Restriction WTP(W)=WTP(C)	Wald statistic	Decision on restriction
River ecology	£12.26=£50.68	37.7	reject
Aesthetics	£12.24=£35.92	29.3	reject
Banksides	£12.74=£57.54	40.5	reject

Note: W = WTP calculated for River Wear, C = WTP for the River Clyde.

Finally, we can examine the size of error that would occur in using the model for one site to predict WTP values for the other site, relative to observed values at this latter site. To illustrate, we use the model estimated for the Wear sample to predict WTP values for each attribute for the Clyde sample. Results are given in Table 6.5. As can be seen, we would significantly underestimate the values that people place on water quality improvements on the River Clyde if we used the model of preferences obtained for the River Wear to predict them (a similar conclusion can be reached if the opposite proposition is tested).

Table 6.5   Using the River Wear sample model to predict WTP values for the River Clyde sample

	R. Clyde values calculated using R. Wear logit model	Actual values from R.Clyde sample	Wald statistic for test in difference, predicted versus actual	Accept/reject null hypothesis of equality
River ecology	12.87	50.68	33.1	reject
Aesthetics	12.84	35.92	26.4	reject
Banksides	13.37	57.54	34.5	reject

5   CONCLUSIONS

In this chapter, we were interested in seeing (a) what values people place on improvements to watercourses such as are envisaged under the Water Framework Directive and (b) whether choice experiments provide encouraging evidence for benefits transfer in this context. With regard to the former point, three attributes were selected to represent the concept of 'good ecological status' under the Directive: river ecology, which represents aquatic life including fish, plants and invertebrates; aesthetics, which represent the amount of litter in the river; and the quality of banksides both in terms of vegetation and in terms of erosion. For the River Wear, we found that people place insignificantly different values on these three aspects of the quality of rivers. One possible interpretation of this is that all three are seen as equally valid indicators of a 'healthy river', which is all that people really care about. For the River Clyde, larger differences were found, with aesthetic improvements being valued appreciably lower than either river ecology or bankside conditions. This result shows a clear difference in preferences between the two samples.

The second purpose of this chapter was to carry out tests of benefit transfer. This was thought to be important, since the Water Framework Directive will impose a considerable burden on regulators to compare the costs and benefits of river basin management plans. Finding acceptably accurate means of benefit transfer will be a vital component of this task. We used an identical survey instrument to value identical improvements on two rivers which are both classified as being of 'fair' quality currently. However, all three benefit transfer tests were rejected: preferences and values differ significantly across the two samples. This is a similar finding to that reached by Morrison, Bennett and Blamey (2002), who largely reject transferability of values and preferences in a choice experiment study of wetlands conservation in Australia. We found that people living near the Clyde valued improvements to their local river more highly than people in Durham valued identical improvements on their local river, despite the fact that the former sample had lower incomes than the latter. This is surprising to the extent that the demand for environmental quality is typically assumed to increase with higher incomes; however, people living near the Clyde appear willing to exchange a larger fraction of their income for local environmental improvements than people living near the Wear.

Finally, work clearly needs to progress on finding acceptable methods of benefit transfer for water quality improvements under the Water Framework Directive, since it is hard to see how it can be fully implemented in Europe without such a benefit transfer system being set up. Choice experiments do seem promising in this regard, since they can incorporate variations in both environmental quality and socio-economic characteristics across sites, which would seem *a priori* to be the biggest drivers of differences in value. The present study shows that simple choice experiments may not be capable of delivering such benefit transfers within conventional limits of statistical significance. However, it may well be that policy-makers will view much lower levels of accuracy as acceptable in practice. The question is: how close is close enough?

ACKNOWLEDGEMENTS

This paper is based on data collected during a study for the UK Department of the Environment, Food and Rural Affairs. We thank Maggie Dewar for research assistance.

NOTES

1. Sewage treatment is privatised in England but remains a public service in Scotland.
2. For a copy of the questionnaire, please contact the corresponding author.

REFERENCES

Adamowicz, W., J. Louviere and M. Williams (1994), 'Combining stated and revealed preference methods for valuing environmental amenities', *Journal of Environmental Economics and Management*, **26**, 271-92.
Barton, D. (2001), 'The Transferability of Benefits Transfer', PhD thesis, Aas: Agricultural University of Norway.
Bateman, I., R. Carson, B. Day, M. Hanemann, N. Hanley, T. Hett, M. Jones-Lee, G. Loomes, S. Mourato, E. Ozdemiroglu, D.W. Pearce, R. Sugden and J. Swanson (2002), *Economic Valuation with Stated Preference Techniques: A Manual*, Cheltenham, UK and Northampton, MA, USA: Edward Elgar.
Bennett, J. and R. Blamey (2001), *The Choice Modelling Approach to Non-Market Valuation*, Cheltenham, UK and Northampton, MA, USA: Edward Elgar.
Bergland, O., K. Magnussen and S. Navrud (1995), *Benefit Transfer: Testing for Accuracy and Reliability*, Discussion Paper #D-03/1995, Department of Economics and Social Sciences, Aas: The Agricultural University of Norway.
Brouwer, R. (2000), 'Environmental value transfer: state of the art and future prospects', *Ecological Economics*, **32** (1), 137-52.
Burton, M., S. Marsh and J. Patterson (2000), 'Community Attitudes Towards Water Management in the Moore Catchment', Paper presented at the Agricultural Economics Society Conference, Manchester.
Chow, G. (1960), 'Tests of equality between sets of coefficients in two linear regressions', *Econometrica*, **28**, 591–605.

Desvouges, W., F. Johnson and H. Banzhaf (1998), *Environmental Policy Analysis with Limited Information*, Cheltenham, UK and Northampton, MA, USA: Edward Elgar.

Garrod, G. and K. Willis (1996), 'Estimating the benefits of environmental enhancement: a case study of the River Darrent', *Journal of Environmental Planning and Management*, **39** (2), 189–203.

Georgiou, S., I. Bateman, M. Cole and D. Hadley (2000), *Contingent Ranking and Valuation of Water Quality Improvements*, CSERGE discussion paper 2000-18, University of East Anglia.

Greene, W. (1993), *Econometric Analysis*, New York: Macmillan.

Hanley, N., S. Mourato and R. Wright (2001), 'Choice modelling approaches: a superior alternative for environmental valuation?', *Journal of Economic Surveys*, **15** (3), 435–462.

Hanley, N., F. Schlapfer and J. Spurgeon (2003), 'Aggregating the benefits of environmental improvements: distance-decay functions for use and non-use values', *Journal of Environmental Management*, **68**, 297–304.

Heberling, M., A. Fisher and J. Shortle (2000), 'How the Number of Choice Sets Affects Responses in Stated Choice Surveys', Mimeo, Cincinnati: US EPA.

McFadden, D. (1974), 'Conditional Logit Analysis of Qualitative Choice Behaviour', in P. Zarembka (ed.), *Frontiers in Econometrics*, Academic Press: New York.

Morrison, M., J. Bennett and R. Blamey (2002), 'Choice modelling and tests of benefits transfer', *American Journal of Agricultural Economics*, **84** (1), 161–70.

Ready, R., S. Navrud, B. Day, R. Doubourg, F. Machado, S. Mourato, F. Spanninks and M. Rodriquez (2001), 'Benefits Transfer: Are Values Consistent Across Countries?', mimeo, Dept. of Agricultural Economics, Penn State University.

Scottish Executive (2002), *Costs and Benefits of Implementation of the EU Water Framework Directive (2000/60) in Scotland*, Report to the Scottish Executive, Edinburgh by WRc.

Shrestha, R. and J. Loomis (2001), 'Testing a meta analysis model for benefit transfer in international outdoor recreation', *Ecological Economics*, **39** (1), 67–84.

WRc (1999) *Potential Costs and Benefits of Implementing the Proposed Water Resources Framework Directive*, Final report to DETR, London.

7. Testing Benefit Transfer with Water Resources in Central Queensland, Australia

John Rolfe, Adam Loch and Jeff Bennett

1   INTRODUCTION

Several techniques are available for estimating the value of environmental and social impacts where the information is not directly available from market information. These include related market techniques, such as the travel cost and hedonic pricing methods, and stated preference techniques such as the contingent valuation method (CVM) and choice modelling (CM). There are often demands for results of non-market valuation experiments to be transferred from an original study to another application, but there is some uncertainty about how accurate that benefit transfer process might be (Loomis 1992). Questions about benefit transfer (BT) relate particularly to the stated preference valuation techniques, where there are concerns that any inaccuracies or biases in the values may become exacerbated in the transfer process (Brookshire and Neill 1992).

For BT to be accepted, the two main requirements are that the values estimated in the first study are free of major biases, and that the benefit transfer process does not generate substantially more bias. Much of the development work for techniques such as the CVM has concentrated on the first issue. The difficulty for the CVM is that because it does not specifically relate respondent choices to the characteristics of the site in question, it is difficult to identify how well values can be transferred to other locations where the circumstances may be slightly different. CM has more advantages than CVM in analysing a benefit transfer process because the probability of choice is related more specifically to the attributes of the site and the population in question.

In a BT process, the key factors that are expected to influence values are the extent to which both the original and target sites are similar, and the extent to which a similar population is involved. Values may also depend on whether the framing of the issues involved is similar across the source and target case studies. Examples of framing issues include quantity and scale effects. A quantity effect can occur when the quantity of an environmental or social impact varies between source and target settings, while a scale effect can occur when the context in which an item is presented changes. Their combined influence can be termed a scope effect.

Scope effects may influence how respondents view and frame the problem. This may be because, when environmental issues are presented at different levels of scope, respondents automatically consider different substitutes or quantities of natural resource levels for framing purposes, leading to a variation in the *a priori* expected results. For example, analysts may be interested in determining what value respondents would place upon a kilometre of healthy waterway. The trade-offs could be presented using different scales:

- a single river;
- a catchment with several rivers;
- all rivers/catchments in a state; and
- all rivers/catchments in a country.

The trade-off could also be presented using different quantities, for example:

- 1 kilometre;
- 10 kilometres;
- 100 kilometres; and
- 1 000 kilometres.

Where the frame is couched in terms of change from a larger scale perspective (i.e. more rivers) it is likely that respondents will consider a higher range of substitute choices and accordingly report a lower marginal value for each additional unit of healthy waterways. Similarly, quantity effects may influence the marginal values that respondents report. Where a higher quantity of waterways is considered (i.e. more kilometres) the respondent may again consider the trade-off between a higher number of substitutes and accordingly report a lower value for protecting an additional kilometre of healthy waterways. Conversely, where a respondent's perspective is focused upon a smaller resource base (whether scale or quantity) they may adopt a regional attitude to loss and report a higher marginal value for healthy waterways saved.

In this chapter, the potential for benefit transfer is explored in relation to water resources and irrigation development issues. A series of CM experiments relating to potential further development of water resources in the Fitzroy basin in central Queensland have been performed.

The experiments differ according to the case studies selected and the population groups that have been surveyed. This allows the analyst to test whether a single experiment could have been performed, and then the results extrapolated to account for site and population differences. It also allows tests for the potential impact of scale and quantity differences.

2   CHOICE MODELLING AND BENEFIT TRANSFER ISSUES

Guidelines have been suggested for benefit transfer applications involving non-use values. Boyle and Bergstrom (1992) suggest 'idealistic' technical criteria such as:

- the non-market commodity valued at the study site must be identical to the non-market commodity to be valued at the policy site (both in terms of the characteristics of the good and the nature and extent of the change being valued);
- the populations affected by the non-market commodity at the study site and the policy site hold identical characteristics; and
- the assignment of property rights at both sites must lead to the same theoretically appropriate welfare measurement (e.g. willingness to pay versus willingness to accept).

Some development work has already occurred in relation to using CM for potential benefit transfer applications (Morrison and Bennett 2000; Rolfe and Bennett 2000; van Bueren and Bennett 2004). The richness of data from CM experiments allows analysts to test where differences might be between values for two sites when two separate valuation experiments have been performed. If the values for one experiment could be successfully used to replicate the second experiment and estimate values for the other site, then it appears that potential for benefit transfer exists.

Bennett and Blamey (2001) discuss this in more detail, identifying several justifications for the use of choice modelling as the basis for successful BT. These include:

- CM produces estimates that can be modelled for any scenario alternative that falls within the range of attributes and label space of the experiment. This provides obvious cost advantages, which is relevant to the normal justification for using BT.
- The decomposition of value into component parts (attributes) also assists in the process of BT. Often, BT is inhibited by differences

between the original and transfer sites. Where sites share only some similar descriptive attributes, CM allows the flexibility for the transfer to proceed.

• CM also allows the inclusion of attributes to capture values for socioeconomic issues.

Previous research has raised a number of issues that are important to the application of CM in attempts at BT of environmental values. The process of BT can only ever be as methodologically sound as the estimation technique on which the previous study is based (Atkinson et al. 1992; Smith 1992). Boyle and Bergstrom (1992), Desvouges et al. (1992) and Garrod and Willis (1999) suggest a range of criteria for conducting successful BT. These focus on site and population equivalence as important prerequisites of benefit transfers.

Tests for transferring CM values between different sites and different populations have been carried out by Morrison et al. (1998) in relation to wetland protection, by Rolfe and Bennett (2000) in relation to preserving vegetation, and by van Bueren and Bennett (2004) in relation to land and water degradation. The results indicated that there was potential for BT to occur, but that it may not be appropriate in all situations. Population differences were found to be more substantial than site differences.

3   THE CASE STUDY AREAS

The Fitzroy basin, encompassing 142 000 km², is the second largest externally draining basin in Australia. Beef cattle, grain, irrigated crops and coal are key primary products in the region. The Fitzroy basin has two major irrigation centres: the Emerald irrigation area located on the Comet/Nogoa/Mackenzie river systems and the Dawson valley irrigation area located along the Dawson River. These irrigation areas are approximately the same size and produce mostly cotton, peanuts, citrus and grains.

These two sub-catchments are similar in resource and environmental conditions. About 50 per cent of vegetation has been cleared from the floodplains in both areas, although there are much higher levels of clearing in some soil and vegetation types. Each of the sub-catchment's river systems comprise around 1 000 kilometres of waterways and there is only a slight variance in river health between the two areas. The Comet/Nogoa/Mackenzie has about 50 per cent of its river systems in a healthy condition and the Dawson River has 40 per cent. In addition, if the proposal to build a major storage dam along the Dawson River is approved, there will be little or no water left in reserve for future environment or development purposes in the two areas.

Differences exist between the catchments in terms of demographics. The Emerald district has a more reliable water supply and is home to other major industries such as coal mining and horticulture (which employs many seasonal workers). As a direct result, the population in the Emerald irrigation area is larger and more stable than that of the Dawson irrigation area. The Dawson valley is serviced by a number of smaller towns which appear more susceptible to population losses and/ or economic stagnation.

In the Fitzroy basin, around 50 per cent of floodplain vegetation has been cleared and about 60 per cent of its 2 800 kilometres of waterways are rated in good health. Although the population of the basin is quite stable, there is an underlying pattern of people shifting from rural areas and small townships into the larger centres. However, in contrast to the sub-catchments where approximately 50 000 megalitres remain in reserve, there is a greater amount of potential reserve water available in the lower Fitzroy area — some 300 000 megalitres — although this is largely situated along or around land unsuitable for major irrigated agriculture.

The diversion of further water for irrigation purposes is likely to have some social and environmental consequences. Social consequences include increased regional spending and employment prospects that flow from increasing production, although the scale economies of most irrigation developments limit the job creation potential. Environmental consequences include biophysical effects of the interruption to natural flows in watercourses, the development of land for farming, and potential for run-off to impact on water quality in the system.

To evaluate these issues in economic terms, it is important to be able to estimate values for both production and non-production outcomes. Although the former (such as the value of additional cotton production) can be estimated from market data, the latter (such as community values for protecting vegetation in floodplains) are more difficult to estimate. CM can be employed to estimate these values.

4   DESIGN AND PERFORMANCE OF THE EXPERIMENTS

A series of CM surveys was designed to estimate values for environmental and social trade-offs associated with irrigation development in the Fitzroy basin. It was important that the valuation information could be applied in various formats, particularly at the sub-catchment or project level. For these reasons, the surveys were designed to test a number of hypotheses about benefit transfer issues. The key issue of interest was whether environmental and social values associated with water resource development were consistent across similar sites and population groups. The surveys were also designed to test if choices (and subsequent value estimations) were affected by variations in quantity and scale.

The first key test of interest was to determine if a single population had the same values for environmental and social trade-offs in similar sites. This was achieved by ascertaining values held by the Brisbane population for trade-offs in the Comet/Nogoa/Mackenzie and the Dawson rivers. These are two sub-catchments in the Fitzroy basin that are similar in terms of size, irrigation development and environmental condition.

The second key test was about whether different populations held the same values for environmental and social trade-offs in the Fitzroy basin. Populations of interest included Brisbane as a major capital city centre, Rockhampton as a regional centre near the mouth of the Fitzroy River, and Emerald as a smaller town in an irrigation district. To capture the required data, three versions of the survey were devised. To test for site differences, surveys for the Comet/Nogoa/Mackenzie basin and the Dawson basin were collected in Brisbane. To test for population differences, surveys for the Fitzroy basin were collected in Emerald, Rockhampton and Brisbane.

The objective of the CM experiment was to estimate respondents' preferences for trade-offs between further floodplain development in the Fitzroy basin and environmental and social impacts. To present survey respondents with development and protection alternatives, the issues had to be described in several concise attributes. These were selected with the aid of scientific and policy experts in the basin, and the conduct of a series of focus groups in the towns to be surveyed (Loch, Rolfe and Windle 2001). A social attribute was included to illustrate that some tradeoffs may be non-monetary ones, and it was explained in the survey information that the levels of agricultural development had some impact on regional populations.

For consistency, the same attributes were used as the basis for the choice scenarios generated for the three case study areas. These attributes were:

- payment levy (an annual levy collected through local government rates over 20 years);
- the amount of healthy vegetation left on floodplains;
- the kilometres of waterways that remain in good health;
- the number of people leaving rural or country areas every year; and
- the amount of water kept in reserve for future use.

Attribute levels were selected to be representative of each catchment. The base was selected as the likely level in 20 years' time for each attribute if current trends continued. The other levels for each attribute to be used in the alternative scenarios were set between the current level and the expected future level. This allowed for a variety of different outcomes if various protection measures were implemented. Payment levels for the Fitzroy were set higher than for the two sub-catchments to take account of the increased quantities associated with Fitzroy profiles. The base and alternative levels for each version of the survey are set out in Table 7.1.

Table 7.1   WTP base and attribute levels for the case study areas

Attribute	Fitzroy Levels		CNM Levels		Dawson Levels	
	Base	Alternatives	Base	Alternatives	Base	Alternatives
Payment	0	20, 50, 100	0	10, 20, 50	0	10, 20, 50
Healthy vegetation in floodplains	20%	30%, 40%, 50%	25%	30%, 40%, 50%	10%	20%, 30%, 40%
Kilometres of healthy waterways	1 500	1 800, 2 100, 2 400	400	500, 650, 800	300	400, 550, 700
People leaving country areas	300	275, 325, 350	0	0, 25, 50	300	275, 325, 350
Amount of water in reserve	0%	5%, 10%, 15%	0%	-2%, 2%, 4%	0%	-5%, 5%, 10%

The *a priori* expectations were that respondents would prefer smaller payments, larger amounts of Vegetation, Healthy Waterways and Reserve, and smaller number of People Leaving. In the case of the Reserve attribute, a negative level was used for both the Dawson and Comet/Nogoa/Mackenzie basins to indicate that water could potentially be allocated below the Water Allocation Management Plan limits (the median flow level). In the case of the People Leaving attribute, one smaller level than the status quo was used to indicate the possibility that careful protection of water and environmental resources may protect regional industry and reduce population changes.

Each of the choice sets presented to respondents involved a status quo or base alternative (the expected position in 20 years' time), together with two alternative scenarios that involved some annual payment for increased protection measures. Figure 7.1 demonstrates how a single choice set includes the three alternatives, with labels used to represent the attributes. The experimental design resulted in a series of 25 choice sets to represent the range of possible scenarios that could be constructed from the attributes and levels used. These were blocked into five versions

	Question X: Options A, B and C. Please choose the option you prefer most by ticking ONE box.				
	Twenty-year effects				
How much I pay each year	Healthy vegetation left in floodplains	Kilometres of waterways in good health	People leaving country areas each year	Amount of reserve left unallocated	I would choose
Option A					
$0	20%	1500	300	0%	
Option B					
$40	30%	1800	275	5%	
Option C					
$80	50%	2400	275	10%	

Figure 7.1   Example choice set used in the survey

of the survey, so that five choice sets within a version were presented to respondents.[1]

A drop-off and pick-up approach was used to collect the surveys. Respondents were sampled at random in Emerald, Rockhampton and Brisbane based on a cluster sampling technique.[2] Each survey collector was provided with a set of instructions on respondent selection in each node and the survey process. Collectors made a minimum of two attempts to collect the survey. The surveys were collected at the three locations in November and December 2000.

In Brisbane, 340 completed surveys were collected for the three versions. In Rockhampton, 122 surveys were completed, and there were 149 completed in Emerald. 50.5 per cent of all people approached gave back a fully completed survey. 41.5 per cent of all people approached declined to complete the survey, and 9 per cent of people approached took a survey form and either did not return it to the collector or did not complete it fully.

4.1   Survey Statistics

The socio-demographics of the respondents who completed the surveys are summarised in Table 7.2 below. Results show slight differences between the sample groups that may influence the model results. The models can also be adjusted to substitute other levels for socio-economic variables where samples may not be fully representative of the relevant population. When a benefit function is transferred between populations, it is normal to adjust the socio-demographic levels in a function for the new population.

Table 7.2   Socio-demographics of the survey respondents

Variable	Brisbane	Rockhampton	Emerald
Average age (> 17 years)	43.00 years	43.82 years	39.43 years
Education (%>year 12)	50.78%	58.96%	50.08%
Average Income (household)	$43 125	$37 570	$41 399

5   RESULTS AND ANALYSIS

The choice data from each version of the CM surveys were analysed and modelled using the LIMDEP program. The data were analysed with multinomial logit (MNL) models which relate the probability of choosing a particular scenario to the attributes of the scenario and the characteristics of the respondents. The socio-economic variables were only specified for the two alternatives on offer, so that they indicate in the model how important these variables are in describing the selection of alternatives over the base option. Each of the variables used in the models is specified in Table 7.3.

Table 7.3   Variables used as regressors in CM models

Variables	Description
Cost	Amount that households would pay in extra rates (or rent) each year to fund improvements
Vegetation	% of healthy vegetation remaining in floodplains
Waterways	Kilometres of waterways in catchment remaining in good health
People leaving	Number of people leaving country areas each year
Reserve	% of water resources in catchment not committed to the environment or allocated to industry/urban/irrigation uses
Alternate Specific Constant (ASC)	Constant – reflects the influence of all other factors on choice of protection alternative
Age	Age of respondent (in years)
Education	Education (ranges from 1 = primary to 5 = tertiary degree)
Income	Gross income of household in dollar terms

The models that could be generated from these data were used to test the specific framing issues of interest relating to site, population, scale and quantity factors. These issues are discussed in turn.

5.1 Site Equivalence Results

The site test was aimed at finding whether the scenario values of two similar catchments (Comet/Nogoa/Mackenzie (CNM) and the Dawson) held by the same population (Brisbane) were identical. Model results for the catchments are shown in Table 7.4 below.[3] The models appear robust, with most attributes significant and signed as expected. As expected, coefficients for the Cost and People Leaving attributes are negative, indicating that respondents preferred lower levels. Coefficients for the other attributes are positive, indicating that respondents preferred higher levels.

Table 7.4   Results of MNL models for CNM and Dawson sites

	Comet/Nogoa/Mackenzie		Dawson	
	Coefficient	Standard Error	Coefficient	Standard Error
ASC	-0.828	0.507	-0.215	0.470
Cost	-0.023***	0.004	-0.029***	0.004
Vegetation	0.031***	0.010	0.033***	0.008
Waterways	0.002***	0.001	0.002***	0.001
People leaving	-0.015***	0.004	-0.004***	0.002
Reserve	0.149***	0.032	0.069***	0.011
Education	0.265**	0.104	-0.305***	0.094
Income	0.000***	0.000	0.000***	0.000
Model Statistics				
No. of Observations	435		605	
Log-Likelihood	-338.78		-553.52	
Chi-square (d o f = 7)	222		278	
Adjusted Rho-square	0.20007		0.16167	

Note: *** = P<0.01, ** = P<0.05.

The main way of testing the hypothesis that the models generated are equivalent is through the use of likelihood ratio tests. Differences that exist can then be specified more closely through a comparison of part-worth values, and the potential for different value functions to generate equivalent values can be gained through a comparison of compensating surplus values. The performance of each test is described in turn.

5.1.1 Tests for model equivalence across sites

The hypothesis for the site test can be stated as follows:

$$H0: \beta_{CNM} = \beta_{DAW}$$
$$H1: \beta_{CNM} \neq \beta_{DAW}$$

where β_{CNM} and β_{DAW} are the parameter vectors corresponding to the Comet/Nogoa/Mackenzie and the Dawson data sets respectively.

The key test for the site hypothesis is a likelihood ratio test. Here, the log-likelihood values for the individual models are compared to the log-likelihood value of a combined model to generate a test statistic using the following formula:

$$\chi2 = -2*(LL_{Pooled} - (LL_{Model\,A} + LL_{Model\,B})) \qquad (7.1)$$

The test statistic is approximately chi-square distributed with the degrees of freedom equivalent to the number of parameters added. If the test statistic is larger than the appropriate chi-square statistic, there is a significant difference in the parameter vectors for each model.

The log-likelihood of the joint CNM/Dawson model is -967.11. The test statistic is therefore

$$= -2 \times (-967.11 - (-338.78 - 553.52)) = 149.62 \qquad (7.2)$$

The appropriate chi-square statistic with eight degrees of freedom is 15.507. Therefore it can be concluded that a significant difference does exist between the two models, and that benefit transfer of results would be inacurate.

5.1.2 Part-worth (implicit price) site test

The part-worth tests can be used to identify where differences might be occurring, given that a significant difference in models has been identified above. The relevant hypotheses can be specified as follows:

$$H0: \beta i_{CNM}/\beta m_{CNM} = \beta i_{DAW}/\beta m_{DAW}$$
$$H1: \beta i_{CNM}/\beta m_{CNM} \neq \beta i_{DAW}/\beta m_{DAW}$$

where βi represents non-monetary attribute coefficient, βm represents the coefficient for the monetary attribute, CNM represents the Comet/Nogoa/Mackenzie model, and DAW represents the Dawson model.

A parametric bootstrapping technique (Krinsky and Robb 1986) was used to draw a vector of 1 000 parameter estimates for each of the models. Part-worths were calculated from each parameter estimate. The simple convolutions method of Poe et al. (2001) was then used to estimate the average proportion (over 100 random draws) of part-worth differences that were less than zero. A proportion of less than 5 per cent would be evidence of a significant difference. Results are reported in Table 7.5.

Table 7.5 *Proportion of part-worth differences (CNM-Dawson) less than zero*

	Vegetation	Waterways	People Leaving	Reserve
CNM – Dawson	0.3723	0.52281	0.99698	0.00603

The test suggests that there are no significant differences for the Vegetation and Waterways attributes, but there are significant differences (at the 1 per cent level) for the People Leaving and Reserve attributes. The results show that the CNM model generates significantly lower values for the People Leaving part-worth, and significantly higher values for the Reserve part-worth.

The significant difference in part-worths provides some evidence of marginal value impacts. The levels for People Leaving and Reserve were very different in the two sub-catchments (see Table 7.1), indicating that the part-worth values are sensitive to the absolute values of the levels involved. The higher part-worth values are associated with lower absolute values of the relevant attributes. The results indicate that the models are equivalent in the areas where the case studies were similar, but vary when the attributes have very different levels in the different case studies. This indicates that point benefit transfer may still be appropriate for similar attributes between sites that are not equivalent.

5.1.3 Compensating surplus site test

The third test involves a comparison of compensating surplus values for the two sites. This will help to identify the extent to which benefit functions can be transferred between sites, even if there are some differences in sites. The relevant hypotheses can be specified as follows:

$$Ho: CS_{CNMi} = CS_{DAWi}$$
$$H1: CS_{CNMi} \pi CS_{DAWi}$$

where CS represents compensating surplus, CNM represents the Comet-Nogoa-Mackenzie model, DAW represents the Dawson model, and i represents 1... n alternatives.

The test involves estimation and comparison of compensating surplus for specific alternatives. Because a very large number of scenarios could be described from the attributes and levels used in the experiment, an experimental design process was used to select a representative sample of nine scenarios. For each scenario,[4] the models reported in Table 7.4 were used to generate compensating surplus measures across 1 000 random draws for both the CNM and Dawson sites. The Poe et al. (2001) procedure was then used to identify whether differences between the compensating surplus measures for each model were significant (Table 7.6).

Table 7. 6   Compensating surplus estimates for CNM and Dawson sites

Scenario	Attribute Changes from Base	Proportion of difference less than zero
1	Veg +5%, Water +100k 's, People 0 change, Reserve -2%	0.505
2	Veg +5%, Water +250k 's, People +25, Reserve +4%	0.502
3	Veg +5%, Water +400k 's, People +50, Reserve +2%	0.500
4	Veg +15%, Water +100k 's, People+25, Reserve +2%	0.501
5	Veg +15%, Water +250k 's, People+50, Reserve -2%	0.499
6	Veg +15%, Water +400k 's, People 0 change, Reserve +4%	0.501
7	Veg +25%, Water +100k 's, People+50, Reserve +4%	0.498
8	Veg +25%, Water +250k 's, People 0 change, Reserve +2%	0.504
9	Veg +25%, Water +400k 's, People+25, Reserve -2%	0.503

The results show no significant differences between the consumer surplus estimates generated from the two separate models. This is likely to be because the significant difference between attribute values identified in the part-worth tests may have offset each other in the scenarios. These results support the transfer of benefit functions as being more appropriate than point value transfers. The results also show that the transfer of value functions may still proceed in some instances between similar sites, even if there are significant differences in the benefit functions applying at each site.

5.2 Population Equivalence Results

The population test was aimed at finding whether the values of the local population, the regional city (in the catchment) population and the capital city (out of the catchment) population were identical.

The models generated from the three populations (Table 7.7) appear to be robust. Most attributes are significant and signed as expected. The results indicate that the Rockhampton population did not consider People leaving to be significant, and the Brisbane population did not consider Reserve to be significant. In the socio-economic section there is far greater variance between the models, with none of the attributes consistently appearing as significant across all three populations. Age appears to be significant only for the Emerald and Rockhampton. respondents, while Education and Income were significant factors for Rockhampton and Brisbane residents.

Table 7.7   Results of the multinomial logit models for population

Variables	Emerald Population		Rockhampton Population		Brisbane Population	
	Coeff.	St. Err	Coeff.	St. Err	Coeff.	St. Err
ASC	0.921*	0.511	0.106	0.485	0.044	0.449
Cost	-0.018***	0.002	-0.013***	0.002	-0.020***	0.002
Vegetation	0.023***	0.007	0.024***	0.008	0.034***	0.008
Waterways	0.001***	0.000	0.001***	0.000	0.000*	0.000
People	-0.005***	0.002	-0.003*	0.002	-0.006***	0.002
Reserve	0.016	0.015	0.030*	0.016	0.003	0.016
Age	-0.020**	0.009	-0.021***	0.007	0.001	0.006
Income	0.000	0.000	0.000**	0.000	0.000***	0.000
Model Statistics						
Number of Choice Sets	630		610		650	
Log Likelihood	-604.05		-621.92		-617.42	
Adjusted rho-square	0.12168		0.06584		0.13003	
Chi-square (d o f = 8)	174.16		96.46		193.34	

Note: *** = P<0.01, ** = P<0.05, * = P<0.10.

As with the site hypothesis, the likelihood ratio test can be applied to determine if the models from the different populations are equivalent. The part-worth and compensating surplus equivalence tests can then be used to provide richer information about where differences may exist. These tests are reported in turn.

5.2.1 Tests for model equivalence across populations
The key test for this population hypothesis is a likelihood ratio test. The hypotheses can be stated as follows:

$$H0: \beta_{EMD} = \beta_{ROK}, \beta_{EMD} = \beta_{BNE}, \beta_{ROK} = \beta_{BNE}$$
$$H1: \beta_{EMD} \neq \beta_{ROK}, \beta_{EMD} \neq \beta_{BNE}, \beta_{ROK} \neq \beta_{BNE}$$

where β_{EMD}, β_{ROK} and β_{BNE} are the parameter vectors corresponding to the Emerald, Rockhampton and Brisbane population data sets respectively.

The test is performed by estimating two models separately, and then a combined model. A likelihood ratio test is then performed using the log-likelihoods from each model. For example, the test for differences between the Emerald and Rockhampton models is as follows:

$$\chi^2 = -2*(LL_{Pooled} - (LL_{Emerald} + LL_{Rockhampton})) = 11.24 \qquad (7.3)$$

The test results for each pairwise comparison are shown in Table 7.8.

Table 7.8   Log likelihood tests for differences in population models

Test	Emerald Vs Rockhampton	Emerald Vs Brisbane	Rockhampton Vs Brisbane
LL of Pop A	-604.05	-604.05	-621.92
LL of Pop B	-621.92	-617.42	-617.42
LL of Pop AB	-1231.59	-1227.31	-1251.18
Test result	11.24	11.68	23.68
Degrees of Freedom	10	10	10
Significant difference?	No	No	Yes

The appropriate chi-square statistic with 10 degrees of freedom is 18.307. Therefore it can be concluded that a significant difference exists between the Rockhampton and Brisbane populations. The part-worth and confidence interval tests can be performed to identify more accurately where differences may exist.

5.2.2 Part-worth (implicit price) tests for population differences

The part-worths, together with significance tests, for the three sites of interest can assist in identifying where differences in values may exist between populations. The relevant hypotheses can be specified as follows:

$$H0: \beta i_{FITZ\,A}/\beta m_{FITZ\,A} - \beta i_{FITZ\,B}/\beta m_{FITZ\,B} = 0$$
$$H1: \beta i_{FITZ\,A}/\beta m_{FITZ\,A} - \beta i_{FITZB}/\beta m_{FITZ\,B} \neq 0$$

where βi represents a non-monetary attribute coefficient, βm represents the coefficient for the monetary attribute, FITZ represents the Fitzroy catchment, and A and B represent two of the Emerald, Brisbane and Rockhampton populations.

Again, a parametric bootstrapping technique (Krinsky and Robb 1986) was used to draw a vector of 1 000 parameter estimates for each of the models, and part-worths were calculated from each parameter estimate. The simple convolutions method of Poe et al. (2001) was then used to estimate the average proportion (over 100 random draws) of part-worth differences that were less than zero. A proportion of less than 5 per cent would be evidence of a significant difference. Results are reported in Table 7.9.

Table 7.9   *Proportion of part-worth differences (EMD, ROC, BNE)
less than zero*

	Vegetation	Waterways	People	Reserve
Emerald – Rockhampton	0.779	0.634	0.552	0.835
Emerald – Brisbane	0.768	0.030	0.442	0.280
Rockhampton – Brisbane	0.420	0.027	0.404	0.070

There are significant differences at the 5 per cent level in the part-worth for Waterways between the Emerald and Brisbane populations, and the Rockhampton and Brisbane populations. There are no significant differences between the other part-worths. This suggests that most point benefit transfers between the three populations would be appropriate.

5.2.3 Compensating surplus population test

A comparison of compensating surplus values from the models for the three populations helps to identify whether transferring benefit functions between populations is valid. The relevant hypotheses can be specified as follows:

$$H0: CS_{EMi} = CS_{RRi} = CS_{BBi}$$
$$H1: CS_{EMi} \neq CS_{RRi} \neq CS_{BBi}$$

where CS represents compensating surplus, EM, RR and BB represent the Emerald, Rockhampton and Brisbane models respectively, and i represents $1 \dots n$ alternatives

The test has to be performed across a representative sample of possible scenarios as shown in Table 7.10. Consumer surplus estimates were calculated from the models reported in Table 7.7, and the Poe et al. (2001) test applied to determine if significant differences existed between estimates. Results are reported in Table 7.10.

The results indicate that values held by the three populations are similar, with no significant differences identified between the Emerald and Rockhampton, and Emerald and Brisbane population. There were significant differences at the 5 per cent level between the Brisbane and Rockhampton populations for three out of the nine scenarios. The transfer of benefit functions between these population groups is not fully accurate.

5.3 Framing Tests for Quantity Differences

The issue of whether the presentation of different quantities of an amenity of interest has a significant impact on values can also be tested.

Table 7.10   Proportion of compensating surplus differences less than zero

Scenario	Attribute Changes (from base)	Emerald Rockhampton	Emerald Brisbane	Brisbane Rockhampton
1	Veg +10%, Water +300kms, People –25, Reserve +5%	0.107	0.946	0.996
2	Veg +10%, Water +600kms, People +25, Reserve +15%	0.406	0.639	0.717
3	Veg +10%, Water +900kms, People +50, Reserve +10%	0.347	0.475	0.645
4	Veg +20%, Water +300kms, People+25, Reserve +10%	0.211	0.912	0.980
5	Veg +20%, Water +600kms, People+50, Reserve +5%	0.180	0.779	0.953
6	Veg +20%, Water +900kms, People-25, Reserve +15%	0.438	0.441	0.518
7	Veg +30%, Water +300kms, People+50, Reserve +15%	0.373	0.819	0.873
8	Veg +30%, Water +600kms, People-25, Reserve +10%	0.249	0.747	0.901
9	Veg +30%, Water +900kms, People+25, Reserve +5%	0.223	0.558	0.829

The CM procedure automatically accounts for the variations in levels used within an experiment. However, if the range of quantity changes within a source study is very different from those considered at a target site, it is possible that BT may not be accurate.

Tests for quantity equivalence can be conducted by selecting case studies with similar scale trade-offs (the CNM and Dawson split-samples), and ascertaining if the trade-offs for each attribute are sensitive to the similarities or differences in the levels involved. As shown in Table 7.1, the major differences between the two split-samples could be found in the levels for the People Leaving attribute. The levels used for the Vegetation and Waterways attributes were very similar, while the levels for the Reserve attribute span a wider range for the Dawson split-sample compared with the CNM split-sample.

5.3.1 Part-worth tests

Part-worth tests were used to determine if reported values would be equivalent for similar levels, or differ where the levels involved differed. The hypotheses of interest can be formally stated below as:

$$H0: PW_{\text{Waterways CNM}} = PW_{\text{Waterways Daw}} \qquad H0: PW_{\text{Vegetation CNM}} = PW_{\text{Vegetation Daw}}$$

$$H1: PW_{\text{Waterways CNM}} \neq PW_{\text{Waterways Daw}} \qquad H1: PW_{\text{Vegetation CNM}} \neq PW_{\text{Vegetation Daw}}$$

$$H0: PW_{\text{People CNM}} = PW_{\text{People DAW}} \qquad H0: PW_{\text{Reserve CNM}} = PW_{\text{Reserve DAW}}$$

$$H1: PW_{\text{People CNM}} \neq PW_{\text{People DAW}} \qquad H1: PW_{\text{Reserve CNM}} \neq PW_{\text{Reserve DAW}}$$

where PW = part-worth value, CNM represents the Comet/Nogoa/Mackenzie model, and DAW represents the Dawson model. The performance of these tests using the simple convolutions method of Poe et al. (2001) has been reported in Table 7.5. The results indicate that there are no significant differences for the Vegetation and Waterways attributes, but there are significant differences (at the 1 per cent level) for the People Leaving and Reserve attributes. The results show that the CNM model generates significantly lower values for the People Leaving part-worth, and significantly higher values for the Reserve part-worth.

The People Leaving attribute involved much larger quantity changes in the Dawson model, so the results indicate that people were sensitive to the absolute changes involved. In contrast, the Reserve attribute involved a much smaller initial endowment in the CNM, so the results for this attribute indicate sensitivity to the relative changes involved. Both results confirm that quantity effects are present in the models, indicating that the marginal utility of an attribute change varies as the absolute or relative quantity involved increases. This result suggests that BT between source and target studies where different quantity impacts are involved may be inappropriate.

5.4 Framing Tests for Scale Differences

The study was designed to test for scale differences by using the same population (Brisbane) to assess trade-offs at both a catchment level (Fitzroy) and a sub-catchment level (Comet/Nogoa/Mackenzie and Dawson). The scale tests were aimed at identifying whether the results of the sub-catchment models were consistent with the results of the catchment model.

Normally, if the choice modelling application is conducted using major scale differences, researchers could expect to find differences in value estimates derived from applications conducted on different scale issues (van Bueren and Bennett 2004). In turn, these scale differences make BT difficult to achieve because the appropriate scale factor often remains unclear.

Conversely, if the application is conducted using minor scale differences, then BT should be relatively straightforward. The purpose of this study was to determine if catchment to sub-catchment transfers in the Fitzroy basin represented a minor difference in scale. If the scale differences are not significant, then it can be assumed that the values can be disaggregated from the basin level to sub-catchments without the need for scale factors or multipliers.

5.4.1 Testing if CNM + Dawson = Fitzroy

The test for scale differences focuses on whether value estimates for changes in the Fitzroy catchment are equal to values estimated for the equivalent amount of changes in two major sub-catchments.[5] To avoid quantity effects being confounded with the results, the tests involve equal amounts of each environmental and social attribute. This means that any differences in the values determined should be attributed to the scale of the attributes used. The null hypothesis can be formally stated as follows:

$$H0: V_{CNM} + V_{DAW} = V_{FTZ}$$
$$H1: V_{CNM} + V_{DAW} \neq V_{FTZ}$$

where V = value.

Essentially, the test is whether the value of change A in the CNM basin plus the value of change B in the Dawson basin is equivalent to the value of the A+B change in the Fitzroy basin. Because the Reserve attribute is not significant in the Fitzroy model, the test is limited to changes in the levels for the Vegetation, Waterways, and People Leaving attributes. Testing the hypothesis involved a comparison of compensating surplus values for specific alternatives for the three populations. An experimental design process was used to select a representative sample of nine scenarios. Levels for the Waterways and People attribute in the CNM and Dawson models were simply summed to create levels for the Fitzroy model, while levels for the Vegetation attribute were converted to the appropriate area changes in the Fitzroy[6] (Table 7.11).

Table 7.11 Scenarios used to test for scale differences

Scenario	Attribute	Change in level above base		
		CNM	**Dawson**	**Fitzroy**
1	Vegetation	0.05	0.1	0.055
	Waterways	100	100	200
	People	0	-25	-25
2	Vegetation	0.05	0.1	0.05
	Waterways	250	250	500
	People	25	25	50
3	Vegetation	0.05	0.1	0.055
	Water	400	400	800
	People	50	50	100
4	Vegetation	0.15	0.2	0.125
	Water	100	100	200
	People	25	25	50
5	Vegetation	0.15	0.2	0.125
	Water	250	250	500
	People	50	50	100
6	Vegetation	0.15	0.2	0.125
	Water	400	400	800
	People	0	-25	-25
7	Vegetation	0.25	0.3	0.197
	Water	100	100	200
	People	50	50	100
8	Vegetation	0.25	0.3	0.197
	Water	250	250	500
	People	0	-25	-25
9	Vegetation	0.25	0.3	0.197
	Water	400	400	800
	People	25	25	50

To facilitate the comparison with the CNM and Dawson models, a revised model for the Fitzroy was estimated where Education was included and Age was omitted. Values for the nine scenarios were then estimated, and Poe et al. (2001) tests were used to identify if significant differences existed. The mean values for the CNM + Dawson scenarios were larger than the mean values for the equivalent Fitzroy scenarios (Table 7.12), indicating that some scale effects were present. However, significant differences at the 95 per cent level could only be identified in two of the nine scenarios. This indicates that only limited scale effects could be identified and that most benefit transfers between catchment and sub-catchment levels were appropriate.

Table 7.12   Compensating surplus estimates for CNM + Dawson, and Fitzroy

Scenario	Mean value CNM + Dawson	Mean value Fitzroy	Proportion of compensating surplus differences < 0
1	$77.82	$73.62	0.440
2	$79.30	$57.41	0.140
3	$84.32	$49.01	0.069
4	$53.67	$50.30	0.446
5	$58.68	$37.08	0.151
6	$129.87	$88.19	0.046
7	$33.04	$34.80	0.541
8	$104.23	$81.09	0.151
9	$105.72	$64.87	0.036

6   CONCLUSIONS

Benefit transfer issues are important to the wider application of results from non-market valuation studies. In this chapter, some insights are gained about the potential for benefit transfer to be applied to environmental and social values associated with water resource development. Similar choice modelling experiments have been run to systematically test site and population equivalence in the one study, as well as to test the impact of quantity and scale issues on the way that values are framed. Both point transfers and benefit function transfers have been trialled in the tests.

Three separate tests have been performed on both site and population experiments to determine how suitable benefit transfer might be. First, a likelihood ratio test was used to determine if different models were equivalent. Second, the part-worths (marginal values) were compared between models to ascertain whether the differences between those point estimates were significant. Third, an orthogonal sample of scenario values was estimated from the models and tested to ascertain whether significant differences existed.

The pattern of results was similar for both site and population tests. The results of the likelihood ratio tests indicated that the relevant site and population models were not equivalent. A significant difference in the site models was surprising, given the similarities of the two sites in question. However, the tests for transferring point and value function estimates showed that benefit transfer may still be valid in some situations.

Point transfers appear to be valid between sites where similar characteristics exist. Where differences in resource stocks exist between sites, these values appear to change in line with expectations about shifts in marginal values. The transfer of point estimates between populations appears to be generally robust, but it is unclear from the work presented why there were two exceptions involving protection values for waterways.

The transfer of value functions between sites for an orthogonal set of scenarios appears to be valid in the experiment reported. This may be, in part, because some of the attribute changes may have been offsetting, although there are no significant differences between profiles where no offsetting is present. The transfer of value functions between populations had mixed results, showing that a small proportion of transfers may not be appropriate.

The results of quantity and scale tests indicate that the frame of a valuation experiment may impact on values, suggesting that benefit transfer may be limited when the scope of a good varies between source and target studies. In particular, marginal values are likely to be higher when the quantity of an asset or change being considered is restricted, or when smaller scale trade-offs are being considered. The results of the experiments conducted indicate that benefit transfer may still be appropriate when quantity or scale effects are limited, but that some adjustment may be necessary when larger impacts are involved.

Results of the experiments confirm the comments of Loomis et al. (1995) and Bateman et al. (2002) that benefit transfer is difficult and sometimes contradictory. Yet the results are also encouraging. They show that the detailed models available through CM analysis can be used to effect benefit transfer, and they confirm that both point transfer and value function transfer can be performed in some situations.

ACKNOWLEDGEMENTS

The research reported in this chapter has been supported by the Australian Research Council and the Queensland Department of Natural Resources and Mines. The contribution of Dr Jill Windle to the design and performance of the choice modelling experiments is gratefully acknowledged.

NOTES

1. The efficiency of the experimental design using the multinomial logit model and estimating only main effects is 69.1931 per cent (analysis provided by Associate Professor Deborah Street, University of Technology, Sydney).
2. Several site areas for sampling were selected across the city. Within a site area, a randomised selection process was used (e.g. every fifth house in every third street).
3. Insignificant variables across all models have been omitted. A standard set of variables have been used for the models to facilitate model comparisons.
4. The compensating surplus equation used is as follows:

   $CS = -1/\beta_{COST}$ (β_{Veg}*ΔVeg + β_{Water} *ΔWater + β_{People} *ΔPeople + $\beta_{Reserve}$ *ΔReserve + β_{ASC} + β_{Edu}*Education + β_{Inc}*Income).

   The same population characteristics derived from the 2001 census were used in each model for the socio-economic variables.
5. Although the term 'sub-catchment' is used throughout this chapter, in the actual questionnaires, only the term 'catchment' was used to describe the area of consideration in the various survey sets. Accordingly, respondents could not perceive any size differential when making their choices.
6. The process of setting the sum of scenario changes in the CNM and Dawson models to be equivalent to scenario changes in the Fitzroy model is outlined in Loch et al. (2002).

REFERENCES

Atkinson, S. E., T. D. Crocker and J. F. Shogren (1992), 'Bayesian exchangeability, benefit transfer and research efficiency', *Water Resources Research*, **28** (3), 715–22.

Bateman, I.J., R.T. Carson, B. Day, M. Hanemann, N. Hanley, T. Hett, M. Jones-Lee, G. Loomes, S. Mourato, E. Ozdemiroglu, D.W. Pearce, R. Sugden and J. Swanson (2002), *Environmental Valuation with Stated Preference Techniques,* Cheltenham UK and Northampton, MA, USA: Edward Elgar.

Bennett, J.W. and R.K. Blamey (2001), *The Choice Modelling Approach to Environmental Valuation*, Cheltenham UK and Northampton, MA, USA: Edward Elgar.

Boyle, K.J. and J.C. Bergstrom (1992), 'Benefit transfer studies: myths, pragmatism and idealism', *Water Resources Research*, **28** (3), 657–63.

Brookshire, D.S. and H.R. Neill (1992), 'Benefit transfers: conceptual and empirical issues', *Water Resources Research*, **28** (3), 651–5.

Desvouges, W. H., M.C. Naughton and G.R. Parsons (1992), 'Benefit transfer: conceptual problems in estimating water quality benefits using existing studies', *Water Resources Research*, **28** (3), 675–83.

Garrod, G. and K.G. Willis (1999), *Economic Valuation of the Environment: Methods and Case Studies*, Cheltenham UK and Northampton, MA, USA: Edward Elgar.

Krinsky, I. and A. Robb (1986), 'On approximating the statistical properties of elasticities', *Review of Economics and Statistics*, **68**, 715–19.

Loch, A., J. Rolfe and J. Windle (2001), *Using Focus Groups to Design Choice Modelling Valuation Frameworks for Floodplain Development*, Valuing Floodplain Development in the Fitzroy Basin, Research Report No.3, Emerald: Central Queensland University.

Loch, A., J. Rolfe and J. Bennett (2002), *Scale Effects and Their Importance for Benefit Transfer of Natural Resource Values in the Fitzroy Basin*, Valuing

Floodplain Development in the Fitzroy Basin, Research Report No.5, Emerald: Central Queensland University.

Loomis, J.B. (1992), 'The evolution of a more rigorous approach to benefit transfer: benefit function transfer', *Water Resources Research*, **28** (3), 701–5.

Loomis, J.B., B. Roach, F. Ward and R. Ready (1995), 'Testing transferability of recreation demand models across regions: a study of Corps Engineers reservoirs', *Water Resources Research*, **31** (3), 348–61.

Morrison, M.D. and J.W. Bennett (2000), 'Choice modelling, non-use values and benefit transfer', *Economic Analysis and Policy*, **30** (1), 13–32.

Morrison, M.D., J.W. Bennett, R.K. Blamey and J. J. Louviere (1998), *Choice Modelling and Tests of Benefit Transfer*, Choice Modelling Research Report No. 8, Canberra: University of New South Wales.

Poe, G.L., K.L. Giraud and J.B. Loomis (2001), *Simple Computational Methods for Measuring the Differences of Empirical Distributions: Application to Internal and External Scope Tests in Contingent Valuation*, Staff Paper 2001–05, Department of Agricultural, Resource and Managerial Economics, Cornell University.

Rolfe, J.C. and J.W. Bennett (2000), *Testing for Framing Effects in Environmental Choice Modelling*, Choice Modelling Research Report No. 13, Canberra: University of New South Wales.

Smith, V. K. (1992), 'On separating defensible benefit transfers from smoke and mirrors', *Water Resources Research*, **28** (3), 685–94.

van Bueren, M. and J. Bennett (2004), 'Towards the development of a transferable set of value estimates for environmental attributes', *Australian Journal of Agricultural Resource Economics*, **48**, 1–32.

8. Transferring Mitigation Values for Small Streams

Geoffrey N. Kerr and Basil M.H. Sharp

1 INTRODUCTION

Choice experiments have the flexibility to value a wide range of potential outcomes. A novel use of this attribute of choice experiments is provided in a New Zealand study undertaken to evaluate the adequacy of off-site mitigation. The expense, skills and time involved in undertaking choice studies provide ample motivation for benefit transfer. Consequently, the study was designed to provide a test of benefit transfer, using two separate populations within a region and two types of stream protection sites to test the possibility of benefit transfer, with the view to using study results across the region should the outcome be favourable.

This chapter commences with an introduction to the problem of mitigating development impacts on Auckland streams. A choice model for assessing off-site mitigation is developed and applied to two different cases. Choice model results are then used to evaluate benefit transfer between the two cases studied. The chapter concludes with an evaluation of case study implications for benefit transfer.

2 THE PROBLEM

2.1 Development Impacts on Waterways

Every year, hundreds of hectares of land in New Zealand's Auckland region are disturbed for transportation, housing, industrial, commercial and community amenity purposes. Major development activities are controlled by the Auckland Regional Council, which requires an earthworks consent for each development. Most applications for earthworks consents are associated with small first- or second-order soft-bottomed streams in retired pasture. These streams are usually ecologically degraded before any development occurs. Other developments involve activities in or near relatively pristine waterways, and disturbance or removal of native vegetation, which provides habitat and food sources for both terrestrial and aquatic species.

On-site activities commonly involve construction site earthworks, such as site contouring for residential subdivision development, stream channelisation, armouring and culverting. Impacts include complete loss of waterways (for example, when a stream is piped), and modifications to wildlife habitat, visual amenity and other waterway attributes, as well as off-site impacts, such as sedimentation.

Sedimentation is a particular concern in the Auckland region because of the combination of soils, weather, topography and receiving environment attributes. There is up to 100 times the sediment yield per hectare from construction sites compared with pastoral land. Adverse ecological effects of sediment include: modified or destroyed instream values; modified estuarine and coastal habitats; smothering and abrading of fauna and flora; changes in food sources; and interruption of life cycles. In addition, there may be damage to water pumps and other structures, the quality of water supplies usually diminish, localised flooding can occur, and there is loss of aesthetic appeal.

Projects in the Auckland region involving land disturbance are required to incorporate best-practice erosion and sediment controls. Best management practices include structural techniques such as sediment retention ponds, contour drains and silt fences. Best management practices are not 100 per cent effective and even with appropriately designed and maintained systems in place, significant sediment discharges and other environmental impacts occur. Residual sedimentation can lead to significant cumulative effects within catchments. In a practical sense, stream channels and associated riparian margins are damaged regardless of what normal best management practices are used.

2.2 Mitigation

In addition to requiring best management practices, the Auckland Regional Council has the ability to place conditions on earthworks consents, including specific offsetting mitigation requirements. Offsetting mitigation may augment stream quality at one site to compensate for the adverse environmental effects associated with development at other sites. Enhancement could occur within the catchment undergoing development and/or possibly in other catchments. The idea is to use mitigation to achieve and sustain desired environmental outcomes.

Offset mitigation is a tool used to complement best management practices where some kind of ecological balance can be protected by enhancing stream quality in proximate areas. Requiring the consent holder to provide offset mitigation for the unavoidable damage caused by an activity is well established internationally. Typical examples of offset mitigation include riparian planting and stream bank retirement to offset water quality degradation, planting forests to offset greenhouse gas emissions, and creating or enhancing wetlands or native vegetation to offset impacts of land drainage.

The method for establishing 'appropriate mitigation' in Auckland is far from clear and generally relies on a 'best professional judgement' approach based on ecological indicators such as species diversity, stream cover, flow rate, temperature, and so on. In order for the offset mitigation to function effectively as required by New Zealand's Resource Management (1991) and Local Government Act (2002), the community needs to have confidence in the mitigation process. However, very little is known about the community preferences regarding alternative states of Auckland streams. Without information on community preferences it is not possible for the Auckland Regional Council to identify mitigation that reflects the environmental outcomes the community desires. Consequently, it is highly desirable either to quantify in dollar terms the costs of both the adverse effects at the site of development and the benefits of the offset mitigation, or to identify how the community is willing to trade-off site attributes. Transparent quantification of costs and benefits ensures that the mitigation proposed offers the potential to offset, from both the ecological and the economic perspectives, the adverse effects generated. Choice modelling was employed to identify and evaluate important Auckland stream quality attributes. The following section provides a brief description of the study design. It is followed by the results and an evaluation of benefits transfer, which leads to discussion and conclusions. Kerr and Sharp (2003) provide full details of study design and results.

3   CHOICE MODEL

Choice modelling entails several key steps:

1. Salient attribute identification;
2. Choice model design;
3. Data collection;
4. Data analysis; and
5. Application to policy.

3.1   Salient Attribute Identification

Salient attribute identification was undertaken using discussions with Auckland Regional Council personnel, and using focus groups conducted in the two case study communities (South Auckland and

North Shore). Council staff provided several perspectives. They are extremely familiar with the physical and ecological systems and the impacts of developments upon them. Further, Auckland Regional Council is the agency responsible for environmental management, and council staff receive ongoing feedback from developers, community and environmental groups, placing them in an advantageous position for monitoring community and interest group perceptions and values. Focus groups were important to get direct input from the community about their concerns over stream management, their salient attributes, and their willingness to undertake and ability to complete choice questions about stream management. The likelihood of self-selection to focus groups on the basis of personal preferences *vis-à-vis* stream management was minimal because participants had no prior information on the specific purpose of the focus group meetings. Details of the procedure followed at each focus group meeting are reported in Kerr and Sharp (2002). Responses from the two focus groups were similar, with the following stream attributes mentioned in discussion.

- Water clarity
- Flow of water
- Quality of the stream bank
- Access
- Safety
- Surrounding land use
- Habitat for wildlife
- Natural shape of the stream

Strong views were expressed that the people creating degradation should be held responsible and should be required to pay for mitigation. However, community funding of stream improvement activities was considered to be acceptable if there was an element of 'publicness' associated with enhancement. The focus group studies indicated that stream attributes could be described in relatively simple terms that could be understood by the general population. Participants understood the idea of a choice game and were prepared and able to carefully consider the trade-offs and make meaningful choices. The choice game format used in the focus groups provided the basis for developing the survey questionnaire.

3.2 Choice Model Design

Choice models typically employ a linear utility function of the form:[1]

$$V_k = V(Z_k, Y_k) = \beta_0 + \beta_1 Z_{1,k} + \beta_2 Z_{2,k} + \ldots + \beta_n Z_{n,k} + \beta_Y Y_k \qquad (8.1)$$

where V is the observable component of utility and the Z_i are choice attributes (or transformations of choice attributes) at the study site. Y is the cost to the individual. The subscript k indexes the choice. Attributes differ between choices, but coefficients in the utility function do not. Data analysis entails selection of the vector of coefficients that maximises the probability of obtaining the observed choices. This model allows evaluation of on-site mitigation. The overall impact of site changes that degrade some attributes and improve others (including monetary compensation, Y_k) can be identified by comparing prior and posterior utility (V_k). Alternatively, the utility function can be used to identify mitigation that leaves utility unchanged.

The primary study objective was identification of whether off-site attributes could be used as mitigation for specified on-site environmental changes. Consequently, attributes needed to vary simultaneously at two sites. Extending the utility function to incorporate two sites (suppressing k for clarity) yields:

$$V = \beta_0 + [\beta_{11}Z_{11} + ... + \beta_{n1} Z_{n1}] + [\beta_{12}Z_{12} + ... + \beta_{n2} Z_{n2}] + \beta_Y Y \quad (8.2)$$

Where β_{ij} is marginal utility of attribute i at site j and Z_{ij} is the level of attribute i at site j. On-site mitigation requires that a change in an attribute at site 1 (say Z_{11}) is offset by changes in other attributes at site 1 (i.e. by changing attributes Z_{m1} where m≠1). Off-site mitigation entails changing attributes at the other site. A change in an attribute at site 1 (say Z_{11}) is offset by changes in attributes at site 2 (i.e. by changing attributes Z_{j2} where j includes all attributes at site 2). In order to identify willingness to trade-off attributes between sites, the utility function must include attributes at both sites. This effectively doubles the number of attributes in the utility function compared with single site models. While this model form allows identification of off-site mitigation, an extremely useful by-product is the ability to evaluate the adequacy of on-site mitigation (or a mixture of on-site and off-site mitigation) using the same model. Inclusion of the cost attribute (Y) allows monetary measurement of the non-market costs of development impacts and the non-market benefits of stream enhancements. Knowledge of these values may not be important, particularly if monetary compensation is not relevant or permitted. Auckland Regional Council wanted to measure monetary values of impacts, so it was necessary to include a cost attribute in the choices presented to citizens.

Recent choice studies typically incorporate four to six attributes. With these numbers of attributes, survey designs are available to estimate interaction effects between the attributes. For example, willingness to pay for additional fish species might be expected to depend upon the amount of fish habitat available, suggesting an interaction between number of fish species and available fish habitat. This study did not allow the possibility of interaction effects of this type. The requirement for attributes to vary at two sites, along with the number of attributes that were identified in the focus groups as being potentially significant, and the requirement for a money cost attribute to allow assessment of money values for site attributes, resulted in selection of the ten choice attributes in Table 8.1.

Table 8.1 Choice attributes

Attribute	Attribute values: Natural Stream	Attribute values: Degraded stream
Water Clarity	Clear; Muddy	Clear; Muddy
Native Fish Species	1; 3; 5	2; 3; 4
Fish Habitat	2km; 3km; 4km	1km; 2km; 3km
Native Streamside Vegetation*	Little or none; Moderate; Plentiful	Little or none; Moderate; Plentiful
Channel Form	-	Straightened; Natural
Cost to Household	\$0/year; \$20/year; \$50/year	

Note: * Dummy-coded, with 'Little or none' as the base.

Because of the large number of attributes in the choice sets, the number of choice events faced by each individual was limited to five to reduce fatigue. The fractional factorial, main effects statistical design adopted (Hahn and Shapiro 1966) required six different versions of the survey, with some choice sets occurring in more than one version. In each choice event, survey participants were able to choose between the status quo (clearly labelled as such) and two unlabelled alternatives. The use of at least three alternatives provides more information from each choice event, which improves model fit and the accuracy of coefficient estimates (Rolfe and Bennett 2003). The first choice option presented in each case was the status quo, forming the base. The first alternative to the base in each choice event was developed from the statistical design plan. The second alternative to the base was the foldover of the first alternative.

The payment vehicle was regional council rates. Justification for this vehicle was provided with the following introduction, which was read out by the interviewer. The statement was designed to ensure that survey participants were aware that it is not always possible to identify the people responsible for environmental degradation, yet the community may benefit from improving damaged environments. It also sought to introduce the concepts of opportunity costs through environmental trade-offs.

> Stream restoration and management can be expensive. Sometimes it is obvious who has caused stream changes and they can be made to pay to restore the condition of the stream. In other cases, the changes occurred a long time ago or have been caused by things done for the whole community.

In these cases the condition of streams is a community responsibility. Regional Council rates could be raised to allow extra stream restoration activities to be undertaken. If this happened then costs to your household would increase through your rates bill or, if you are renting your house, through having to pay higher rent to your landlord.

While the condition of some streams continues to decline because of new and ongoing activities, other streams are getting better because of management actions. Stream managers have to decide whether it is better to try to protect streams that have not been changed much, or to restore streams that have already been degraded. Sometimes it is much easier and cheaper to restore streams that have already been degraded. Restoring degraded streams can mean there is less money available to manage other streams, so their condition can decline.

3.3   Data Collection

Data were collected in personal interviews conducted at the respondent's own home by a professional research agency. The sample was obtained by randomly drawing individual names and addresses from registered voters in postal zones 1701 and 1702 (South Auckland) and 1309–1311 (North Shore). This procedure identified 60 start point addresses in each location. Each start point was used to obtain five interviews. From the start point interviewers turned left and followed the pavement, approaching every second house. At least two calls were made to each house where no response was obtained. Response rates were 44 per cent in North Shore and 40 per cent in South Auckland, with 308 interviews completed on the North Shore and 311 completed in South Auckland. Surveying was undertaken in January and February 2003.

The survey drew heavily on design parameters that have proved to be successful in similar Australian studies (Whitten and Bennett 2001). Attribute levels were communicated wherever possible by the use of icons to allow visual identification of the trade-offs being made. In order to ensure that all respondents were reacting to the same stimuli, a two-sided A4 glossy brochure was given to each survey participant to read at their own pace before commencement of choice questioning. The brochure provided photographs of representative stream conditions alongside labelled icons.

Large, coloured show cards were used to present the choice questions. The interviewer described the items on the card and explained the choices that were available to the respondent. Figure 8.1 provides an example of the choice question cards presented to respondents. In order to test for socio-economic effects, data were collected on sex, age, income, education, ethnicity and number of residents in the household. Two questions probed how respondents perceived the difficulty of the choice questions, and another question assessed the interviewers' perceptions of how well the respondents understood the assigned tasks.

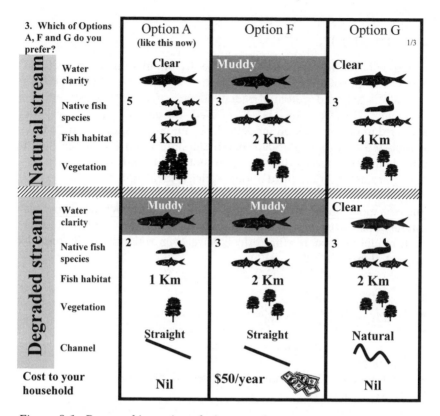

Figure 8.1 Personal interview choice question

3.4 Sample Characteristics

Differences between population and sample distributions were tested using population data from the 2001 census for people 20 years of age or older. The sampling frame was a specific address and the participant was randomly selected from people 20 years or older resident at that address. Consequently, the sample should ideally conform to household level census data. The two surveys obtained responses that are representative of home ownership rates and the sex and age distributions within the populations. People with a university degree were more likely to respond than others. The South Auckland sample was over-representative of people from households with incomes less than $50,000 per year, whereas on the North Shore, the sample closely matched population incomes.

Large households were over-represented in both samples, possibly a result of the higher probability of finding someone at home in a larger household.

4   RESULTS

Site-specific models are reported for the two population groups in Table 8.2. Where possible, the Heteroscedastic Extreme Value model (HEV) was fitted to avoid potential independence of irrelevant alternatives problems. However, the HEV offered no improvement over the standard multinomial logit model (MNL) for North Shore, so the MNL is reported in Table 8.2. Scale parameters are reported for the South Auckland HEV model, but these are not significantly different to the scale parameter for the third option, which is identically set to unity. The models forced inclusion of all stream attributes and the money attribute, but each model includes different interaction effects.[2] While all possible interactions of attributes and socio-economic variables were tested for each model, only significant effects have been retained in the models presented in Table 8.2.

The personal attributes that significantly affect choices are:

- Age (Respondent's age in years);
- People (Number of people in the household);
- Degree (0,1 Dummy: 1 if respondent has a university degree);
- Homeowner (0,1 Dummy: 1 if residence is owned by the inhabitants);
- High Income (0,1 Dummy: 1 if household income exceeds $50,000 per year); and
- Very High Income (0,1 Dummy: 1 if household income exceeds $100,000 per year).

The coefficients on 'Money' are highly significant and of the expected negative sign, indicating that any particular option is less likely to be selected if it costs more. While the low rho-square statistics indicate relatively poor model fits, the significance of stream attribute coefficients is generally strong, with only three of 22 stream attribute coefficients not being significant. The relatively low goodness of fit for these models indicates that there are explanatory factors that have not been included in the models, or that there is considerable underlying inter-personal variance (or both).

Table 8.2   Site-specific models

	Attribute	North Shore	South Auckland
Natural Stream Attributes	Water Clarity (N1)	0.6509***	0.6420***
	Fish Species (N2)	0.1082***	0.0467**
	Fish Habitat (N3)	-0.3969***	-0.0015
	Moderate Vegetation (N4A)	0.2759**	0.1567
	Plentiful Vegetation (N4B)	0.2105**	0.5116***
Degraded Stream Attributes	Water Clarity (D1)	0.7706***	0.5996***
	Fish Species (D2)	0.2640**	0.0939*
	Fish Habitat (D3)	0.1315***	0.2098***
	Moderate Vegetation (D4A)	0.2110	0.3447**
	Plentiful Vegetation (D4B)	0.1977**	0.5258***
	Channel (D5)	0.3213***	0.3042***
	Money	-0.0098***	-0.0095***
Personal Attributes	Age x D2	-0.0050**	
	Age x N3	0.0080***	
	Degree x N3	0.1548*	-0.3144***
	Degree x D1	0.3798**	
	Degree x D5	-0.4428***	
	People x D1	-0.1188**	
	People x N4B		-0.0802**
	Homeowner x D3		-0.2394***
	High Income x D5	0.5985***	
	Very High Income x N4B		0.8449**
	Very High Income x D1		0.6737**
	Very High Income x D2		-0.6100***
	Very High Income x D5		0.6585**
Alternative-Specific Constants	Status Quo	0.2984*	0.5740**
	Second option	0.0185	-0.0955
HEV Scale Parameters	Status Quo	na	1.473
	Second option	na	0.867
N		1331	1281
$LL_{Restricted}$ (LL_R)		-1433.81	-1388.87
$LL_{Unrestricted}$ (LL_{UR})		-1305.79	-1273.40
Rho^2		0.089	0.083

Note: *Significance at 10% level; ** Significance at 5% level; ***Significance at 1% level.

Alternative Specific Constants (ASCs) are significant when factors other than independent variables in the model are important determinants of choice. In each choice situation the first option was labelled as the status quo, while the other two options were unlabelled. The choice models used here arbitrarily set the ASC for the third option to zero. Second-option ASCs are not significant, indicating that there were no perceived differences between the unlabelled alternatives apart from the attributes used to describe them. Status quo ASCs are positive, and significant, indicating a preference for the status quo.[3]

Interaction effects allow detection of the influence of individual or household-specific characteristics (such as respondent age and household income) on the probability of selecting a particular option. Interaction effects were tested in several ways.

- First, interactions of the variables High Income and Very High Income with the variable MONEY tested income effects. The effects were significant in all cases and supported prior beliefs that wealthier respondents would be prepared to pay more for any given environmental enhancement.
- Second, independent variables were interacted with ASCs to test whether personal characteristics influenced choice between the options, particularly between the status quo and either of the two change options. None of these interactions was significant.
- Third, personal characteristics were interacted with each of the site attributes to identify whether particular groups of individuals valued attributes differently. Significant interactions are reported in Table 8.2. Interaction effects vary significantly between models.

The sign of the interaction effect indicates how the population views the importance of the relevant attribute. For example, the North Shore interaction (High Income x D5) is highly significant and positive, indicating that North Shore high income households place a higher value than other households on natural channel form in degraded streams.

In Table 8.3, the part-worth estimates and their 95 per cent confidence intervals for the models in Table 8.2 are presented.

Table 8.3   Part-worths ($/household)

		North Shore mean	95% confidence interval	South Auckland mean	95% confidence interval
Natural Stream	Water Clarity	$66	$43~$110	$67	$42~$114
	Native Fish Species	$11	$6~$20	$5	$0~$12
	Fish Habitat	-$1	-$12~$9	-$3	-$15~$8
	Moderate Vegetation	$28	-$1~$68	$16	-$10~$49
	Plentiful Vegetation	$21	$2~$50	$41	$17~$75
Degraded Stream	Water Clarity	$48	$28~$84	$73	$47~$123
	Native Fish Species	$4	-$6~$17	$0	-$13~$14
	Fish Habitat	$13	$5~$27	$5	-$6~$18
	Moderate Vegetation	$21	-$5~$53	$36	$8~$76
	Plentiful Vegetation	$20	$0~$48	$55	$28~$97
	Channel	$58	$38~$97	$42	$21~$73

Because individual characteristics interact with the site attributes, part-worths are different for different people. For example, 'Channel' is valued at \$94 by people living on the North Shore who have very high income, but is valued at \$33 by other North Shore residents. In Table 8.3, personal characteristics have been set to their population means. Consequently, the North Shore Channel part-worth in Table 8.3 (\$58) reflects the proportion of the North Shore population in the very high income category.

Several part-worths are not significantly different from zero. 'Water Clarity', 'Channel' and 'Plentiful Streamside Vegetation' part-worths are significant in all cases. The abundance of 'Native Fish Species' is significant on natural streams, but not for degraded streams. Availability of 'Fish Habitat' is only significant on North Shore degraded streams. 'Moderate Streamside Vegetation' is significant only on South Auckland degraded streams.

Marginal rates of substitution between any two attributes can be identified from the coefficients in Table 8.2. The increase in attribute i required to offset a one unit decrease in attribute j is the ratio $\beta j/\beta i$. For example, on the North Shore it is necessary to increase native fish habitat by about 0.8 km on a degraded stream to offset the loss of one native fish species on a natural stream $[\beta_j/\beta_i = N2/D3 = 0.1082 \div 0.1315 = 0.823]$. Marginal rates of substitution are relevant guides for policy where mitigation occurs through manipulation of the natural environment. Of course, there is an infinite combination of attributes that yield the same level of utility, allowing design of alternative mitigation scenarios. Part-worths are necessary for identifying monetary mitigation (compensation) measures.

4.1 Understanding

Application of choice modelling to evaluate mitigation is novel. Because the large number of attributes involved places a significant burden on respondents, and the existence of two streams in the one model is conceptually more difficult to grasp than comparing two different types of sites (such as a forest and a wetland), the question of respondent understanding arises. Related is the ease or difficulty of making choices between three alternatives with ten attributes each. These potential concerns have been addressed by inclusion of two self-evaluation questions and one interviewer evaluation question, each measured on a one-to-ten scale, with one being extremely easy to make choices and extremely understandable.

Differences between locations are not significant for respondent-evaluated understanding or respondent-evaluated ease of making choices. However, interviewer evaluation response distributions do differ between North Shore and South Auckland. While interviewers rated understanding moderately highly, they judged North Shore interviewees to have had better understanding. Responses are consistent across all three measures. Respondents typically found choices moderately easy to make, with median scores of four and modal scores of two for both locations. In general, most respondents appear to have understood the choice task quite well.

In order to detect any potential biases because of differences in understanding, part-worths have been estimated for three groups of North Shore respondents. The groups are:

- respondents who evaluated their own understanding with a score of three or less (very high understanding);
- respondents who evaluated their own understanding with a score of five or less (moderate understanding); and
- all respondents, regardless of level of understanding.

There are no significant differences between estimated part-worths for the three groups. While the reduced numbers in the very high understanding group result in broad confidence intervals, point estimates are very similar. There is no evidence to suggest that use of information from respondents with lower levels of understanding has systematically biased results. Whilst it is acknowledged that the choice tasks presented to survey respondents were relatively difficult, most respondents appear to have understood what was requested of them and have been able to make well-reasoned choices.

5   BENEFIT TRANSFER

In this case study, two separate populations within the same metropolitan area have been used. The populations differ in several respects. People living on the North Shore are generally more affluent and better educated than South Auckland residents. While age and sex distributions and home ownership rates are very similar, North Shore households are more likely to consist of only one or two people. Large households are common in South Auckland. The ethnic mixes of the two communities are also different. These two diverse communities were chosen to test for potential differences in values, and to provide a test of value transfer between communities. Each population was asked to value streams in their own area[4] (one natural stream, one degraded stream, each stream type defined to have the same characteristics in each location). The same streams may differ in value by location simply because of availability of complements and substitutes. Consequently, differences in values between populations reflect differences in people, and in study site values. For simplicity, the aggregates of these effects are referred to as differences between populations.

In this example, benefit transfer is based upon the underlying assumption that people with the same characteristics in different locations possess similar values for the same items in the same context. Tests of the underlying assumption are frequently undertaken by assessing convergent validity – testing whether benefits measured at one site are the same as those predicted at another. As with non-market valuation method convergent validity tests, it is important to control for as many factors as possible in order to remove explainable reasons for differences. Some of the sources of difference include (Boyle and Bergstrom 1992; Brouwer 2000; Brouwer and Spaninks 1999; Desvousges et al. 1992; Loomis 1992; Oglethorpe et al. 2000; Shrestha and Loomis 2001):

1. The nature of the valued sites themselves;
2. The changes valued at each of the sites;
3. Valuation methods (e.g. hedonic, contingent valuation, choice model);
4. Time of study (season or year);
5. Availability of substitutes and complements for each of the sites; and
6. Differences in the people valuing the sites (e.g. demographic, social, economic, cultural).

The choice model study of Auckland streams valued identical changes to streams with identical characteristics at each site. Furthermore, identical methodology was employed concurrently at each site to avoid elicitation method and temporal impacts that could have affected estimated values. Population differences arising from the influences of age, sex, ethnicity, household size, home ownership and education can be statistically controlled. Substitutes, complements, and other contextual differences cannot be controlled using the Auckland study design. Because it removes sources of differences numbers 1 to 4 above, and provides partial control over number 6, the Auckland study provides an excellent opportunity to measure the convergent validity of benefit measures across sites and populations.

The three principal methods of transferring benefits from a study site or sites to a policy site are direct transfer, benefit function transfer, and meta-analysis. In direct transfer, mean values estimated at the study site, or several study sites, are used directly at the policy site, without adjustment to reflect policy site characteristics. For benefit function transfer, a valuation function derived at the study site is applied to the policy site using policy site parameters. Benefit function transfer provides control over site and/or population differences, and is generally thought to be more accurate than direct benefit transfer (Rosenberger and Loomis 2003; VandenBerg et al. 2001). Meta-analysis is another form of valuation function benefit transfer. It uses results from valuation studies completed at many sites to identify statistically the influences of site and personal attributes. Direct transfer and benefit function transfer are both possible using the Auckland Stream study results, but there are insufficient data to apply meta-analysis.

5.1   Transferring the Auckland Benefit Estimates

The simplest convergent validity test of benefit transfer accuracy is comparison of benefit estimate confidence intervals for the two populations. This is a test of direct benefit transfer. It is a weak test because it fails to account for any of the potential reasons that benefits could differ between sites. However, non-overlapping confidence intervals can indicate potential problems with benefit transfer. There are no cases where North Shore and South Auckland part-worth confidence intervals do not overlap substantially (Figure 8.2).[5] Only one item (Degraded Stream Plentiful Vegetation) has part-worth confidence intervals that come close to non overlap. Consequently, this test does not signal concerns about benefit transfer of part-worths.

The overlapping confidence intervals test is relatively weak. The probability of drawing two results in the opposite tails of the distributions is much less than the significance level of the individual confidence intervals (in this case 5 per cent) (Poe et al. 1994). Consequently, it is possible for confidence intervals to overlap even if differences in part-worths are significantly different from zero. Figure 8.3 depicts confidence intervals for part-worth differences between populations. Rather than reporting two separate distributions for part-worths, each developed independently using a Monte Carlo procedure (as in Figure 8.2), a single distribution of part-worth differences is developed by subtracting the vector of Monte Carlo part-worths for one population from the vector of Monte Carlo part-worths for the other population (Poe et al. 2001).

Again, none of the distributions of part-worth differences is significantly different from zero at the 5 per cent level, although 'Degraded Stream Plentiful Vegetation' is significantly different at the 10 per cent level. These results mean that it is not possible to reject homogeneity of benefit estimates between locations. However, large variability of value estimates at each site suggests the need for caution – larger samples might produce significant differences. Further, non-significant benefit differences do not imply that benefit estimates at one site are good predictors of benefits at the other site.

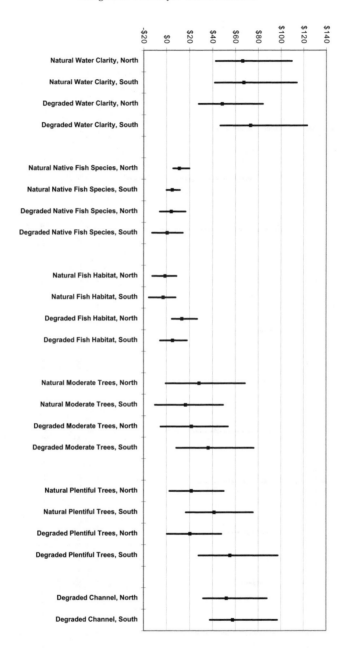

Figure 8.2 Part-worth 95 per cent confidence intervals

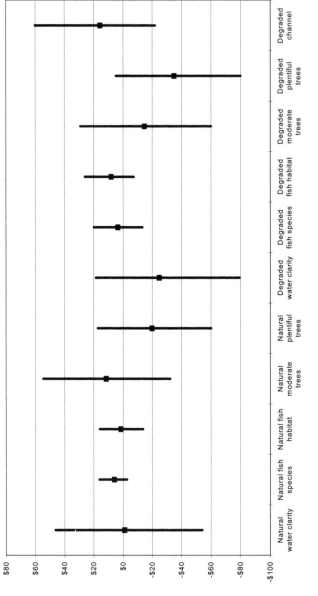

Figure 8.3   Part-worth difference (North – South) 95 per cent confidence interval

5.2   Point Benefit Direct Transfers

An alternative measure of the merits of direct benefit (part-worth) transfer validity is the percentage error in using one population point estimate to predict another population point estimate[6] (Rosenberger and Loomis 2003; VandenBerg et al. 2001). Errors arising from using point estimates from one population to predict point estimates in another population using the direct transfer approach (Table 8.4) show wide variability, with errors ranging from 2 per cent to 704 per cent. These error magnitudes are similar to those found in other studies (Rosenberger and Loomis 2003).

Table 8.4   Direct and valuation function point benefit transfer errors

		North Shore Part Worth (NSPW)	South Auckland Part Worth (SAPW)	Direct Transfer		Function Transfer	
				Error in predicting SAPW from NSPW	Error in predicting NSPW from SAPW	Error in predicting SAPW from NSPW	Error in predicting NSPW from SAPW
Natural Stream	Water Clarity	$66.23	$67.26	-2%	2%	-2%	2%
	Native Fish Species	$11.01	$4.89*	125%	-56%	125%	-56%
	Fish Habitat	-$1.32*	-$2.89*	-54%	119%	-12%	314%
	Moderate Vegetation	$28.08*	$16.42*	71%	-42%	71%	-42%
	Plentiful Vegetation	$21.42	$41.31	-48%	93%	-48%	114%
Degraded Stream	Water Clarity	$48.38	$73.12	-34%	51%	-38%	59%
	Native Fish Species	$4.10*	$0.51*	704%	-88%	704%	-169%
	Fish Habitat	$13.38	$5.25*	155%	-61%	155%	-67%
	Moderate Vegetation	$21.47*	$36.11	-41%	68%	-41%	68%
	Plentiful Vegetation	$20.12*	$55.09	-63%	174%	-63%	174%
	Channel	$57.65	$41.94	37%	-27%	39%	-21%

Note: Population means of independent variables are used throughout.
*   Not significantly different from zero at 5 per cent level.

Care should be exercised in interpreting these results. Several part-worths are not significantly different from zero. Consequently, a small change in one part-worth can result in large percentage differences. Further, even changes in sign may not be significant. When consideration is given only to cases in which both part-worth point estimates are significantly different from zero, the errors are somewhat smaller. Benefit transfer errors in these cases range from 2 per cent to 114 per cent.

5.3   Point Benefit Function Transfers

The picture for point benefit function transfers of part-worths, which apply the models in Table 8.2 using study population parameters, is very similar to that for point benefit direct transfers.[7] Consequently, function transfer part-worth difference confidence intervals are not reported here.[8] Again, there is overlap on all measures. However, when either benefit function is used to produce part-worths for the other location, the differences in part-worths for 'Degraded Stream Plentiful Vegetation' are significant at the 8 per cent level. South Auckland residents appear to place higher value than North Shore residents on 'Degraded Stream Plentiful Vegetation'.

Whether the, apparently, large errors in Table 8.4 are an indictment of benefit transfer is debateable. On the one hand, it is apparent that very large percentage errors can occur from use of transferred point estimates. However, it should be acknowledged that the confidence intervals for individual study sites are large – meaning that use of point estimates at study sites is risky. Comparison of two uncertain values introduces the opportunity of compounding that error. Just as very low errors from point estimate transfers can arise by chance and consequently do not guarantee that benefit transfer is valid, large percentage errors in transferring point estimates do not necessarily indicate that benefit transfer is invalid.

Whereas the simple overlapping confidence interval test offers an unjustified, overly enthusiastic endorsement of benefit transfer, errors associated with transfer of point benefit estimates are likely to provide an overly pessimistic view of the reliability of benefit transfer because they do not account for the confidence intervals surrounding both sets of benefit estimates. Benefit difference confidence intervals provide an approach that is intermediate to these extremes by recognising point differences and their confidence intervals concurrently. Consequently, benefit difference confidence intervals provide better indicators of the reliability of benefit transfer. Using the benefit difference approach with valuation function benefit transfer indicates significant differences (albeit at a low level of confidence) between populations for the value of 'Degraded Stream Plentiful Vegetation'.

5.4   Pooled Models

Further tests of benefit transfer are provided by pooled models, which allow detection of population differences. Pooled models allow for site-specific differences in attribute coefficients and in the role of socio-economic characteristics for each population. The different interaction variables occurring in each model in Table 8.2 indicate that location differences are likely to occur, with only Degree x N3 being significant in Table 8.2 for both groups. Here, the potential use of pooled models for benefit transfer purposes is explored with the aid of two tests.

Test 1:
The hypothesis that one utility function applies to both populations is tested by fitting the same model to each group, as well as to the pooled responses from both groups (Table 8.5).

Table 8.5   Pooled and independent models

	Attribute	North Shore	South Auckland	Pooled
Natural Stream	Water Clarity (N1)	0.6035***	0.6940***	0.6412***
Attributes	Fish Species (N2)	0.0984***	0.0517*	0.0779***
	Fish Habitat (N3)	-0.3447***	-0.1621	-0.2664***
	Moderate Vegetation (N4A)	0.2268*	0.1998	0.1980**
	Plentiful Vegetation (N4B)	0.0497	0.6627***	0.3288***
Degraded Stream	Water Clarity (D1)	0.6473***	0.8107***	0.6606***
Attributes	Fish Species (D2)	0.2298*	0.1145	0.1939**
	Fish Habitat (D3)	0.1683**	0.2052**	0.1945***
	Moderate Vegetation (D4A)	0.1735	0.3750**	0.2519***
	Plentiful Vegetation (D4B)	0.1629*	0.5854***	0.3318***
	Channel (D5)	0.2843***	0.3999***	0.3414***
	Money	-0.0092***	-0.0104***	-0.0092***
Personal	Age x D2	-0.0041*	-0.0004	-0.0028
Attributes	Age x N3	0.0069***	0.0037	0.0058***
	Degree x N3	0.1358	-0.4023**	0.0170
	Degree x D1	0.3582**	0.1393	0.2182*
	Degree x D5	-0.4202***	-0.2229	-0.3579***
	People x N4B	0.0369	-0.1128**	-0.0429
	People x D1	-0.0864*	-0.04657	-0.0477*
	Homeowner x D3	-0.0735	-0.2286**	-0.1447**
	High Income x D5	0.5055***	-0.0989	0.2724***
	Very High Income x N4B	0.1828	1.0363*	0.3877**
	Very High Income x D1	-0.0053	0.8662**	0.1344
	Very High Income x D2	-0.0783	-0.7153**	-0.2025**
	Very High Income x D5	0.2913	0.9144*	0.5272***
ASC	Status Quo	0.4417**	0.4706	0.4393**
	Second option	0.1154	-0.2026	0.0321
HEV Scale	Status Quo	1.4645	1.0943	1.2845
Parameters	Second option	1.1302	0.7605	1.0041
Relative scale parameter				0.934
N		1331	1256	2587
LL_R		-1433.811	-1361.700	-2797.702
LL_{UR}		-1302.836	-1242.487	-2579.131
Rho^2		0.091	0.088	0.078
LR test of pooled versus separate models		$\chi^2 = 67.616$	$P(\chi^2,30) = 1.01 \times 10^{-5}$	
Swait–Louviere test of relative scale parameter		$\chi^2 = 0.410$	$P(\chi^2,1) = 0.522$	

Note: *Significance at 10% level; ** Significance at 5% level; ***Significance at 1% level.

The interactions specified in these models include all significant interactions identified in the individual population models fitted in Table 8.2. A method proposed by Swait and Louviere (1993) was used to identify the optimal relative scale of error terms for the two data sets in the pooled model. The relative scale parameter is very close to one. The Swait–Louviere test result indicates that allowing non-uniform errors did not significantly improve model fit relative to the naïve pooled model that assumes identical errors. A likelihood ratio test measures the significance of improvement in fit from use of separate models. The test statistic is distributed χ^2 with degrees of freedom equal to the number of estimated parameters. The result is highly significant.

$$\chi 2 = -2*(LL_{Pooled} - (LL_{North\,Shore} + LL_{South\,Auckland})) = 67.616 \qquad (8.3)$$

Together, these results indicate that different utility functions apply to the two populations and that the differences occur in the estimated coefficients, not in the scale factor (Swait and Louviere 1993). Different utility functions imply that transferring valuation functions between populations may lead to estimation errors.

Test 2:
A pooled model is developed that includes location dummy variables interacted with site attribute and personal characteristics. This type of model has the advantage that it concurrently produces population-specific coefficients within a single model. Coefficient differences between populations are automatically identified without the need for comparison of separate model coefficients, part-worths or their confidence intervals. The location-related interactions take two forms. Two-way interactions (e.g. South x N2) show the direct impact of location on the value of the attribute. Three-way interactions (e.g. South x Degree x N3) show differences by location in the way personal characteristics influence the values of specific attributes. Results are reported in Table 8.6. As with Test 1, the Swait–Louviere procedure was used to identify the relative scale parameter, which at 0.990 is not significantly different from one. A likelihood ratio test $[\chi^2 = -2*(LL_R - LL_{UR})]$[9] indicates that location variables are highly significant as a group.

Five personal characteristics (High Income, Age, Degree, Homeowner, Household Size) affect attribute values independent of location. Three attribute part-worths differ between locations, independent of personal characteristics. The value of 'Natural Stream Fish Species' abundance is greater for North Shore residents, while South Auckland residents place higher values on 'Plentiful Vegetation' at both types of stream. The significant two-way interactions between attributes and location (South x N2; South x N4B; South x D4B) indicate that, despite overlapping

Table 8.6 Pooled model with location variables

	Attribute	Coefficient
Natural Stream Attributes	Water Clarity (N1)	0.6514***
	Fish Species (N2)	0.1169***
	Fish Habitat (N3)	-0.2718***
	Moderate Vegetation (N4A)	0.2038**
	Plentiful Vegetation (N4B)	0.2098**
Degraded Stream Attributes	Water Clarity (D1)	0.7429***
	Fish Species (D2)	0.0644*
	Fish Habitat (D3)	0.2041***
	Moderate Vegetation (D4A)	0.2662***
	Plentiful Vegetation (D4B)	0.2228**
	Channel (D5)	0.3318***
	Money	-0.0097***
Personal Attributes	High Income x D5	0.5536***
	Age x N3	0.0063***
	Degree x D5	-0.3021***
	Homeowner x D3	-0.1593***
	People x D1	-0.0549**
Location Variables	South x N2	-0.0720**
	South x N4B	0.3665**
	South x D4B	0.2687**
	South x Degree x N3	-0.4040***
	South x People x N4B	-0.0982***
	South x High Income x D5	-0.5868***
	South x Very High Income x N4B	0.9624**
	South x Very High Income x D1	0.8234**
	South x Very High Income x D2	-0.6119***
	South x Very High Income x D5	0.7734**
Alternative-specific constants	Status Quo	0.4357**
	Second option	-0.0362
HEV Scale Parameters	Status Quo	1.2471
	Second option	0.9299
Relative scale parameter		0.9900
N		2587
$LL_{Constant\ only}$		-2797.702
$LL_{No\ location\ variables}$		-2591.157
$LL_{Full\ model}$		-2557.716
Rho^2		0.086
LR test of location variables	$\chi^2 = 66.882$ $P(\chi^2,10) = 1.77\text{x}10^{-10}$	
Swait–Louviere test of relative scale parameter	$\chi^2 = 0.010$ $P(\chi^2,1) = 0.9203$	

Note: *Significance at 10% level; ** Significance at 5% level; ***Significance at 1% level.

95 per cent confidence intervals, part-worths for 'Natural Stream Fish Species' and 'Plentiful Vegetation' on both stream types are significantly different at the 95 per cent confidence level.

There are seven three-way interactions that differentiate the impact of personal characteristics by location. Of particular note is the diverse influence on 'Degraded Stream Channel' form because of income. High Income causes increased willingness to pay for a more natural channel form on the North Shore (β = 0.5536), but has no significant effect in South Auckland (β = 0.5536 - 0.5868 = -0.0332). However, South Auckland displays a strong impact from Very High Income that does not occur in North Shore.

Table 8.7 reports site-specific part-worth estimates and 95 per cent confidence intervals for each location from the pooled model. In each case, results are modelled for a 45-year-old respondent with a university degree from a high-income, home-owning household of three people.

Table 8.7   Part-worths – pooled model ($/household)

45-year-old homeowner with a degree. Hhld. income more than $50,000 p.a. 3 people in household.		North Shore	95% confidence interval	South Auckland	95% confidence interval
Natural Stream	Water Clarity	$67	$49 ~ $94	$67	$49 ~ $94
	Fish Species	$12	$7 ~ $18	$5	$0 ~ $10
	Fish Habitat	$1	-$6 ~ $9	-$40	-$68 ~ -$16
	Moderate Vegetation	$21	-$1 ~ $45	$21	-$1 ~ $45
	Plentiful Vegetation	$22	$3 ~ $43	$29	$10 ~ $54
Degraded Stream	Water Clarity	$59	$43 ~ $86	$59	$43 ~ $86
	Fish Species	$7	$0 ~ $15	$7	$0 ~ $15
	Fish Habitat	$5	-$4 ~ $14	$5	-$4 ~ $14
	Moderate Vegetation	$27	$8 ~ $50	$27	$8 ~ $50
	Plentiful Vegetation	$23	$4 ~ $44	$51	$28 ~ $77
	Channel	$60	$34 ~ $92	$0	-$33 ~ $32

The shaded cells in Table 8.7 highlight attributes for which part-worths are invariant between populations irrespective of personal characteristics. 'Degraded Stream Water Clarity' and 'Degraded Stream Fish Species' do not differ in the case reported in Table 8.7 because their differential effects only occur for very high-income households. The simple non-overlapping confidence interval test indicates highly significant differences between populations for 'Degraded Stream Channel Form' and 'Natural Stream Fish Habitat' part-worths. The other three part-worths that are affected by personal characteristics exhibit confidence interval overlaps.

The values in Table 8.8 have been derived from a Monte Carlo simulation of the differences in part-worths for the five attributes in Table 8.7 that differ by location. In each case the estimated South Auckland part-worth has been subtracted from the estimated North Shore part-worth to yield a simulated distribution of part-worth differences. In only one case (Natural Stream Plentiful Vegetation) does the 95 per cent confidence interval include zero. These results indicate that, even after controlling for personal characteristics, North Shore residents in this demographic profile place significantly higher values on abundance of 'Natural Stream Fish Species', availability of 'Natural Stream Fish Habitat', and 'Degraded Stream Channel Form'. South Aucklanders value 'Degraded Stream Plentiful Vegetation' more highly than do North Shore residents.

Table 8.8   Pooled model part-worth differences

45-year-old homeowner with a degree. Household income more than $50,000 p.a. 3 people in household.	Part worth differences (North minus South)	95% confidence interval
Natural Stream Fish Species	$7	$1 ~ $15
Natural Stream Fish Habitat	$42	$17 ~ $70
Natural Stream Plentiful Vegetation	-$7	-$30 ~ $14
Degraded Stream Plentiful Vegetation	-$28	-$58 ~ -$3
Degraded Stream Channel	$60	$29 ~ $100

Differences arise irrespective of personal characteristics because of the significant two-way interaction variables (South x N2, South x N4B and South x D4B) in Table 8.6. While part-worth differences occur regardless of personal characteristics, differences vary by demographic profile. Consequently, the non-significance of 'Natural Stream Plentiful Vegetation' in Table 8.8 is not inconsistent with the model in Table 8.6. For example, changing household income to more than $100,000 per annum (while leaving all other characteristics unchanged) produces significant part-worth differences for this attribute, as well as for 'Degraded Stream Water Clarity' and 'Degraded Stream Fish Species' abundance.

6   CONCLUSIONS

This study has used choice modelling to identify community willingness to trade-off stream attributes. People have understood the tasks asked of them and have given consistent responses that have allowed estimation of utility functions, marginal rates of substitution, and stream attribute part-worths. The values estimated allow the design of mitigation to offset damages in Auckland streams. Part-worth estimates provide the information necessary for the assessment of mitigation options. Thus community values can be associated with degradation/mitigation options. A range of mitigation scenarios can be evaluated, provided cost data are available, to identify the cheapest mitigation option available to offset project impacts.

A limitation of the existing approach may be the use of a linear utility function without interactions between site attributes. The identity between willingness to pay and willingness to accept compensation measures imposed by the linear utility function is not consistent with theoretical or empirical results (Horowitz and McConnell 2002). Errors introduced by this restriction are likely to be small when part-worths are small relative to income. They are also likely to be avoided to a certain extent by the design of the study. By definition, natural stream attributes could only get worse when moving from the status quo, while degraded stream attributes could only improve. Consequently, the framing of the study predisposes it to estimate willingness to accept measures for damages to the natural stream, and willingness to pay measures for enhancements to the degraded stream. This is consistent with the policy question frame.

The study provides important insights into benefits transfer. Overlapping part-worth confidence intervals indicate similar values between the two populations, but provide an overly optimistic view of benefits transfer when compared to confidence intervals of attribute part-worth differences. Point estimate transfers, whether direct or benefit function transfers, resulted in some very large errors. However, point transfers do not account for uncertainty in the estimates at either site and so percentage errors of point transfers provide poor tests of benefit transfer. Tests of part-worth differences and two pooled model tests were used to overcome deficiencies in overlapping confidence interval and point estimate tests. Part-worth difference tests identified significant differences (albeit at low levels) in one part-worth using both direct and benefit transfer approaches.

Two different pooled model tests have been used to show that the same utility function does not apply to both populations. Because it has a larger sample size and the ability to control for other factors, tests based on the pooled model with location variables have more power to identify differences than do tests based on independently estimated models for each site. In addition, pooled models identify the sources of part-worth differences. Part-worth difference distributions from the pooled model that includes location effects are significantly different from zero, consistent with the significance of location variables in the model. The pooled models indicate that errors will arise from transfer of benefits between locations. Those errors were not identified by overlapping confidence interval or part-worth difference tests based on independent models.

Studies of the type conducted here have the luxury of values being identified for both the original and target sites (or populations). When benefit transfer is undertaken for policy purposes it is not known what the true value at the policy site is, or even the range of values that include the true value. If that information were available, there would be no need for benefit transfer. In that situation it is not possible to compare value distributions or point estimates of value, or to fit pooled models. The analyst has three options – direct transfer of benefits, transfer of valuation functions, or not to transfer benefits at all. Significant part-worth differences remaining in the pooled model after controlling for socio-economic effects suggest that there are unaccounted-for differences between values in the two population groups. Such differences may arise because of contextual differences, unaccounted-for socio-economic differences, or simply because people living at the two locations value stream attributes differently. These results caution against benefit transfer.

What would happen if valuation functions or point estimates were transferred in these cases? It is not possible to provide an unambiguous answer to that question, as it depends on the policy proposal being evaluated. When off-site mitigation is undertaken, several attributes may change at each stream, which means that errors may compound – or they may cancel each other out. While the potential to be wrong is moderated in this situation, the implications of being wrong may be very serious. It is apparent that the use of point estimates has the potential to produce highly biased results. The implications when confidence intervals are developed for welfare changes are less likely to be problematic, but, because errors may compound across several attributes, still have the potential to provide extremely misleading indicators of welfare change. Overall, the evidence presented here adds weight to the growing literature that has identified large potential errors from benefit transfer, even under close-to-ideal conditions.

ACKNOWLEDGEMENTS

We gratefully acknowledge the assistance of Jeff Bennett, John Rolfe, Chris Hatton and Graeme Ridley in designing and reviewing this study. This chapter was completed while Geoff Kerr was a Visiting Fellow at the Asia Pacific School of Economics and Government (APSEG) at the

Australian National University, Canberra. We are extremely appreciative of the encouragement and support offered by APSEG.

NOTES

1. In order to clarify the nature of the changes involved in using a choice experiment to evaluate off-site mitigation, socio-economic effects have been suppressed.
2. While the experimental design precludes interactions between site attributes, it does not curtail interactions between site attributes and individual respondent characteristics.
3. The hypothesis that the status quo is preferred to either of the options entailing change was tested by utilisation of models that included an ASC on the status quo and no ASC on either of the other options. Results mirrored those in Table 8.2, indicating a significant preference for the status quo, with no significant change to other coefficients. Since these alternative models contain less information, the more general models that allow detection of all order effects are presented in Table 8.2.
4. People living in North Shore valued North Shore streams and people living in South Auckland valued South Auckland streams.
5. Also, there are no cases in which degraded and natural stream attribute part-worth confidence intervals do not overlap. Differences in attribute values between stream types are not addressed here.
6. Percentage error is defined as 100 x ('Estimate' – 'Actual')/'Actual', where 'Estimate' is the point measure of benefits at the study site and 'Actual' is the point measure of benefits at the policy site.
7. Valuation function benefit transfers result in some predictions better than, and some predictions worse than, direct benefit transfers.
8. The benefit function transfer analogue of the direct transfer estimates in Figure 8.4.
9. LL_{UR} is the log likelihood of the full (31 parameter) model that includes location variables. LL_R is the log likelihood of the same excluding the ten location variables.

REFERENCES

Boyle, K.J. and J.C. Bergstrom (1992), 'Benefit transfer studies: myths, pragmatism and idealism', *Water Resources Research*, **28** (3), 657–63.

Brouwer, R. (2000), 'Environmental value transfer: state of the art and future prospects', *Ecological Economics*, **32**, 137–52.

Brouwer, R. and F.A. Spaninks (1999), 'The validity of environmental benefits transfer: further empirical testing', *Environmental and Resource Economics*, **14**, 95–117.

Desvousges, W.H., M.C. Naughton and G.R. Parsons (1992), 'Benefit transfer: conceptual problems in estimating water quality benefits using existing studies', *Water Resources Research*, **28** (3), 675–83.

Hahn, G.J. and S.S. Shapiro (1966), *A Catalogue and Computer Programme for the Design and Analysis of Symmetric and Asymmetric Fractional Factorial Experiments*, Report No. 66-0-165, New York: General Electric Research and Development Centre.

Horowitz, J.K. and K.E. McConnell (2002), 'A review of WTA/WTP studies', *Journal of Environmental Economics and Management*, **44** (3), 426–47.

Kerr, G.N. and B.M.H. Sharp (2002), *Community Perceptions of Stream Attributes: Focus Group Results*, Report to Auckland Regional Council. Agribusiness and Economics Research Unit, Canterbury: Lincoln University.

Kerr, G.N. and B.M.H. Sharp (2003), *Community Mitigation Preferences: A Choice Modelling Study of Auckland Streams*, Agribusiness and Economics Research Unit Research Report No. 256, Canterbury: Lincoln University.

Loomis, J.B. (1992), 'The evolution of a more rigorous approach to benefit transfer: benefit function transfer', *Water Resources Research*, **28** (3), 701–5.

Oglethorpe, D., N. Hanley, S. Hussain and R. Sanderson (2000), 'Modelling the transfer of the socio-economic benefits of environmental management', *Environmental Modelling and Software*, **15**, 343–56.

Poe, G.L., E.K. Severance-Lossin and M.P. Welsh (1994), 'Measuring the difference (X-Y) of simulated distributions: a convolutions approach', *American Journal of Agricultural Economics*, **76**, 904–15.

Poe, G.L., K.L. Giraud and J.B. Loomis (2001), *Simple Computational Methods for Measuring the Differences of Empirical Distributions: Application to Internal and External Scope Tests in Contingent Valuation*, Staff Paper 2001–05, Department of Agricultural, Resource and Managerial Economics, Cornell University.

Rolfe, J. and J.W. Bennett (2003), 'WTP and WTA in Relation to Irrigation Development in the Fitzroy Basin, Queensland', Paper presented to the 47th annual conference of the Australian Agricultural and Resource Economics Society, Fremantle, Western Australia, 12–14 February.

Rosenberger, R. and J.B. Loomis (2003), 'Benefit Transfer' in P.A. Champ, K.J. Boyle and T.C. Brown (eds) *A Primer on Nonmarket Valuation*, Dordrecht: Kluwer Academic Publishers, pp. 445–82.

Shrestha, R.K. and J.B. Loomis (2001), 'Testing a meta-analysis model for benefit transfer in international outdoor recreation', *Ecological Economics*, **39**, 67–83.

Swait, J. and J. Louviere (1993), 'The role of the scale parameter in the estimation and comparison of multinomial logit models', *Journal of Marketing Research*, **30**, 305–14.

VandenBerg, T.P., G.L. Poe and J.R. Powell (2001), 'Assessing the Accuracy of Benefits Transfers: Evidence from a Multi-site Contingent Valuation Study of Groundwater Quality', in J.C. Bergstrom, K.J. Boyle and G.L. Poe (eds) *The Economic Value of Water Quality*, Cheltenham UK and Northampton, MA, USA: Edward Elgar, pp. 110–20.

Whitten, S.M. and J.W. Bennett (2001), *Non-market Values of Wetlands: A Choice Modelling Study of Wetlands in the Upper South East of South Australia and the Murrumbidgee River Floodplain in New South Wales*, Private and Social Values of Wetlands Research Report No.8, School of Economics and Management, Canberra: University of New South Wales.

9.   Transferring the Environmental Values of Wetlands

Stuart M. Whitten and Jeff Bennett

1   INTRODUCTION

The management of wetlands located on private lands is a contentious and topical issue in Australia and worldwide. Conflict is focused on aspects of resource management that are perceived to generate benefits and costs that extend beyond the current landowner and are seemingly not considered by the landowner within existing decision mechanisms. These resources generate private and social values that include both use and non-use values. Wetland policies that are designed to help resolve conflicts between beneficiaries of wetland outputs should be based on sound estimates of the relative values generated by wetlands.

Different wetland types and the same wetland type in different locations can produce differing mixes of outputs. The benefits and harms generated by estuarine wetlands differ significantly from those provided by freshwater wetlands, which differ from those provided by desert lakes and so forth. In addition, a benefit in one location may be a harm in another. For example, increased waterfowl populations could be beneficial (pest control) or harmful (consuming pasture) or even both – but to different individuals (pasture consuming waterfowl that are recreationally hunted).

Estimation of marginal changes to non-use values associated with alternative wetland management options is complex, time-consuming and expensive. Therefore, estimation of the full array of benefits and harms of all wetland types in all locations would be prohibitively time-consuming and repetitive. In this chapter the focus is on the potential for benefit transfers from two existing case studies of non-use wetland values in the Upper South East (USE) of South Australia (SA) and the Murrumbidgee River floodplain (MRF) between Wagga Wagga and Hay in New South Wales (NSW), Australia.

Benefit transfers remain a contentious issue because of the differences in environmental services being considered, the values held by differing populations, and the rigour of the valuation study being transferred. Debate about the appropriateness of benefit transfer continues, despite a number of writers developing protocols for benefit transfer, including Desvousges, Naughton and Parsons (1992), Brouwer (2000), and Rosenberger and Loomis (2001). Three particular issues have been raised in recent contributions to the literature that will be addressed in this chapter:

1. Extrapolating benefits across surveyed populations (Morrison 2000);
2. Transferring benefits to other populations (Morrison and Bennett 2000; Morrison, Bennett, Blamey and Louviere 2002; van Bueren and Bennett 2004; Morrison and Bennett 2004; and Rolfe and Windle 2005); and
3. Transferring benefits across sites (Morrison and Bennett 2000; Barton 2002; Morrison, Bennett, Blamey and Louviere 2002; and van Bueren and Bennett 2004).

The chapter is structured as follows. In section 2 the context for potential benefit transfer from the case study wetlands is set out via a discussion of characteristics of the case study wetlands and the nature of the resultant non-use values that are generated. The non-market valuation exercise, including the choice modelling questionnaire, sampling procedure, and results for the two case studies are described in section 3 in preparation for the benefit transfer exercise. Section 4 comprises a discussion of the implications from the choice model results for extrapolating benefits across the surveyed population, transferring the estimated benefits to other populations and finally transferring benefits across sites. A brief summary of the main conclusions for benefit transfer then completes the paper.

2   NATURE OF THE CASE STUDY WETLANDS AND VALUES

The estimation of the value of marginal changes to non-use benefits generated by the wetlands discussed in this chapter is nested within a wider project to inform wetland policy development and implementation. An integrated bio-economic model for the values generated by wetlands was developed to estimate the relative values generated by alternative wetland management strategies (Whitten and Bennett 2005). These estimates of the benefits enjoyed by society were then used as a basis for designing appropriate wetland policies. These benefit estimates explicitly include a range of non-use values that were estimated via application of the choice modelling technique. These include the option values associated with future potential uses, existence values from the knowledge that healthy wetland ecosystems remain, including the continued existence of flora and fauna species, and bequest values for the passing of these values to future generations.

The two case study areas for which bio-economic models were estimated, including estimates of non-use values, were the USE region of SA and the MRF in NSW. The approximate locations of the case study areas are shown in Figure 9.1.

Figure 9.1   Location of case study areas

2.1   The Upper South East of South Australia

In the USE of SA, large areas of wetlands have been cleared and/or drained and converted to pasture for agricultural production. Sixty-three thousand hectares of healthy wetlands, or less than 7 per cent of the original wetland area, remain in the region. The reduction in wetland area is further threatened by the impacts of dryland salinity. Dryland salinity has resulted from landscape scale replacement of native vegetation with alfalfa and then, following the impact of the alfalfa aphid in the late 1970s, annual pasture species. The change in species has progressively increased groundwater recharge within the region and thus caused elevated groundwater levels in and around wetlands.

The array of values generated by USE wetlands is shown in Table 9.1. The conversion of the landscape to pastoral production was motivated by the private values so obtained. However, the private and social values generated by natural wetlands in the region have been significantly reduced. The area of healthy wetlands and remnant vegetation, the number of threatened species that benefit and the number of ducks hunted were used to describe the changes to social values.[1] Other values commonly associated with wetlands, such as groundwater recharge, are either not associated with USE wetlands or are not anticipated to change as a result of changes to wetland management in the region.

Table 9.1   Values estimated for changes to USE wetland management

	Wetland owner (private) values	**Social values**
Use values that change	Pasture production	Hunting
	Hunting	Public tourism and recreation
	Tourism	Private tourism and recreation
	Recreation	
	Costs of management	Beautify regional landscapes
Non-use values that change	Not estimated[a]	Healthy wetlands
		Healthy remnant vegetation
		Threatened species protection
		Duck hunting
Change to values not significant[b]	Firewood/timber production	Natural fire break
	Water supply	Water quality benefits
	Irrigation drainage	Fishing
	Fishing	Groundwater re/discharge
	Attract pest-eating birds	Flood mitigation

Notes:
a   Note that wetland owners receive the non-use social values as private values but changes to these values were not estimated.
b   Changes to some of these values may be significant at the farm scale but were not estimated.

2.2   The Murrumbidgee River Floodplain in New South Wales

Many wetlands on the MRF between Wagga Wagga and Hay have been subject to degradation as a result of land and water management practices. In the MRF, relatively few wetlands have been drained, but many wetlands on the floodplain have been droughted while those closely linked with the river have been over-flooded as floodwater is stored and released for irrigated crop and pasture production. Wetlands in the MRF have also been degraded by logging, grazing and to a lesser extent, irrigation drainage management practices.

As in the USE region, the change in land and water management was motivated by the private values generated from irrigation, grazing and timber production. The social values of wetlands have been lowered via reduced bird and fish breeding and reductions in water quality and wetland health.

The array of values for which values are estimated in the MRF is shown in Table 9.2. The overarching non-use values for each region are the same (existence, option and bequest values) but are defined using different attributes in the MRF. These non-use attributes are the area of healthy wetlands, the population of native birds, and the population of native fish.[2]

Table 9.2   Values estimated for changes to MRF wetland management

	Wetland owner (private) values	Social values
Use values that change	Pasture production	Public tourism and recreation
	Firewood/timber production	Beautify the regional landscape
	Costs of management	
	Water supply	
	Drainage storage/basin	
Non-use values that change	Not estimated[a]	Healthy wetlands
		Native birds present
		Native fish present
Change to values not significant[b]	Tourism	Natural fire break/hazard
	Fishing	Water quality benefits
	Attract pest-eating birds	Fishing
	Recreation	Groundwater recharge
		Flood mitigation
		Private tourism and recreation
		Number of farmers in region[c]

Notes:
a   Note that wetland owners receive the non-use social values as private values but changes to these values were not estimated.
b   Changes to some of these values may be significant at the farm scale but were not estimated.
c   Values for change to farmers leaving were estimated due to impacts perceived by respondents as identified in focus groups.

3   CHOICE MODELLING ESTIMATES OF WETLAND VALUES

The choice modelling technique (CM) was used to estimate the value of marginal changes to the non-use value attributes shown in Tables 9.1 and 9.2. It is anticipated that these attributes will also have captured some aesthetic values associated with changes to the appearance of the regional landscape in the MRF and USE and future option values for duck hunting in the USE. These non-use values of wetlands represent the option values associated with future potential (unknown) uses, existence values from the knowledge that healthy wetland ecosystems and the values they support remain, and bequest values for the passing of these values to future generations.

Benefit transfer of environmental values depends on confidence in the empirical rigour of the initial study and similar types and quantities of the environmental good in question among other factors. The nature of the values estimated, along with the empirical rigour of the CM valuation exercise, is in part the focus in this section.

3.1   Questionnaire Design

The questionnaire was designed to facilitate a mail-out, mail-back format. Questionnaire design followed the basic design parameters recommended by Bennett and Adamowicz (2001) including a letter of introduction and the following questionnaire elements:

- preamble including background and contextual information (framing information);
- statement of the problem and potential solution;
- introduction to the choice sets;
- the choice sets;
- debriefing questions;
- socio-economic and attitude-based questions; and
- opportunity for additional feedback.

An initial draft questionnaire was designed, based on questionnaire designs from Blamey et al. (1997) and Morrison, Bennett and Blamey (1997). This design was refined following feedback from several rounds of focus groups. Focus group discussions targeted the preamble, statements of the issue and solution, and the choice sets.

The attributes used to describe the changes to the non-use values in the questionnaire are summarised for the two case study areas in Table 9.3. The monetary cost is included as an attribute to indicate the trade-offs between the resources required to produce the environmental attributes and alternative resource use options. Note the inclusion of 'number of farmers leaving' in the MRF to account for respondent perceptions of the impacts of wetland management change on farm livelihoods.

Table 9.3   USE and MRF survey attributes

Attributes for USE survey	Attributes for MRF survey
• Cost to the respondent • Area of healthy wetlands • Area of healthy remnants • Threatened species that will benefit • Number of ducks hunted	• Cost to the respondent • Area of healthy wetlands • Population of native water and woodland birds • Population of native fish • Number of farmers leaving

The choice sets are a crucial element of any CM application and are the vehicle used to obtain respondent information on their trade-offs between alternatives. The final design is shown in Figures 9.2 and 9.3 for the USE questionnaire. Key features of the design are:

1. The labels 'What I pay' and 'What I get' clarify the trade-offs facing respondents;
2. The choice options are read horizontally; and
3. Icons represent the attribute levels. The icon levels were shown in a 'Symbol key' that folded out to allow respondents to view it while completing the choice sets (shown for the USE in Figure 9.2).

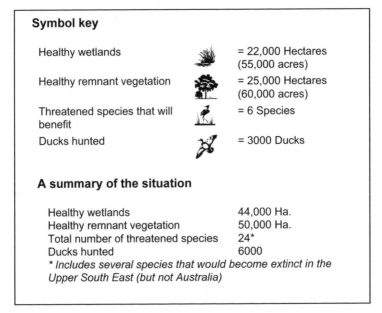

Figure 9.2   Foldout symbol key used in questionnaire

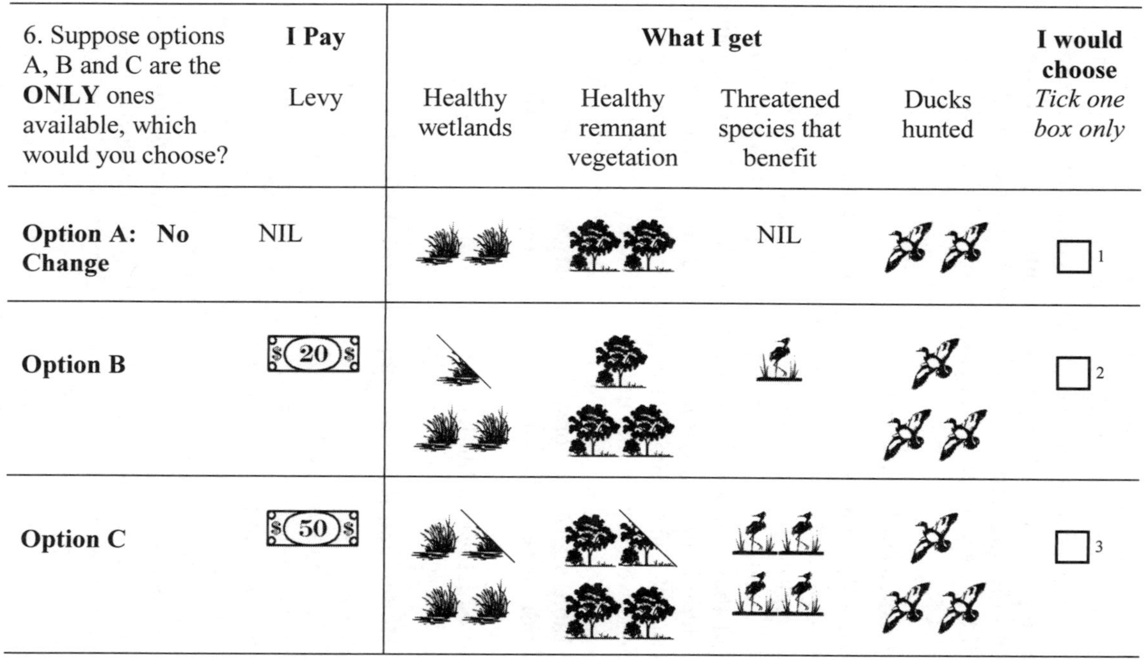

6. Suppose options A, B and C are the ONLY ones available, which would you choose?	I Pay Levy	What I get Healthy wetlands	Healthy remnant vegetation	Threatened species that benefit	Ducks hunted	I would choose *Tick one box only*
Option A: No Change	NIL			NIL		☐ [1]
Option B	20					☐ [2]
Option C	50					☐ [3]

Note: The symbols were related to the quantitative numbers in the preamble of the survey and respondents were reminded of the key to the symbols in the introduction to the choice sets.

Figure 9.3 Choice set design for USE questionnaire

The levels used in the choice sets are an important attribute in benefit transfer exercises because value estimates are generally only considered valid for the range in which they are estimated due to the impacts of diminishing marginal utility from additional units of a good. The attribute levels used in the USE and MRF CM questionnaires are shown in Table 9.4. The scale of management changes differs significantly between the two case study regions. For example, it is readily apparent from the levels in Table 9.4 that the wetland area for which a management change is considered differs by an order of magnitude in the MRF compared to the USE.

3.2   Survey Response Characteristics

A total of 4 800 questionnaires about the future management of wetlands on the MRF (2 800) and USE (2 000) were sent to households in the Murrumbidgee region of New South Wales, the Australian Capital Territory, and Adelaide and Naracoorte in SA in February 2001. It should be noted that a major dryland salinity and flood management scheme that included improving some wetlands management was being undertaken in the USE at the time of the questionnaire being distributed and water reforms were continuing in NSW including within the MRF.

Basic data on the sample, response rates and sample characteristics are shown in Table 9.5. A response rate of just over 30 per cent was achieved for both surveys. This rate compares favourably with other mail-out CM surveys in Australia. Respondents tended to self-select, being older, more highly educated, more likely to be male and wealthier than the Australian average (ABS 1997).

3.3   Choice Models and Resultant Implicit Price Estimates

Nested logit models (NLM) were estimated for the MRF and USE following tests of preliminary models showing violations of the assumption of independence of irrelevant alternatives (IIA violations).[3] The results for the USE and MRF are shown in Tables 9.6 and 9.7 respectively. In each case the explanatory power of the models is very high with adjusted rho-squares of 32.9 per cent and 33.6 per cent respectively.

The way in which the attributes are entered in the two models differs significantly. In the USE model, initial models produced a statistically insignificant coefficient for the 'area of healthy wetlands' attribute. Interacting wetlands with the results from a question designed to identify whether respondents generally supported or opposed conservation effectively splits this variable into two statistically significant components depending on attitudes towards conservation. A similar response was found with respect to the number of ducks hunted. In this case the

Table 9.4 *Attribute levels used in the USE and MRF questionnaires*

Attribute	Unit of measurement	Levels used in questionnaire			
MRF		Status quo	Level 1	Level 2	Level 3
Area of healthy wetlands	Hectares	2 500	5 000	7 500	12 500
Population of water and woodland birds	Percentage of pre-1800 bird numbers	40	60	70	80
Population of native fish	Percentage of pre-1800 fish numbers	20	30	40	60
Number of farmers leaving	Number	0	5	10	15
Cost to the respondent (income tax levy)	One-off dollar cost per household in 2000-01[a]	0	20	50	200
USE		Status quo	Level 1	Level 2	Level 3
Area of healthy wetlands	Hectares	44 000	55 000	66 000	77 000
Area of healthy remnant vegetation	Hectares	50 000	75 000	87 500	100 000
Threatened species that will benefit	Number	0	6	12	24
Ducks Hunted	Number	6 000	3 000	9 000	12 000
Cost to the respondent (income tax levy)	One-off dollar cost per household in 2000-01[a]	0	20	50	200

Note: [a] Australian dollars

Table 9.5 *CM questionnaire sample and underlying population characteristics*

Characteristic	ACT	Wagga Wagga	Griffith	Adelaide	Naracoorte	Aggregate
MRF Sample						
Response rate	33.7%	33.0%	22.0%	34.1%	N.A.	33.7%
Median age	48	49	52	52		50
Sex (% Male)	61.8%	55.8%	66.2%	60.2%		60.9%
Median income	$52,000 to $77,999	$36,400 to $51,999	$36,400 to $51,999	$36,400 to $51,999		$36,400 to $51,999
Tertiary educated	52.3%	28.4%	26.0%	42.5%		37.9%
USE Sample						
Response rate	33.0%	N.A.	N.A.	32.1%	28.7%	30.8%
Median age	48			49	50	50
Sex (% Male)	50.5%			59.9%	61.1%	58.1%
Median income	$52,000-$77,999			$36,400 to $51,999	$36,400 to $51,999	$36,400 to $51,999
Tertiary educated	46.1%			29.7%	16.0%	27.4%

ABS 1996 census data	ACT	Wagga Wagga	Griffith	Adelaide	Naracoorte	Australia
Median age	39	39	41	43	43	42
Sex (% Male)	48.7%	48.5%	50.3%	47.8%	51.0%	48.9%
Median income	$48,699	$32,850	$33,163	$30,971	$28,647	$34,322
Tertiary educated	23.9%	8.9%	6.1%	10.4%	5.1%	11.0%

Notes: Response rate adjusted for non-delivered questionnaires, age and percentage male for individuals 18 years and over, income is median annual income. For all samples, the sample is significantly different from the population at the 95 per cent level of confidence except ACT Gender.

'number of ducks hunted' parameter was interacted with the results of a question asking respondents whether they had hunted ducks. In the USE model, all attributes are entered into the model linearly. In the MRF model, the best performing functional form had all attributes except 'cost to respondents' and 'number of farmers leaving' in a $1/x$ format, thus allowing for diminishing marginal returns to additional conservation outcomes.

Table 9.6   USE nested logit model results

Model statistic		
N (choice sets)	2385	
Log Likelihood	-1337.703	
Adjusted rho-square (%)	32.882	
Utility functions		
Alternative specific constant equals 1 for option 2 else zero	0.20E+0	**
Cost – size of one-off levy on income via income tax	-0.13E-1	**
Area of healthy wetlands (hectares)	-0.16E-4	**
Area of healthy remnant vegetation (hectares)	0.12E-4	**
Number of threatened species that benefit	0.63E-1	**
Number of ducks hunted	-0.57E-4	**
Interaction term combining pro-conservation respondents and wetland area	0.36E-4	**
Interaction term combining duck hunters and number of ducks hunted	0.97E-4	**
Branch choice equations		
Alternative specific constant equals 1 for options 2 and 3 else zero	7.62E+0	**
Log of respondent income	-0.68E+0	**
Dummy variable equals 1 for respondents intending to visit else zero	-0.51E+0	**
Age of respondent	-0.15E-1	**
Dummy variable equals one for respondent reporting they were confused about survey design or information else zero	0.38E+0	**
Dummy variable equals one for respondent indicating they either do not trust government to make levy one-off or protested against the payment vehicle on other grounds else zero	2.36E+0	**
Dummy variable equals 1 for ACT respondents else zero	-0.34E+0	*
Inclusive value parameters[a]		
Inclusive value parameter – Support	0.99E+0	**
Inclusive value parameter – No support (fixed parameter)	1.00E+0	

Notes:
The dependent variable is the ratio of the probability of the choice being made given the choice options.
* denotes significance of parameter at the 10% level, ** denotes significance at the 5% level.
a The nested logit model includes additional parameters for each choice set partition (i.e. nesting level). These inclusive values (alternatively termed logsum or expected maximum utility) are the scale parameters in each level of the model. The upper level scale parameter is normalised to 1 and that for the lower level left free to be estimated (for more information see Louviere, Henscher and Swait, 2000).

Table 9.7   MRF nested logit model results

Model statistics		
N (choice sets)	3148	
Log Likelihood	-2400.30	
Adjusted rho-square (%)	33.58	
Lower level choice equations		
Alternative specific constant equals 1 for option 2 else zero	1.20E-01	**
Cost – size of one-off levy on income via income tax	-0.12E-01	**
1 / Area of healthy wetlands (hectares)	-7.83E+03	**
1 / Number of native birds as a percentage of pre-1800 numbers	-5.10E-01	**
1 / Number of native fish as a percentage of pre-1800 numbers	-3.28E-01	**
Number of farmers who leave as a result of management changes	-0.70E-01	**
Upper level choice equations		
Alternative specific constant equals 1 for options 2 and 3 else zero	5.81E+00	**
Log of respondent income	-3.45E-01	**
Dummy variable equals 1 for respondents intending to visit else zero	-4.44E-01	**
Age of respondent	1.01E-01	**
Dummy variable equals 1 for tertiary education else zero	-2.16E-01	*
Dummy variable equals 1 for respondent indicating they either do not trust government to make levy one-off or protested against the payment vehicle on other grounds else zero	1.55E+00	**
Dummy variable equals 1 where respondent indicated levy is not a good idea else zero	2.11E+00	**
Dummy variable equals 1 for Griffith respondents else zero	5.39E-01	**
Dummy variable equals 1 for Adelaide respondents else zero	-2.28E-01	
Inclusive value parameters[a]		
Inclusive value parameter – No support (fixed parameter)	1.00	
Inclusive value parameter – Support	4.65E-01	**

Notes:
The dependent variable is the ratio of the probability of the choice being made given the choice options.
* denotes significance of parameter at the 10% level, ** denotes significance at the 5% level.
a The nested logit model includes additional parameters for each choice set partition (i.e. nesting level). These inclusive values (alternatively termed logsum or expected maximum utility) are the scale parameters in each level of the model. The upper level scale parameter is normalised to 1 and that for the lower level left free to be estimated (for more information see Louviere, Henscher and Swait, 2000).

All USE coefficients except 'area of healthy wetlands' have the expected sign.[4] The negative cost coefficient indicates that respondents are less likely to choose options as cost increases. Likewise, respondents are less likely to choose options with larger numbers of ducks hunted, but more likely to choose options with larger numbers of endangered species protected and larger areas of healthy remnant vegetation. The positive 'interaction term combining pro-conservation respondents and wetland area' indicates that respondents who indicated that they favour conservation over development also value increased wetland area. The positive 'interaction term combining duck hunters and number of ducks hunted' coefficient indicates that duck hunters value increased duck-hunting harvests.

The MRF coefficients for all of the attributes in the choice sets are significant at the 1 per cent level and have the expected sign. The negative cost coefficient indicates that respondents are less likely to choose options as cost increases. Likewise, respondents are less likely to choose options with more farmers leaving. The negative coefficients for wetland area, birds and fish are a reflection of the functional form and indicate respondents are more likely to pay for options with more healthy wetlands, birds and fish, but at a decreasing rate.

Respondents to both USE and MRF questionnaires who indicated they were confused by the questionnaire, did not trust the government, or protested against the payment vehicle (the levy) are more likely to support the 'no change' option in the choice sets and hence possess a positive coefficient when predicting the likelihood of supporting 'no change'. The significance of these variables indicates that, despite the careful design and proofing of the survey, a statistically significant element of respondent confusion and protest against the payment vehicle remained. Individuals with higher incomes are more likely to support the proposal, hence a negative income coefficient.[5] Intended visitors are expected to support changed management as a reflection of their option values for future visits, again a negative coefficient is expected. Education, gender and location dummies were insignificant with the exception of the Canberra dummy. Section 4 contains a more detailed discussion of the implications of these variables for benefit transfer.

The NLM results can be used to estimate two types of values:

1. Implicit prices – the willingness to pay for a unit change in a single attribute; and
2. Compensating surplus – the change in welfare, measured in dollars, resulting from a change in management.

In theory, both measures can be of use in benefit transfer exercises. However, valid transfer of compensating surplus measures requires that the same group of attributes be impacted in the new location as that from which the values are transferred. Since this will occur very rarely, only implicit price estimates are discussed further.

3.4   Implicit Price Estimates

Implicit prices (IP) are the marginal rates of substitution between the non-marketed attributes and the monetary attribute in the NLM. The marginal rates of substitution are derived as the partial differentiation of the attribute of interest with respect to utility as represented by the monetary attribute. Hence, they are estimated as the ratio of the coefficient of a non-monetary attribute and the coefficient of the monetary attribute in the USE NLM models as follows:

$$IP = \beta_{\text{non-monetary attribute}} / \beta_{\text{monetary attribute}}$$

In the more complex 1/x functional form used in the MRF NLM, the implicit price is related to the level of the attribute supplied and is defined as follows:

$$IP = - (-\beta_{\text{non-monetary attribute}} / \text{attribute level}^2) / \beta_{\text{cost}}$$

Implicit price and confidence intervals for the USE and MRF attributes are presented in Table 9.8.[6] The results indicate that, on average, USE respondents are willing to pay $0.92 for an extra 1 000 hectares of remnant vegetation and $4.81 to benefit an additional threatened species. USE respondents who indicated they were pro-conservation were willing to pay $2.73 more for an additional 1 000 hectares of wetlands than other respondents. That is, $1.51 for an additional 1 000 hectares of healthy wetlands. Remaining USE respondents were willing to pay -$1.22 and the average willingness to pay across the whole sample was -$0.61 per additional 1 000 hectares of healthy wetlands.

MRF IPs are calculated at the mid-point of the levels for the area of healthy wetlands and populations of native birds and fish because the 1/x functional form allows them to vary across the level of the attribute. On average, respondents to the MRF questionnaire were willing to pay (per household as a one-off payment) $11.39 for an extra 1 000 hectares of healthy wetlands, $1.15 for a 1 per cent increase in the population of native wetland and woodland birds and $0.34 for a 1 per cent increase in the population of native fish. A result of the CM survey with important policy implications is the high willingness to pay respondents had to avoid farmers having to leave the land as a result of changes to wetland management ($5.73 per farmer).

The marginal rates of substitution can also be used to estimate the trade-offs between differing attributes. For example, USE respondents are willing to trade-off:

1 additional threatened species benefits	=	5 219 ha of extra remnant vegetation	=	2 684 fewer ducks hunted

Although not discussed further, these trade-offs can be useful in identifying equivalent benefits within the region if, for example, an 'offset' policy is being considered.

Table 9.8   Estimates of USE and MRF attribute values

CM attributes	Implicit price[b]	95% Confidence Interval	
		Upper	Lower
MRF attributes[a]			
Area of healthy wetlands (/1 000 ha)	$11.39	$13.92	$8.97
Population of native wetland and woodland birds (/1% pre 1800 pop.)	$1.15	$1.68	$0.63
Population of native fish (/1% pre-1800 pop.)	$1.68	$2.12	$1.17
Number of farmers leaving (/farmer)	-$5.73	-$4.46	-$7.15
USE attributes			
Area of healthy wetlands (non-conservation oriented/1 000 ha)	-$1.22[c]	-$0.53	-$1.92
Area of healthy wetlands (pro-conservation oriented/1 000 ha)	$1.51	$2.35	$0.66
Area of healthy wetlands (average/1 000 ha)	-$0.27[c]	$0.05	-$1.24
Area of healthy remnant vegetation (/1 000 ha)	$0.92	$1.54	$0.25
Threatened species that benefit (/specie)	$4.81	$5.70	$3.94
Number of ducks hunted (non-hunters/1 000)	-$4.35	-$2.62	-$6.07
Number of ducks hunted (hunters/1 000)	$3.01[c]	$7.35	-$1.34
Number of ducks hunted (average/1 000)	-$3.19	$0.06	-$3.49

Notes:
a   One-off average willingness to pay per household, calculated at the mid point of the questionnaire levels for the area of healthy wetlands and populations of native birds and fish.
b   MRF prices at the midpoint of the survey levels.
c   Not significant at the 95 per cent level of confidence.

4   IMPLICATIONS FOR BENEFIT TRANSFER

In this section the focus is on the implications of the choice modelling results for benefit transfer of the implicit price estimates reported in Section 3.[7] The implications of the results in this study for benefit transfer can be divided into three main areas as outlined in the introductory discussion. The first of these is concerned with issues of extrapolation within the surveyed population, and specifically the implications of the representativeness of the respondent population. The second issue relates to the implications from these case studies for transferring benefits to other populations and whether the values from geographically distinct respondent populations differ for individual attributes or overall. The third benefit transfer issue relates to the potential for benefit transfer across sites and specifically the evidence for whether transfers should be limited to those involving similar types and quantities of environmental goods.

4.1   Issues of Extrapolation within Surveyed Populations

The value estimates generated by the choice model are an artefact of the sample selected and the subsequent set of responses. Samples are selected to be representative of the population from which they are drawn. However, different sub-sets of the population may systematically derive different values from the wetlands for which changes to management are being valued. Individuals within the sample also decide whether or not to respond to the questionnaire, thus self-selecting the respondent group within the sample. Therefore, extrapolation to the surveyed population may be biased. While the potential bias may relate to specific wetland attributes, or to the package of values as a whole, the discussion here relates only to specific wetland attributes.

In order to identify whether values systematically vary across a sample, there needs to be a means of differentiating between respondent groups holding different values. A highly correlated social or economic characteristic can be used to split the sample into groups holding different values. Specifically, where data has been collected on a potential identifying characteristic, this can be included as an explanatory variable in the choice model. Interacting the explanatory variable directly with the attribute for which values are expected to vary allows estimates of difference in values held by the two groups. The resultant parameter estimates can be used to calculate implicit price estimates for each group that can then be weighted to reflect the population mean rather than the sample mean.

Two examples of potential systematic variation in values as a result of distinct respondent groups are demonstrated in the results from the USE choice modelling exercise. These relate to attributes for the 'number of ducks hunted' and 'area of healthy wetlands'. In the first example, duck hunters are expected to place a positive value on the number of ducks hunted because wetlands provide the necessary habitat for ducks, while non-duck hunters are expected to place a neutral or negative value on ducks hunted. Duck hunters are concentrated in the USE. Therefore, it is expected that the response rate of duck hunters will be higher than the general population and their values for ducks hunted, in particular, will be higher than the remainder of the population. The results for the 'number of ducks hunted' variable are shown in Table 9.9. Individuals who had hunted ducks were willing to pay an additional $3.01 per additional 1 000 ducks hunted, whereas those who had never hunted ducks wanted compensation of $4.35 per additional 1 000 ducks hunted. Stokes (1990) notes that the total number of duck hunting licences has declined from 21 000 to around 7 000 between 1970 and 1990. Within the same period the population grew by about 20 per cent from 1.2 to 1.4 million people (South Australian Government 2004). Allowing that many past hunters may not have hunted every year (say only one in two years) the maximum proportion of the population that have hunted ducks at some stage in their life would be around 5 per cent of the total SA population.[8] Hence, the weighted average implicit price for SA residents increases from -$3.08 to -$3.99 after adjusting for sample biases. Thus the required compensation for each 1 000 ducks hunted increases by nearly 25 per cent.

Table 9.9   Sample versus population implicit prices

	Sample proportion	**Sample value**	**Population proportion**	**Population value**
Number of ducks hunted				
Duck hunters	17.4%	$3.01	5%	-$3.19
Never duck hunted	82.6%	-$4.35	95%	-$4.35
Weighted average (SA)		-$3.08		-$3.99
Area of healthy wetlands				
Favour conservation	34.8%	$1.51	18.6%	$1.51
Remainder	65.2%	-$1.22	81.4%	-$1.22
Weighted average		-$0.27		-$0.72

Note: The IP refer only to SA residents, not to the full sample reported in Table 9.8.

A similar exercise can be undertaken for the 'area of healthy wetlands' variable. SA respondents who indicated they were 'pro-conservation' were willing to pay $1.51 per additional 1 000 hectares of healthy wetlands, while ambivalent or pro-development respondents required compensation of $1.22.[9] About 35 per cent of USE questionnaire respondents favoured conservation, generating an average implicit price of -$0.27. However, the overall SA response to a similar question posed by the ABS found approximately 19 per cent of the population could be considered pro-conservation, generating a weighted value of -$0.72 per 1 000 hectares of healthy wetlands.[10]

4.2   Benefit Transfers Across Populations

4.2.1   Variation due to differences in population composition
The values held for wetlands may also vary systematically across different geographic populations. This variation could be due to differences in the

population composition (such as a higher proportion of the population who hunted ducks) or more generic factors such as distance from the wetlands being valued and general variations in taste. Evidence of both forms of systematic geographic variation in values is discussed here with respect to the USE CM model results.

Two examples of the impact of differences in population composition are reported in Table 9.10. The first example shows that there is significant variation in the (negative) values generated by duck hunting in the USE within the ACT, Adelaide and Naracoorte sub-samples, and when extrapolated to the populations from which the samples are drawn. Over a quarter of respondents to the Naracoorte sample report that they had hunted ducks, which generated an average sample willingness to pay of -$2.34. Less than 10 per cent of Adelaide and ACT sample respondents reported hunting ducks, generating sample willingness to pay of -$3.78 and -$3.85 respectively. Similar results are exhibited when extrapolating results to the Naracoorte and Adelaide populations following the discussion above, whereby an average of -$3.53 is estimated for the Naracoorte population and -$4.15 for the Adelaide population.

Table 9.10 Population composition and IP estimates

	Naracoorte	**Adelaide**	**S A**	**ACT**
Number of ducks hunted				
Sample				
Duck hunter proportion	27.4%	7.8%	17.4%	6.9%
Weighted IP/1 000 ducks	-$2.34	-$3.78	-$3.08	-$3.85
Population[a]				
Duck hunters	11.2%	2.7%	5%	n.a.
Weighted IP/1 000 ducks	-$3.53	-$4.15	-$3.99	n.a.
Area of healthy wetlands				
Sample				
Pro-conservation	25.4%	34.7%	30.2%	48.0%
Weighted IP/1 000 ha	-$0.53	-$0.27	-$0.40	$0.09
Population[b]				
Pro-conservation	n.a.	n.a.	18.6%	20.7%
Weighted IP/1 000 ha	n.a.	n.a.	-$0.72	-$0.66

Note:
a   Duck hunter population estimates calculated by extrapolating a 5 per cent estimate that have hunted at some stage between Adelaide and SA country using Stokes (1990). This extrapolation is likely to underestimate the proportion of the Naracoorte region population who have hunted ducks because this is a key duck-hunting node in SA. No information is available for ACT population of duck hunters.
b   Pro-conservation population estimates calculated by extrapolation using ABS (1997) data. Note that population data are only available for SA total.

The second example of the impact of population composition in Table 9.10 relates to estimates of the values generated by the area of healthy wetlands in the USE. Sample values differ greatly, with the ACT sample estimate being positive and all others negative. Similarly, population values are quite different to sample values as was the case for the number of ducks hunted. For example, the ACT population estimate for the average willingness to pay for an additional 1 000 hectares of healthy wetlands is negative while the sample estimate is positive. It should be noted that none of these values is statistically different from zero at the 95 per cent level of confidence, nor is there a large difference in the population estimate for SA and the ACT (-$0.72 versus -$0.66).

4.2.2 Geographic variation in consumers' surplus estimates

Variation in the estimated change to consumers' surpluses for a bundle of changes to wetland management can also vary systematically across populations. These variations relate jointly to the values generated by changes to wetland values and therefore cannot be separated into specific implicit price influences. That is, they are not interacted with individual attributes, as was the case for USE duck hunting and wetland area estimates.

Two such variables for which such variation is estimated in the reported case studies are probability of visitation, reflecting option values for future recreation use values, and taste or location, representing location-specific variation in values. Option values for future visitation are related to the distance from the wetlands, while taste is specific to the population from which the estimates are generated. The impact of probability of visitation and location on aggregate consumers' surplus estimates is shown for the USE and MRF in Table 9.11.

Respondents who intended to visit USE wetlands in the future are willing to pay $38.81 more than respondents who do not intend to visit or who are unsure of their visit intentions. Weighting this by the proportion of respondents intending to visit the wetlands in the future, we find that the intention to visit wetlands increases the local community's (Naracoorte) willingness to pay by $9.46 ($34.47 – $25.01) over the sample average, while ACT residents are estimated to value wetlands $15.12 ($9.89 – $25.01) less than the sample average due to fewer intended visits. In a similar vein, ACT residents are estimated to value the USE wetlands $25.71 more than other survey respondents. This variation is attributed to different tastes with respect to environmental outcomes.

Table 9.11   Sub-populations and consumers' surplus estimates

Population proportion	Weighting	WTP impact
USE case study		
Estimated visit option value for USE	100%	$38.81
Naracoorte weighted visit option value	88.8%	$34.47
Adelaide weighted visit option value	61.0%	$23.69
ACT weighted visit option value	25.5%	$9.89
Sample average visit option value	63.7%	$25.01
ACT location variable	100%	$25.71
MRF case study		
Estimated visit option value for MRF	100%	$36.39
ACT weighted visit option value	53.2%	$19.35
Griffith weighted visit option value	81.5%	$29.67
Wagga Wagga weighted visit option value	81.5%	$29.66
Adelaide weighted visit option value	25.4%	$9.26
Sample average visit option value	63.4%	$23.09
Griffith location variable	100%	-$44.13
Adelaide location variable	100%	$18.62

Note: The 'visit option value' may not reflect the true option value held for
maintaining the option of a visit, as intending visitor's tastes may also differ
from the remainder of the sample.

A similar story is told by the MRF data with respondents intending
to visit the wetlands in the future willing to pay $36.39 more than other
respondents. As the intention to visit declines with distance from the
wetlands, the impact is greatest for residents in the MRF (Griffith and
Wagga Wagga residents) and least for those furthest away (Adelaide).
However, downstream residents exhibited positive impact due to location
(Adelaide residents are willing to pay $18.62 more) while residents in the
Murrumbidgee Irrigation Area (Griffith) are willing to pay $44.13 less.

4.3   Benefit Transfer Across Sites

4.3.1 Types of values generated and benefit transfer

The first issue in transferring benefit estimates to other wetlands is
identifying whether the values generated by both wetland sites are
equivalent. At first glance it may seem that the values generated by all
wetlands are similar, particularly all wetlands in inland south eastern
Australia. However, the background research to estimating the values
of wetlands in the USE and MRF indicates that this is not the case. To
understand the source and implications of these differences for benefit
transfer, it is worthwhile to briefly revisit the biophysical drivers and the
values generated by the case study wetlands.[11]

In the USE, the remaining wetlands are a chain of isolated vegetation islands in a sea of land used for agriculture. The specific goals of changing wetland management in this context are to increase the production of valued wetland outputs by:

• facilitating a wetting and drying cycle closer to the historic regime;
• improving the health of native vegetation by reducing grazing and weed competition; and
• increasing native fauna populations by reducing feral animal and domestic livestock competition.

In order to achieve these goals, three broad management strategies were identified:

1. Rehabilitation of degraded wetland areas;
2. Re-creation of some wetlands where they have been drained, especially where they would link existing wetlands; and
3. Rehabilitation of surrounding remnant vegetation and re-creation of linkages between remnant vegetation and wetlands.

The major MRF biophysical drivers are the same as in the USE, with the additional goal of restoring interaction between floodplain wetlands and the Murrumbidgee River. However, the management strategies that were identified are quite different and involve:

1. Reintroducing floods to some wetland areas while allowing other wetlands close to the river to dry more often;
2. Reducing the impact of grazing in wetlands and buffer areas; and
3. Reducing the impact of timber harvesting in wetlands.

Although the wetland management goals are similar in the two areas, the strategies to implement them are quite different and are more indicative of the biophysical differences between the two areas. The large area of wetlands and remnant vegetation in the USE together with a mix of highly ephemeral and more permanent wetlands means that wetlands are important in the maintenance of flora and fauna species within the region. The relatively small area of wetlands in the MRF relative to agricultural lands means that the total population of wetland birds present is influenced by wetlands characteristics, but that the species mix is dependent on events outside of wetlands, and in some cases outside of the case study area. MRF wetlands are important in maintaining native fish populations in the Murrumbidgee River, but there is no such fish population of importance in the USE due to variations in salt concentrations in wetlands as they fill and dry and the lack of a permanent river channel.

Thus, despite the broad similarities in wetland management goals, the non-market values generated by wetlands in the two case studies are quite different. For example, the only common non-monetary attribute for which CM values are estimated is the 'area of healthy wetlands'. That is, while the values generated by USE and MRF wetlands overlap, they are not identical.[12] Therefore, any benefit transfer exercise will need to carefully identify and distinguish between the different values that are generated by any proposed management changes.

The ability of CM to estimate separate implicit prices for each non-monetary attribute is a useful asset in transferring benefits because implicit prices from several different studies can potentially be combined to cover the range of non-market values generated by a specified management change. The positives of this approach should be tempered by caution in ensuring that the range of values is clearly identified, potentially involving both a literature review of the biophysical relationships and focus groups examining the resultant values. Caution should also be exercised to ensure that double counting does not arise.

4.3.2 Quantities of outputs and benefit transfer

The second key issue in transferring benefits to other wetlands is whether the size of the change for which benefit estimates are needed is equivalent. Economic theory suggests that diminishing marginal returns will be generated by progressive increases in normal goods. Thus, diminishing marginal returns to change can also be expected for most wetland outputs.

As an example, consider the scale of benefits resulting from management changes in the USE and MRF as shown in Figure 9.4. The total area for which management changes are considered in the USE is over three times that of the MRF (33 000 ha versus 10 000 ha). However, the management changes in the MRF increase the area of healthy wetlands by a factor of four compared to less than doubling the area in the USE. Therefore, we can anticipate two general conclusions:

1. The value of an additional hectare of healthy wetlands will be much lower in the USE case study; and
2. Diminishing marginal returns to wetland area may be apparent in the MRF case study.

The two anticipated impacts are clearly shown in the CM results. Additional healthy wetlands in the USE region generate a positive marginal return for segments of the population who identify as preferring conservation ($1.51 per 1 000 ha) and a negative value to the remainder of the population (-$1.22 per 1 000 ha). This can be compared to a willingness to pay of $11.39 per 1 000 ha at the midpoint of the MRF.

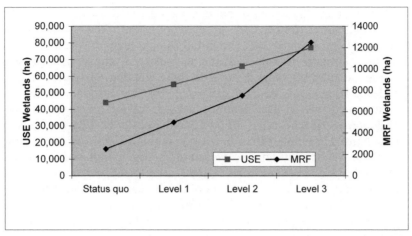

Figure 9.4   Scale of healthy wetlands for which estimates are considered

In the MRF, the best performing model incorporated a diminishing marginal returns structure for the area of healthy wetlands.[13] At the status quo level, the willingness to pay was $102.53 per additional 1 000 hectares, while at the maximum level in the questionnaire the willingness to pay was $4.10 per additional 1 000 hectares. Furthermore, the willingness to pay at the maximum wetland area ($4.10) is much higher than the USE average willingness to pay.

The implications of these results for benefit transfer are clear – the size of the benefits generated is related to the change in attribute size. Hence, not only should the attribute descriptors be carefully selected, so too should the size of the attributes for which benefits are to be transferred.

5   CONCLUSIONS

It may be expected that the values generated from inland wetland systems are relatively similar and can therefore readily be extrapolated across populations or transferred for use in estimating the benefits associated with changing wetland management in other locations. In this chapter we have shown that this is not necessarily the case. A number of complications to benefit transfer arise from the characteristics of the respondent sample, systematic variations across geographically distinct populations and samples, and the equivalence in quality and quantity of the values generated by wetlands. Evidence of these influences on wetland values was demonstrated in this chapter using case studies of wetlands in the USE of SA and on the MRF in NSW.

Three areas that should be considered when extrapolating the values estimated from a CM survey were noted. First, while care is usually taken to ensure that the initial sample invited to respond to a CM questionnaire is unbiased, the self-selected sample that chooses to respond may be skewed towards those holding particular values. Evidence from the USE case study suggests that respondents tended to be more likely to have hunted ducks or favour conservation over development. Hence, values for additional areas of healthy wetlands or ducks hunted are higher than in the population from which the sample is drawn. Second, systematic variations across population segments will need to be corrected when extrapolating to additional populations because some segments of the population may systematically value some attributes more highly. There may also be additional tastes or preferences that systematically differ between different populations but which do not relate to specific attributes. These elements should also be corrected for when extrapolating to additional populations.

Consideration of benefit transfer to other wetland systems should also take into account whether the population characteristics are similar. Two further issues should also be considered. First, are the values for which benefit transfer is considered sufficiently similar in the target system? Evidence from the two case study areas suggests that even where wetland management goals are similar, the values generated may be quite different. Second, is the scale of management changes similar in both wetland systems? Consideration should include the absolute and relative scale of change that is considered, because both may be important in deciding whether benefit transfer is valid.

NOTES

1. These non-use attributes were defined following input from wetland scientists and workshopping the issues in focus groups held in Canberra and Adelaide.
2. These non-use attributes were defined following input from wetland scientists and workshopping the issues in focus groups held in Canberra and Griffith.
3. The NLM is structured to create a separate branch choice equation for the 'no change' option and the remaining alternatives. For more information, see Whitten and Bennett (2005) and Louviere, Henscher and Swait (2000).
4. A potential explanation for a negative wetland coefficient is that many respondents may be recalling the (undesirable) appearance of saline wetlands that can be seen from the major roads through the region.
5. The expected sign of the coefficient depends on which branch of the nested logit model the socio-economic coefficients are placed. If variables were placed on the change options rather than the 'no change' option, then the expected sign would be the opposite to those reported in the text.
6. To estimate confidence intervals a random draw (of 200 in this case) of parameter vectors is made from a multivariate normal distribution with the mean and variance equal to the ß vector and the variance-covariance matrix from the estimated nested logit model (Krinsky and Robb 1986).

7. Extrapolation of compensating surplus estimates from bundles of wetland management changes are not discussed in this section because they are only relevant to the specific bundle being considered. However, much of the discussion in this section is relevant if benefit transfer of such bundles is being considered for an equivalent set of wetland values at another site.
8. Assuming 70 per cent of a population of 1.2 million are over 18 of which 42 000 have hunted ducks.
9. Respondents were designated pro-conservation or pro-development based on their response to the question: When thinking about issues where there are trade-offs between conservation and development do you? 1. Favour development, 2. Favour conservation, or 3. Favour development and conservation equally.
10. ABS (1997) report that 18.6 per cent of SA residents (discarding 'can't decide' and 'don't know') indicate that 'environmental protection is more important than economic growth'.
11. A more complete discussion of the biophysical drivers and resultant wetland resource allocation strategies can be found in Whitten and Bennett (2005).
12. The lack of overlap in wetland attributes also precludes any formal testing of values across the two case studies with the exception of 'area of healthy wetlands' for which values are clearly significantly different.
13. Similar models of diminishing marginal returns to additional change in the USE were not estimated due to the interaction of healthy wetlands with development preference, and duck hunting with the number of additional ducks hunted.

REFERENCES

Australian Bureau of Statistics (1997), *1996 Environmental Issues: People's Views and Practices, ABS Catalogue No. 4602.0*, Canberra: Australian Bureau of Statistics.

Barton, D.N. (2002), 'The transferability of benefit transfer: contingent valuation of water quality improvements in Costa Rica', *Ecological Economics*, **42**, 147–164.

Bennett, J. and W.L. Adamowicz (2001), 'Some Fundamentals of Environmental Choice Modelling', in J. Bennett and R. Blamey (eds), *The Choice Modelling Approach to Environmental Valuation*, Cheltenham, UK and Northampton, MA, USA: Edward Elgar, pp. 37–72.

Blamey, R.K., J.C. Rolfe, J.W. Bennett and M.D. Morrison (1997), *Environmental Choice Modelling: Issues and Qualitative Insights*, Canberra: The University of New South Wales.

Brouwer, R. (2000), 'Environmental value transfer: state of the art and future prospects', *Ecological Economics*, **32**, 137–152.

Desvousges, W.H., M.C. Naughton and G.R. Parsons (1992), 'Benefit transfer: conceptual problems in estimating water quality benefits using existing studies', *Water Resources Research*, **28**, 675–683.

Krinsky, I. and A.L. Robb (1986), 'On approximating the statistical properties of elasticities', *Review of Economics and Statistics*, **72**, 189–90.

Louviere, J.J., D.A. Henscher and J.D. Swait (2000), *Stated Choice Methods: Analysis and Application*, Cambridge: Cambridge University Press.

Morrison, M. (2000), 'Aggregation Biases in Stated Preference Studies', *Australian Economic Papers*, **39**, 215–230.

Morrison, M.D. and J.W. Bennett (2000), 'Choice modelling, non-use values and benefit transfer', *Economic Analysis and Policy*, **30** (1), 13–32.

Morrison, M. and J. Bennett (2004), 'Valuing New South Wales rivers for use in benefit transfer', *The Australian Journal of Agricultural and Resource Economics*, **48**, 591–611.

Morrison, M.D., J.W. Bennett and R.K. Blamey (1997), *Designing Choice Modelling Surveys Using Focus Groups: Results from the Macquarie Marshes and Gwydir Wetlands Case Studies*, Canberra: The University of New South Wales.

Morrison, M., J. Bennett, R. Blamey and J. Louviere (2002), 'Choice Modeling and Tests of Benefit Transfer', *American Journal of Agricultural Economics*, **84**, 161–170.

Rolfe, J. and J. Windle (2005), 'Valuing options for reserve water in the Fitzroy Basin', *The Australian Journal of Agricultural and Resource Economics*, **49**, 91–114.

Rosenberger, R.S. and J.B. Loomis (2001), *Benefit transfer of outdoor recreation use values: A technical document supporting the Forest Service Strategic Plan (2000 revision)*, Gen. Tech. Rep. RMRS-GTR-72, Fort Collins, CO: U.S. Department of Agriculture, Forest Service, Rocky Mountain Research Station.

South Australian Government (2004), www.sacentral.sa.gov.au/information/saybpopulation.pdf, accessed 6 July 2004.

Stokes, K.J. (1990), *Report of the Task Force Enquiring into Duck Hunting in South Australia*, Adelaide: Task Force Enquiring into Duck Hunting in South Australia.

van Bueren, M. and J. Bennett (2004), 'Towards the development of a transferable set of value estimates for environmental attributes', *The Australian Journal of Agricultural and Resource Economics*, **48**, 1–32.

Whitten, S. and J. Bennett (2005), *Private and Social Values of Wetlands*, Cheltenham, UK and Northampton, MA, USA: Edward Elgar.

10. Generalising Environmental Values: The Case of the National Land and Water Resources Audit in Australia

Martin van Bueren and Jeff Bennett

1   INTRODUCTION

Sound policies for natural resource management require a comprehensive assessment of the costs and benefits of alternative options. But the high cost of commissioning surveys to estimate community preferences means that decisions are often made without satisfactory account being taken of the trade-offs involved. At best, value estimates are transferred from other studies. This introduces the risk of bias but provides indicative measures of the magnitude of environmental values. At worst, non-market values are left out of benefit-cost analyses altogether and simply put in the 'too hard basket'. In Australia, billions of dollars are being invested in national and regional programmes to address the impacts of land and water degradation. Given the scale of investment, it is imperative that suitable techniques are developed for incorporating community preferences into cost-benefit assessments of these programmes.

In 1999 the Australian Commonwealth Government initiated the National Land and Water Resources Audit, a four-year programme to assess the physical condition of the nation's natural resources — both in terms of their current state and future trend. Australia is facing various forms of resource degradation, including salinity, biodiversity decline, soil erosion, waterway eutrophication and species loss. Part of the Audit's objective was to develop methods and indicators for identifying

The material presented in this chapter has some overlap with the publication by van Beuren, M. and Bennett, J. 2004 'Towards the development of a transferable set of value estimates for environmental attributes', *Australian Journal of Agricultural and Resource Economics*, 48 (1), pp. 1 – 32. Permission to publish this chapter has been kindly granted by Blackwells Publishing.

degradation problems that deserve priority attention. This called for information on how society values different environmental assets at the broad national level and at a more tightly defined regional level. The goal of the study reported in this chapter was to estimate values for a set of generic attributes that could subsequently be used to examine the net welfare impact of various environmental policies designed to target one or more of the degradation problems.

2   OVERVIEW OF APPROACH

Choice modelling (CM) was chosen as the tool for estimating non-market values. As explained in previous chapters, CM is capable of producing value estimates that are suitable for benefit transfer. It provides a degree of control over the valuation context or frame because respondents are presented with a set of options or resource use outcomes that are characterised by multiple attributes. Instead of a single attribute change being presented for valuation, respondents are asked to make trade-offs between changes in multiple attributes, which reflects the 'real world' context in which people make trade-off decisions in the presence of substitutes. CM also allows estimated values for the choice options to be disassembled into component 'part-worths' or implicit prices for each attribute. Upon transfer, these implicit prices can be reassembled according to the expected outcomes of the environmental programme under investigation.

While CM facilitates benefit transfer, the transfer process is susceptible to bias if the context in which the values were estimated is substantially different from the context where they are to be applied. The valuation frame is a composite of a number of factors including, for example:

- the number and type of attributes that a respondent is aware of at the time of valuing the policy options. Regular embedding is said to occur when the values for a particular attribute decrease when a respondent is provided with an increasingly larger array of substitutes (Randall and Hoehn 1996; Bennett et al. 1998). A 'distance effect' is said to occur when values for attributes that have a 'use value' decline with distance from the respondent's place of residence;
- the scale of environmental change presented to respondents. A scope effect is said to occur when values diminish at the margin for progressively higher levels of environmental improvement. Changes in scope are often accompanied by a widening or narrowing of the array of substitutes — resulting in a mix of embedding and scope effects (Rolfe 1998);

- the institutional setting in which the policy changes are to be implemented; and
- various aspects of the questionnaire that provide cues to the respondent.

In addition to these framing factors, benefit transfer may induce error if differences in population characteristics are not accounted for. Some of these characteristics, such as socio-demographics, can be controlled for by incorporating individual-specific variables in the utility function. However, there are many population characteristics that are difficult to measure and explicitly account for — for instance, social norms and parochial attitudes cannot readily be measured. Because framing and population factors have the potential to influence value estimates and consequently cause problems for benefit transfer, it is imperative to find out the magnitude of these influences and put in place procedures to correct for the potential bias that would otherwise result in the transfer process.

Thus, the primary focus of this study was to measure the effect of frame and population characteristics on community values by undertaking a set of CM experiments that control for these factors. In brief, our approach was to select a standard set of generic attributes to describe the outcomes of a wide range of possible environmental policies at the national and regional level. CM questionnaires were developed for the different frames (regional and national) and the attribute levels were adjusted to match the scale of changes being envisaged in each context. An annual environmental levy was used as a payment vehicle for estimating household willingness to pay for environmental improvements. Questionnaires were administered to several different populations, including a random sample of the national population and samples from capital cities and regional centres. The research design allowed the systematic testing for differences in implicit prices derived from different populations and frames. The test results were used to develop scaling factors for calibrating the value estimates for benefit transfer.

3   RESEARCH DESIGN

Figure 10.1 sets out the structure of the research design and the tests employed. The segments of the triangle represent the different frames — that is, the national survey and the two regional surveys (Region A and Region B). The circles represent the different populations that were sampled, namely, the national population, the population of each region and the populations of the State capital cities corresponding to the two States in which the regions were located. In total, seven separate choice

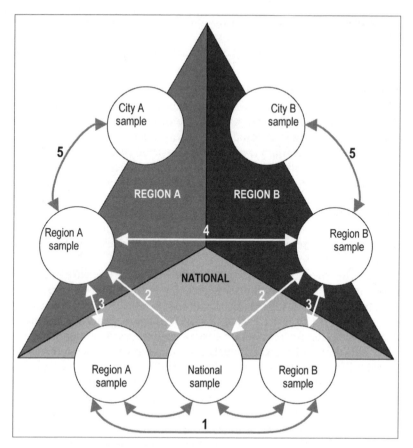

Figure 10.1 Research design and benefit transfer tests

models were estimated, corresponding to the various combinations of frame and population depicted by the intersections in Figure 10.1.

This research design facilitated a number of implicit price equivalence tests for different model pairs, as indicated by the numbered arrows. The tests indicate the validity of transferring value estimates from one frame/population to another. In total, five benefit transfer tests were undertaken:

1. The equivalence of values across the regional and national populations for attributes in the national frame. This tested for population effects, as the frame was held constant and the population varied.
2. The transferability of national estimates to the case study regions. This tested whether values held by the national population for

attributes in the national context are equal to those held by regional populations for attributes in their local area. In this test both frame and population differ.
3. The equivalence of values estimated for attributes in the national frame versus a regional frame, holding population constant.
4. The equivalence of values held by regional households for attributes in each of the two case study regions. In this test both frame and population differ.
5. The equivalence of city and regional populations' values for attributes in a given case study region. In this test the regional frame is held constant and the population is varied.

The national frame, which presented respondents with attribute trade-offs from national level policies, was issued to a random sample of households from the national population and households from the main township in each of the two case study regions. The two regions selected for the study were the Great Southern Region (GSR) of Western Australia and the Fitzroy Basin Region (FBR) of Queensland. A sample of households in the townships of Albany in the GSR and Rockhampton in the FBR were issued with a national questionnaire. The regional questionnaires, which presented respondents with regional policy outcomes, were administered to households residing in these same two towns plus two city samples, which were drawn from the capital cities of the states in which each region was located. Perth and Brisbane are the capital cities corresponding to the GSR and FBR respectively.

The case studies were selected to provide insights into how the national value estimates would need to be calibrated if they were to be transferred to each of the regions. Owing to the wider frame of reference associated with the national questionnaire and the greater scale of changes involved, it was hypothesised that the national implicit price estimates would be smaller than the regional estimates. Furthermore, the values estimated for attributes in each case study region were expected to differ because the environmental degradation issues in each region are markedly different and there is evidence to suggest that Queensland people have different attitudes towards the environment from Western Australians.[1]

4   ATTRIBUTE SELECTION AND QUESTIONNAIRE DESIGN

The questionnaires were developed in consultation with members of the public using structured focus groups. In total, 65 people attended seven focus group meetings over a period of two months. Participants were recruited from a cross-section of the community in each study location. The meetings were used primarily to gain an understanding of public awareness of environmental and social issues associated with land and water degradation and to check communication aspects of the questionnaire.

The discussions amongst members of the focus groups formed the basis for selecting generic attributes suitable for use in the CM application. The aim was to select attributes that were sufficiently general to cover a wide range of circumstances — and thus suitable for benefit transfer — yet specific enough to be meaningful to respondents and relevant for policy. Another selection criterion for choosing the attributes was the minimisation of 'jointness of provision' or causality between the attributes. This arises when changes in the level of one attribute are perceived by respondents to be related to changes in another. To avoid the econometric problems induced by causality, respondents were informed in the questionnaire that there are many plausible reasons why attributes could vary independently of one another, and examples were given to illustrate this point.

In the focus group sessions, participants were asked to list the environmental factors, experiences and opportunities that they felt were important to protect. People commonly identified factors that either imparted use or non-use values. Finally five attributes were selected, including three environmental attributes, a 'social impact' attribute and a money attribute (Table 10.1). The restoration of waterways for fishing and swimming (Water) and the improvement of countryside aesthetics through the repair of degraded farmland (Aesthetics) were defined as use values. In the questionnaire, respondents were told that programmes to improve countryside aesthetics would 'make degraded land more attractive by repairing eroded land and protecting native bush'. The emphasis was on visual appearance rather than the non-use aspects of biodiversity protection. Non-use values were represented by the Species attribute, defined as the number of endangered native species protected from extinction.[2] A social impact attribute (Social) was included because the focus group discussions indicated that people were concerned about the potential link between environmental protection and the prosperity of rural townships. It was recognised that some types of environmental programmes could disadvantage rural people by requiring farmers to give up agricultural land to conservation measures. Other programmes were viewed as having good outcomes for rural townships. In background information accompanying the questionnaire, respondents were provided with concise descriptions of each attribute, together with the current levels of each attribute.

Table 10.1   Attributes selected for the choice modelling questionnaire

Attribute	Variable name	Unit of measurement
Endangered native species	Species	The number of species protected from extinction.
Countryside aesthetics	Aesthetics	The area of farmland repaired and bush protected (ha).
Waterway health	Water	The length of waterways restored for fishing or swimming (km).
Country communities	Social	The net loss of people from country towns each year.
Environmental levy	Cost	Annual household levy ($).

5   SCENARIOS

Two types of scenario were presented as choice options to respondents:

- a '**status quo**' scenario whereby the current level of investment in environmental programmes could continue over the next 20 years (at no extra cost to the respondent); and
- a '**levy option**' scenario whereby respondent households would be required to pay an annual levy in return for environmental improvements over and above what could be achieved under the status quo. The levy ranged between $20 and $200 per annum.

Changes in attribute levels resulting from these scenarios were communicated to respondents by measuring all changes relative to a 'do nothing' reference point defined as the outcomes that would eventuate under a policy of zero investment in the environment. Although this is a hypothetical policy, it served as a benchmark to communicate what improvements are likely to eventuate under alternative levels of environmental expenditure — the status quo level and other higher levels funded by a levy. Figure 10.2 is an illustrative example of how the outcomes were measured. In this example, the 'status quo' option would ensure 50 additional species are protected relative to the 'do nothing' scenario. In contrast, selecting the 'levy option' would ensure that 140 species are protected, again relative to the 'do nothing' reference point. Note that all scenarios involved more species becoming endangered over the 20-year period. Selecting the levy option merely slows down the rise in the number of species that are endangered.

Under the levy options, all of the environmental attributes were defined to improve compared to the 'status quo'. However, for the social attribute, both positive and negative outcomes were formulated. This takes account of the possibility that some types of environmental programmes funded by a levy could accelerate the migration of people

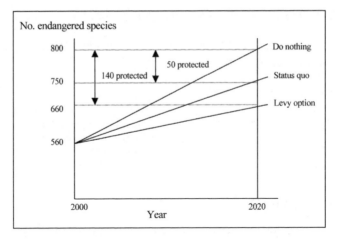

Figure 10.2 An example of scenario outcomes for endangered species

from country communities (for example, the conversion of farmland into long rotation forestry), while other programmes could stem migration losses, relative to the 'status quo' case.

Attribute levels were selected based on available information about the current status of each attribute and how these attribute levels could change under different funding programmes. Scientists and natural resource managers were consulted to ensure that the various scenario outcomes were feasible. Three levels were assigned to each attribute, the upper and lower levels being chosen so as to encompass the range of potential outcomes that could eventuate from alternative policies.

Each questionnaire consisted of five choice sets with three alternatives per choice set — a constant status quo option (A) and two different levy options (B and C) that varied across the choice sets. A sample choice set is shown in Figure 10.3. The levels of the different attributes were combined systematically to make up the options according to an experimental design.[3] The alternatives were not labelled with specific policy names as the questionnaire sought to estimate community values for attribute changes rather than particular policies or processes to achieve the outcomes. Previous studies have found that the inclusion of a policy label, such as 'Revegetation Programme', can deflect respondents' attention away from the attribute outcomes by encoding additional information in the label (Blamey et al. 2001). Where this is the case, the transferability of attribute values is hampered because the impact values are not captured fully by the attribute set.

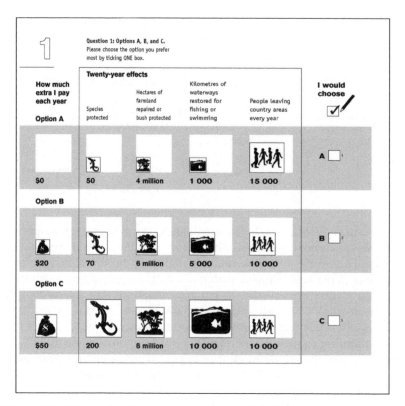

Figure 10.3 Example of a choice set used in the CM questionnaire

6 SURVEY ADMINISTRATION

The questionnaire was pre-tested over two days using a door-to-door, drop off and pick up method. Twenty five households from metropolitan Sydney were selected for the pre-test. The households were drawn from a broad range of socio-economic strata. The pre-tests involved detailed, face-to-face debriefing sessions after the respondents had completed the questionnaire. Only minor modifications were made to the questionnaire following the pre-testing phase, as debriefs with the respondent households did not reveal any significant communication problems.

The final version of the questionnaire was administered as a mail-out/mail-back survey in accordance with the research design outlined in Figure 10.1. The population samples were drawn at random from 'Australia on Disk', a telephone directory sourced database of the Australian population. In total, a sample of 10 800 households was drawn for the study. Table 10.2 summarises the breakdown of household numbers in each sub-sample, together with the percentage of 'usable' responses that were obtained.

Table 10.2 Sample sizes and per cent usable returns (in parenthesis)

	Questionnaire frame		
Population sample	National	Great Southern	Fitzroy Basin
National	3 200 (17%)	-	-
Albany	1 200 (17%)	1 200 (16%)	-
Rockhampton	1 200 (14%)	-	1 200 (16%)
Perth	-	1 400 (18%)	-
Brisbane	-	-	1 400 (13%)

The survey was in-field for approximately six weeks and reminder cards were sent to those respondents who had not responded within the first two weeks. The overall response rate after allowing for undeliverable mail-outs was 16 per cent, which equated to 1 569 completed questionnaires.[4] Response rates around the 20 per cent mark are not uncommon for environmental CM and reflect the complexity of the choice task, particularly when respondents are asked to value non-market goods that are unfamiliar to them.[5] The relatively poor response rate could also be a reflection of the low order of priority placed on the environment by the Australian community. The Australian Bureau of Statistics estimates that only nine per cent of Australians rank environmental problems as their top social issue (ABS, 1999).

In order to diagnose the reason for the low response rate, a follow-up telephone survey of 340 non-respondents was undertaken approximately four months after the survey close-off date. The survey yielded 203 usable replies. The follow-up survey revealed that:

- 55 per cent of respondents said they did not recall receiving the questionnaire, which could be interpreted as a zero level of interest in the subject matter and hence a zero willingness to pay;
- 20 per cent recalled receiving the questionnaire but did not complete it because they were not interested in the subject matter; and
- the remaining 25 per cent said they received the questionnaire and were interested in the subject material but did not complete it because they were either 'too busy to respond' or 'thought the survey did not ask the right questions'. Of this group, about half (47 per cent) said 'yes or maybe' to the idea of supporting an environmental levy.

We conclude from these results that approximately 75 per cent of non-respondents hold zero values for the environmental improvements stipulated in the CM questionnaire, while the other 25 per cent implicitly place some value on protecting the environment. We assume that the values held by these non-respondents are the same as those held by respondents. The results suggest that the value estimates derived from the CM questionnaire could safely be extrapolated to 37 per cent of the population, calculated as the 16 per cent who responded plus the proportion of non-respondents who implicitly hold non-zero, positive values.[6]

7   SAMPLE REPRESENTATIVENESS

It is evident that the survey instrument induced some self-selection bias. For example, the respondent samples contain a significantly higher proportion of males and a higher proportion of people with tertiary qualifications than the population from which the samples were drawn (Table 10.3).

While it is clear that the samples are not representative of the population with respect to some socio-economic characteristics, the CM technique allows value estimates derived from the sample to be corrected for this bias. This is achieved by extrapolating benefit function estimates rather than point estimates — such as mean willingness to pay. The inclusion of socio-economic variables in the benefit function hence allows the standardisation of the implicit prices.

Table 10.3   Comparison of sample means to population means

	National	Perth	Brisbane	Albany	Rock'ton
Sample characteristics					
Median age group	45-54	45-54	45-54	45-54	45-54
Per cent male	62	60	64	57	57
Median weekly h/hold income	700–1 000	700–1 000	700–1 000	500–700	500–700
% with tertiary degree	35	30	35	23	26
% green supporters[a]	24	24	22	27	13
Population characteristics[b]					
Population size (over 15 years)	15 038 339	1 064 190	1 287 004	12 432	46 031
Mean persons per h/hold	2.6	2.6	2.6	2.3	2.5
Median age	35	34	34	37	33
Median weekly h/hold income	700–800	800–1 000	800–1 000	500–600	600–700
% male (over 15 years)	49	49	48	46	48
% with tertiary degree	11	12	12	7	8

Notes:
[a]   Defined as respondents that donate money to environmental organisations or are a member of such an organisation.
[b]   Population means sourced from Australian Bureau of Statistics 2001 census.

8   MODEL SPECIFICATION

A nested structure was used to model respondents' choices of alternative options.[7] This structure assumes that the respondent makes two separate decisions — an upper level decision either to support an environmental levy or retain the status quo (SQ) and, conditional on supporting the levy, a lower level decision which involves the choice between two different levy options. The utility function associated with the upper level choice was hypothesised to be influenced by the respondent's socio-economic characteristics (Age, Sex, Income), environmental disposition (Green), and whether or not the respondent was confused by the background information (Confuse). Environmental disposition was measured by asking whether the individual was a member of an environmental organisation or donated money to environmental causes. Confusion was measured using a binary variable to indicate whether or not respondents found the background information and survey confusing. The probability of the levy being supported was expected to increase with income and pro-environment sentiment, but decrease for respondents who reported confusion. In addition to these individual-specific variables, the choice between retaining the status quo or paying a levy was assumed to be influenced by a constant term (ASC) and an inclusive value (IV) which is a measure of expected utility from the alternatives nested beneath the upper level choice.[8] Each of these variables is defined in Table 10.4.

Table 10.4 Description of individual-specific explanatory variables

Variable	Description
ASC	Alternative specific constant for the levy option, assigned a value of 1 for options B and C, and zero otherwise.
Sex	Respondent's gender, assigned a value of 0 for females and 1 for males.
Age	The midpoint of the respondent's age category.
Income	The midpoint of the respondent's before-tax household income category.
Green	Dummy variable assigned a value of 1 for respondents who are members of, or donate to, an environmental organisation and 0 otherwise.
Confuse	Dummy variable assigned a value of 1 for respondents who reported that they found the background information confusing, 0 otherwise.
IV	Inclusive value representing the expected utility from alternatives in the lower level of the nest.

The utility functions for the upper level alternatives are as follows:

$$V_{levy} = ASC + \beta_1 Sex + \beta_2 Age + \beta_3 Income + \beta_4 Green + \beta_5 Confuse + \alpha_1 IV_{levy}$$ (10.1)

$$V_{SQ} = \alpha_2 IV_{SQ}$$ (10.2)

At the lower level of the nest, the utility associated with the SQ option and each levy option was assumed to be influenced by the attributes and their corresponding levels. Thus, the utility for option j is given by:

$$V_j = \beta_6 Species + \beta_7 Aesthetics + \beta_8 Water + \beta_9 Social + \beta_{10} Cost$$ (10.3)

9   RESULTS

Of those respondents who returned a questionnaire, the majority (89 per cent) answered all five choice sets, while a small proportion (8 per cent) only answered a subset of the five questions. Three per cent of respondents did not complete any of the choice sets. Seventeen per cent of respondents reported confusion about the survey. A majority (80 per cent) of respondents who answered all the choice questions opted for a levy option in at least one of the choice sets. The remaining 20 per cent consistently selected the status quo option.

Parameter estimates for each of the seven nested logit models describing the data relationships emerging from different combinations of questionnaire frame and population sample are reported in Table 10.5. All seven models exhibit a satisfactory goodness of fit, with Likelihood Ratio Indices (LRI) ranging between 0.17 and 0.27. In the majority of models, the environmental attributes (Species, Aesthetics, and Water) are statistically significant and have positive signs, which indicates that increases in the levels of these attributes add to an individual's utility. The signs on Social and Cost are significant and negative across all models, indicating that utility is reduced by increases in the levy and higher levels of population loss from country areas.

The individual-specific socio-demographic variables (Sex, Age, Income, Green, and Confuse) are also significant in explaining respondent choices. The probability of choosing a levy option is shown, in most models, to increase with a respondent's income and pro-environment disposition. The positive sign on income supports the theoretical validity of the models, as willingness to pay should be accompanied by an ability to pay. Confuse is a significant variable in all but one of the models. Its negative sign agrees with the *a priori* expectation that respondents who were confused by the questionnaire were more inclined to choose the

Table 10.5 Parameter estimates

Model	1	2	3	4	5	6	7
Frame	National	National	National	GSR	FBR	GSR	FBR
Population	National	Albany	Rockhampton	Albany	Rockhampton	Perth	Brisbane
Model statistics							
N (choice sets)	2 329	860	720	765	818	1 046	823
Log Likelihood	-2 182.04	-809.84	-639.17	-681.09	-803.16	-976.78	-761.39
LRI	0.23	0.20	0.24	0.27	0.17	0.23	0.23
Lower level choice equation							
Species	5.49E-03 **	2.38E-03 *	2.88E-03 *	1.29E-02 **	4.26E-03	1.13E-02 **	1.72E-02
Aesthetics	6.05E-08 **	1.84E-07 **	2.05E-07 **	1.51E-06 **	8.10E-07 **	1.24E-06 **	1.11E-06 **
Water	6.33E-05 **	4.59E-05	7.58E-05 **	1.30E-03 **	1.04E-03 **	8.05E-04 **	6.71E-04 **
Social	-6.93E-05 **	-9.47E-05 **	-6.76E-05 **	-4.59E-04 **	-1.15E-03 **	-6.34E-04 **	-8.78E-04 **
Cost	-8.13E-03 **	-8.77E-03 **	-1.04E-02 **	-8.24E-03 **	-5.14E-03 **	-8.89E-03 **	-8.54E-03 **
Upper level choice equations							
ASC	-2.85E-01	-1.87E-01 **	2.76E+00 **	-1.65E+00 **	1.28E+00 **	2.54E+00 **	2.39E+00 **
Sex	-3.04E-01 **	5.01E-01 **	-6.52E-01 **	4.26E-01 **	-7.11E-01 **	-2.43E-01	-2.89E-01 *
Age	7.06E-03 *	-1.56E-02 **	-3.23E-02 **	1.42E-02 *	-8.14E-03	-3.83E-01 **	-4.47E-01 **
Income	1.92E-05 **	8.54E-06 **	1.76E-05 **	2.94E-05 **	7.08E-06 **	-5.71E-03	9.65E-02 **
Green	2.43E-01 *	5.13E-01 **	5.82E-01	1.47E+00 **	1.77E-01	-1.39E-01	-3.22E-01
Confuse	-6.49E-01 **	-6.92E-01 **	-1.01E+00 **	-9.11E-01 **	-6.09E-01 **	-3.62E-01 *	omitted
Inclusive value parameters							
IV status quo	1	1	1	1	1	1	1
IV levy	3.43E-01 **	3.84E-01 **	1.97E-01	2.13E-01	2.19E-01	0.3595 **	0.0618

Notes: * denotes significance of parameter at the 10% level, ** denotes significance at the 5% level.

status quo option. Age and Sex are significant in some of the models but the effect of these variables on choice is inconsistent.

10   IMPLICIT PRICES

Attribute implicit prices estimated using the national survey (model 1) are reported in Table 10.6, together with a 95 per cent confidence interval for each estimate. The confidence intervals were calculated using a technique developed by Krinsky and Robb (1986). The results indicate that, on average, respondent households are willing to pay 67 cents per annum over the next 20 years for every species that is protected from extinction. Improvements in landscape aesthetics are valued at 7 cents per 10 000 hectares of countryside restored, while a similar amount (8 cents) is estimated as the value for the restoration of each 10 kilometres of waterway. The implicit price of social decline is a 9 cents cost for every ten people that leave country areas. These estimates assume non-diminishing values for additional improvements in attribute levels. While a non-linear relationship would be expected, at least beyond a certain level of improvement, transforming the data to allow for non-linearity did not improve the model fit. Therefore, it is concluded that implicit prices are constant for changes in the attributes over the range of levels used in the choice sets.

Table 10.6   Attribute implicit prices ($/household/year) derived from the national model

Attribute	Units	Mean implicit price	95% confidence interval
Species	$ per species protected	0.67	0.47 – 0.88
Aesthetics	$ per 10 000 ha restored	0.07	0.02 – 0.14
Water	$ per 10 km restored	0.08	0.04 – 0.16
Social	$ per 10 persons leaving	-0.09	(-0.11) – (-0.07)

The implicit prices provide a basis for assessing the size of benefits associated with a 'package' of environmental improvements or, alternatively, the cost associated with a decline in environmental quality or rural population at the national level. For illustrative purposes, Table 10.7 outlines a particular scenario involving improvements in waterway health, countryside aesthetics and species protection. Using the implicit price estimates, the changes are valued at $174.40 per household each year for 20 years. Assuming the value estimate can be safely extrapolated to 37 per cent of the population, the aggregate benefit of the improvements is $471 million per year, based on an Australian household population of approximately 7.2 million.

Table 10.7   Aggregate benefits from a package of national environmental improvements

Attribute	Change by 2020	Attribute implicit price	Annual value of change ($/hhold)
Water	12 000 km restored	$0.008 per km	$96.00
Aesthetics	4.5 M ha rehabilitated	$7.00 per M ha	$31.50
Species	70 species protected	$0.67 per spp.	$46.90
			$174.40

11   BENEFIT TRANSFER TESTS

Five benefit transfer (BT) tests were performed to gain an insight into how values change across different populations and frames of reference.

BT Test 1: Consistency of Values Across Different Populations for Attributes in the National Frame

This test examines the influence of population effects on values. It tests for the equivalence of values across regional and national populations for attributes in the national frame. The three relevant sets of implicit prices are sourced from the following models:

- model 1: the national sample and frame;
- model 2: the Albany sample and national frame; and
- model 3: the Rockhampton sample and national frame.

The implicit prices estimated from each of the three models are compared in Figure 10.4. The error bars represent the 95 per cent confidence intervals. Attribute values are deemed to be equivalent if the error bars overlap, signifying no statistical difference. For example, the values for Water and Social are not statistically different across the samples because the error bars associated with each attribute value overlap. However, it is found that the national sample of respondents value Species significantly higher than the two regional samples. Aesthetics is valued significantly lower by the national sample relative to the Albany sample, but the values held by Rockhampton respondents for this attribute are not statistically different to those of the national sample. We can conclude from these results that values are dependent on the population sampled, at least for some attributes.

BT Test 2: Transferability of Estimates from a National to Regional Context

This test examines whether the implicit prices estimated for attributes in the national context are equivalent to those obtained in the regional case studies. Unlike BT Test 1, both frame and population vary in this comparison. The implicit prices under examination are derived from the

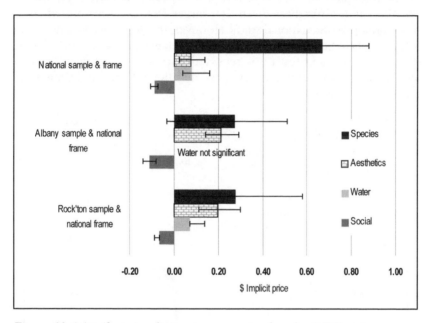

Figure 10.4 Attribute implicit prices examined under BT Test 1

following models:

- model 1: the national sample and frame;
- model 4: the Albany sample and GSR frame; and
- model 5: the Rockhampton sample and FBR frame.

The test results show that attribute values estimated in the regional contexts are significantly higher than those estimated in the national context — by a factor of two to 26 times, depending on the attribute in question (Figure 10.5). The magnitude of value difference provides a guide to the scaling adjustments that would need to be made if the national estimates were transferred to a regional context (see Table 10.8 for scaling factors). At least three reasons could be responsible for the different value estimates. The case studies differ from the national study in terms of the respondents frame of reference, the population sampled and the scope of changes presented for valuation. The results support the *a priori* expectation of regular embedding; that is, consumers place a lower value on attributes when framed in a wide, national context versus a narrow, local context. It could also be the case that people identify more closely with changes occurring in their local district compared to changes at the national level. Alternatively, a scope effect could be responsible for the value differences given that larger changes were presented to respondents in the national study. However, this test does not allow firm conclusions to be drawn about the predominant cause of the differences. BT Test 3, the next test to be reported, serves to disentangle framing effects from population differences so that the influence of framing can be assessed in isolation.

Table 10.8 Scaling factors for calibrating the national estimates for transfer to a regional context

Attribute	Scaling factor
Species	x 2
Aesthetics	x 20 – 25
Water	x 20 – 25
Social	x 6 – 26

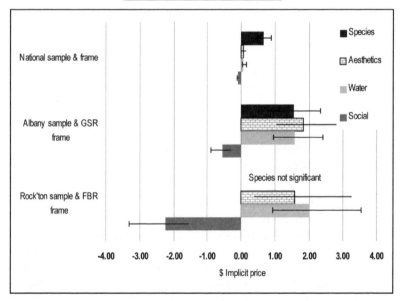

Figure 10.5   Attribute implicit prices examined under BT Test 2

BT Test 3: The Relative Importance of Framing

This test examines the equality of attribute values in a regional and national context, estimated using separate samples drawn from the same regional population. The objective of the test is to gauge the extent of the framing effect, holding population constant. Implicit prices are sourced from the following models:

- model 2: Albany sample and national frame; versus
- model 4: Albany sample and GSR frame

and;

- model 3 Rockhampton sample and national frame; versus
- model 5 Rockhampton sample and FBR frame.

The test results indicate that respondents have significantly higher values when attributes are framed in a regional context (Figure 10.6). The scale of differences is similar to the findings from BT Test 2, which suggests that framing effects (due to scope or context differences) are the primary cause of the differences rather than population effects.

BT Test 4: Consistency of Values Across Case Study Regions

This test examines whether attribute values differ between the two case study regions. Whilst the same set of attributes is evaluated in each case study, the frame in which these attributes are 'embedded' is substantially different. Furthermore, the characteristics of each case-study population are likely to be different. Some of this variation in population characteristics is controlled for by the socio-economic variables included in the utility functions, but attitudinal differences remain unaccounted for. The test was performed using implicit prices from the following models:

- model 4: Albany sample and GSR frame; versus
- model 5: Rockhampton sample and FBR frame.

The implicit prices for these models are shown in Figure 10.6. The results show that values are significantly different between the two case studies for some attributes. Respondents from Rockhampton hold significantly higher values for social impacts in their local region relative to the values held by Albany respondents. Conversely, Species is not valued by Rockhampton respondents in the FBR but is considered a significant attribute by Albany respondents in the GSR. Interestingly, these value disparities do not occur when these attributes are embedded in a national frame (see Figure 10.4). It appears that some attributes are viewed in a different light when respondents are asked to consider attribute trade-offs at a local level. The results of this test also demonstrate that the value estimates obtained in one region do not necessarily reflect community values in a different region, although there is a degree of consistency for some attributes.

BT Test 5: Consistency of Values Across City and Regional Respondents

The purpose of this test is to examine whether regional respondents have different values for attributes in their local area to urban dwellers in the State capital city. This is another test of population effects because the frame is fixed but population is allowed to vary. Implicit prices from the following models are compared:

- model 4: Albany sample and GSR frame; versus
- model 6: Perth sample and GSR frame

and;

- model 5: Rockhampton sample and FBR frame; versus
- model 7: Brisbane sample and FBR frame.

The implicit prices are compared in Figure 10.7. The test results show that implicit prices for the environmental attributes are statistically equivalent for regional and city households. While the direction of results

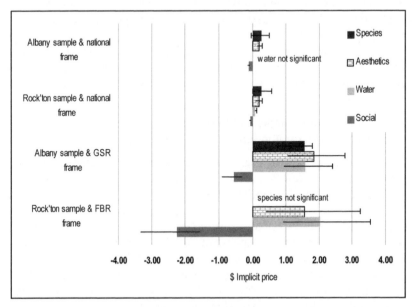

Figure 10.6 Attribute implicit prices examined under BT Tests 3 and 4

is for values to be lower in the city samples (suggesting lower use values), this difference is not statistically significant. The results imply that it is safe to aggregate environmental values from respondents in regional areas to city populations within the same State. Importantly, there is no evidence of values declining with distance from either of the case study regions. Parochialism does not appear to have played a significant role in influencing values in the regional communities. In the case of social impacts, Rockhampton respondents have significantly higher values for this attribute than Brisbane city households — indicating that local residents of Rockhampton have greater concerns about the prosperity of their region than city people. The same trend was not evident in the GSR study.

12   BENEFIT TRANSFER GUIDELINES

The results of the benefit transfer tests demonstrate that community values for environmental and social attributes are dependent on the context in which changes are made and the type of population valuing the changes. Thus it is critical to ensure that the value estimates selected for assessing a particular policy are suitably calibrated before transferring benefits. The following guidelines apply:

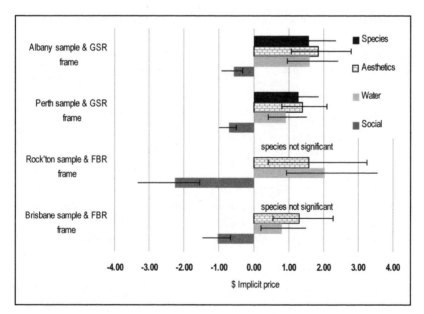

Figure 10.7 Attribute implicit prices examined under BT Test 5

- For environmental policies that have an Australia-wide impact, the national model implicit price estimates (Model 1) should be used and aggregated to the national household population — as per the example in Table 10.7.
- In situations where the impacts of a policy are limited to a particular region within a single State (or possibly spanning two adjoining States), the national implicit price estimates from Model 1 should be scaled up using the scaling factors in Table 10.8. The scaling adjustment is required to reflect the higher values attached to attributes in a regional frame. The benefits should only be aggregated to households residing in the same State(s) as the region where the changes are expected to occur.
- As an example of national-to-regional transfer, consider the case of a proposal to redress land and water degradation in a region in New South Wales (Table 10.9). Under the proposal, 20 000 hectares of rural land will be rehabilitated, 160 kilometres of waterways will be restored, three additional species will be protected and 50 additional people will leave the region each year because the proposal involves lower farming intensities. To value these impacts, the national implicit price estimates are scaled up to fit the regional context, which produces a total annual benefit of $29.72 per household.

Table10.9   Transfer and calibration of national value estimates to assess a regional policy

Attribute	Change by 2020	Calibrated national prices	Regional prices	Annual value of impact ($/hhold)
Water	160 km restored	($0.008) x 20	$0.16 per km	$25.60
Aesthetics	20 000 ha rehabilitated	($0.07) x 20	$1.40 per 10 000 ha	$2.80
Species	3 species protected	($0.67) x 2	$1.34 per species	$4.02
Social	50 people leaving pa	(-$0.09) x 6	$0.54 per 10 persons	-$2.70
				$29.72

- The national estimates serve as a 'base source' of implicit prices, which can be adjusted to fit different policy frames. Naturally, value estimates from the regional case study models would be a better source of estimates for assessing policies that were specifically targeted at those regions.
- If multiple regional policies are to be implemented, and each policy affects a similar set of attributes, it would be inappropriate to assess these separately using the 'scaled up' value estimates and to add up

the benefits to arrive at a total national benefit. This would ignore the influence that regular embedding has on peoples' preferences. The correct course of action would be to use the national value estimates (Model 1) and aggregate these to the relevant household population.

- The transfer tests provide guidance on the 'geographic extent of the market' or how widely the values should be extrapolated. The results suggest that values for regional impacts can be extrapolated to city populations as values were found to be statistically equivalent for the two population types. This result is perhaps due to the generic nature of the attributes selected for this study because other research has found that values are sensitive to parochialism displayed by local populations (Rolfe et al. 2000) and that use values tend to be lower for populations living at distance from the site of interest (Pate and Loomis 1997; Sutherland and Walsh 1985).

13 CONCLUSION

This study provides policy makers with estimates to make a first pass assessment of the non-market values associated with land and water degradation in Australia. The implicit prices estimated using the CM technique allows policy analysts to examine a wide range of different scenarios by 'packaging up' the attribute implicit prices according to the attribute changes that are expected to take place as a result of a proposed resource use change. The values should be regarded as 'order of magnitude' type estimates for evaluating broad regional and national policies — not specific management plans at a local level.

The benefit transfer tests demonstrate how important it is to take account of framing and population characteristics when transferring value estimates. The results show unequivocally that implicit price estimates sourced from the national study are lower than those derived from the regional case studies. One possible reason for the value differences is regular embedding. That is, respondents could be cognisant of a larger array of environmental issues in the national frame and, hence, associate smaller values to the attributes under investigation. Alternatively, a scope effect could be responsible for the differences. That is, the small changes in attribute levels presented to respondents in the case study questionnaires are valued more highly at the margin than the large changes in the national study.

It is clear that the challenge of benefit transfer is greatest when source values are required for evaluating welfare impacts at a localised level where values are highly dependent on the context in which the environmental outcomes are embedded. For example, this study found that populations from different States have similar values for attributes in the national context, but in the regional context the values are markedly different — at least for some of the attributes investigated. Further research is needed to understand the limits of benefit transfer and what options are available for improving its validity.

NOTES

1. A survey by the Australian Bureau of Statistics (ABS) indicated that Western Australian residents have a greater awareness of environmental problems than any of the other States, and Queenslanders have the lowest levels of awareness (ABS 1999).
2. In an information leaflet accompanying the questionnaire, respondents were told that the species referred to in the questionnaire were those that are currently listed as 'endangered' on the official register of endangered species. The types of species on this list only include vertebrates and macro-invertebrates. Thus insects and micro-organisms are excluded.
3. A fractional factorial experimental design was used to assign attribute levels to the alternatives. The resultant alternatives were assigned to five blocks such that each respondent was only presented with the alternatives that comprise one block of the fractional factorial.
4. 1 079 questionnaires were undeliverable (returned to sender).
5. For instance, Whitten and Bennett (2004) recorded response rates between 22 and 34 per cent in their mail-out/mail-back CM survey. However, some mail-delivered CM applications have recorded higher response rates. For instance, Bennett and Morrison (2001) were able to achieve response rates of around 40 per cent.
6. The total number of non-respondents was 8 152. Of this group, the follow-up survey suggests that 25 per cent (or 2 038) have non-zero values. This proportion, when expressed as a percentage of the total number of delivered questionnaires (9 721) is 21 per cent. When this is added to the 16 per cent of people who responded to the survey, the total proportion of the population to which the results can be safely extrapolated is 37 per cent.
7. Initially a multinomial logit model was used to describe the data relationships. However, this specification was shown to result in breaches of the Independence of Irrelevant Alternatives (IIA) assumption. See Kling and Herriges (1995) for more details on nested logit models.
8. The IV coefficient for the levy alternative (a1) is an estimated parameter, while the a2 coefficient on the status quo IV was restricted to one.

REFERENCES

ABS (Australian Bureau of Statistics) (1999), *Environmental Issues: People's Views and Practices,* Catalogue 4602.0, Canberra.

ABS (Australian Bureau of Statistics) (2001), *Regional Population Growth, Australia and New Zealand,* Catalogue 3218.0, Canberra.

Bennett, J. and M. Morrison (2001), 'Estimating the Environmental Values of New South Wales Rivers', *Proceedings of the 3rd Australian Stream Management Conference,* Brisbane, pp. 29–34.

Bennett, J., M. Morrison and R. Blamey (1998), 'Testing the validity of responses to contingent valuation', *Australian Journal of Agricultural and Resource Economics,* **42** (2), 131–48.

Blamey, R., J. Louviere and J. Bennett (2001), 'Choice Set Design', in J. Bennett and R. Blamey (eds), *The Choice Modelling Approach to Environmental Valuation,* Cheltenham UK and Northampton, MA, USA: Edward Elgar, pp. 133–56.

Kling, C.L. and J.A. Herriges (1995), 'An empirical investigation of the consistency of nested logit models with utility maximisation', *American Journal of Agricultural Economics,* **77,** 875–84.

Krinsky, I. and A.L. Robb (1986), 'On approximating the statistical properties of elasticities', *Review of Economics and Statistics,* **72,** 189–90.

Pate, J. and J. Loomis (1997), 'The effect of distance on willingness to pay values: A case study of wetlands and salmon in California', *Ecological Economics,* **20,** 199–207.

Randall, A. and J. Hoehn (1996), 'Embedding in market demand systems', *Journal of Environmental Economics and Management,* **30** (3), 369–80.

Rolfe, J. (1998), *Complexities in the Valuation of Natural Resources and the Development of the Choice Modelling Technique,* unpublished PhD thesis, Canberra: University of New South Wales.

Rolfe, J., J. Bennett and J. Louviere (2000), 'Choice Modelling and its potential application to tropical rainforest preservation', *Ecological Economics* **35,** 289–302.

Sutherland, R.J. and R. Walsh (1985), 'Effect of distance on the preservation value of water quality', *Land Economics,* **61,** 281–91.

Whitten, S. and J. Bennett (2004), *The Private and Social Values of Wetlands,* Cheltenham UK and Northampton, MA, USA: Edward Elgar.

11. Valuing Aboriginal Cultural Heritage across Different Population Groups

John Rolfe and Jill Windle

1 INTRODUCTION

In recent decades, increased emphasis on sustainable development has prompted a more holistic and comprehensive approach to natural resource management issues. In terms of resource economics, this has meant greater interest in including and assessing impacts that are not reflected in normal market processes. There have been substantial advances in the use of non-market valuation techniques to predict community preferences for different environmental outcomes, and the inclusion of such analyses in evaluations such as cost-benefit analysis is becoming more commonplace. However, the application of such techniques to social and cultural heritage issues is much rarer.

One outcome is that economists have only limited involvement in many debates over social and cultural heritage issues, even when they involve natural resource assets. For example, it has been argued in a regional context that sustainable development should encompass all the interests of regional stakeholders (Dore and Woodhill 1999; Dovers and Mobbs 1999; Gray and Lawrence 2001), without explaining how competing interests should be evaluated, prioritised and awarded. The dichotomy between paradigms that identify and articulate needs, and paradigms that rationalise how those needs can be satisfied is perhaps sharpest for indigenous people and cultural heritage issues. In this chapter, these issues are explored in relation to Aboriginal people in Australia.

While many Aboriginal people in northern Australia live on traditional lands and maintain strong traditional cultures, a large proportion of Aboriginal people, particularly in southern Australia, live in more urbanised settings. In view of this graduation of Aboriginal people living between very traditional and very Western cultures, two broad questions can be raised. The first is whether all Aboriginal people view preservation of cultural heritage as a dominant concern, given that these populations also have demands for health, education and other services. The second issue is whether Aboriginal people in urban settings have very different views about cultural heritage and natural resource management from other Australian people in urban areas. If they do, then it is important that their values are not ignored.

At the economic evaluation level, a key issue is how preferences for Aboriginal cultural heritage can be assessed. Many developments involving natural resources may also impact on cultural heritage items, as well as having social and environmental impacts. Preferences for Aboriginal cultural heritage protection are likely to involve non-use values, as many sites lie on private land that is not directly accessible. The involvement of non-use values means that stated preference techniques need to be employed to assess the trade-offs people prefer to make.

For both Aboriginal and non-Aboriginal people, development proposals will involve consideration of a number of different issues. At a specific proposal level, development options may hinge on trade-offs between a small number of factors. In these cases the contingent valuation method (CVM) may be appropriate. At a more general level, trade-offs between several factors may need to be simultaneously considered. In this case the choice modelling (CM) technique may be more appropriate. Where trade-offs between development options and Aboriginal cultural heritage are being considered at a generic regional level, then CM is the most appropriate methodology. Generally, there has been very little economic analysis, including CM studies, that has examined these issues. Consequently, it is very unclear how values for resource management trade-offs and Aboriginal cultural heritage protection differ between Aboriginal and general community groups.

In this chapter, values for the protection of Aboriginal cultural heritage items are reported. CM has been used in a series of case studies assessing the trade-offs between development benefits and environmental and social losses in the Fitzroy Basin in central Queensland. One of these studies has included the impact on Aboriginal cultural heritage sites as one of the attributes used in the choice set. Two tests for benefit transfer are reported. The first test examines if the local regional (Rockhampton) Aboriginal, and general community, and the remote urban (Brisbane) general community groups hold similar values for the protection of Aboriginal cultural heritage sites. The second test examines if the Aboriginal and general community groups value resource management trade-offs in the same way.

2   BACKGROUND

2.1   Water Resource Development in the Fitzroy Basin, Central Queensland

The Fitzroy River Basin is the second largest, externally draining catchment in Australia (after the Murray-Darling). The basin extends over 142 000 km² in central Queensland and is dominated by agriculture (grazing, dryland cropping, irrigated cotton and horticulture) and by mining (coal production of 100 million tonnes/year, magnesite, nickel and historically gold and silver). The major river systems that make up the Fitzroy Basin include the Fitzroy, Dawson, Comet, Nogoa, Connors, Mackenzie and Isaac rivers. The basin is home to around 185 000 people, or 5.3 per cent of the State's population. The major regional centre, Rockhampton, has a population of 59 475. About 4.4 per cent of the total population and 3.6 per cent of the over-18-year-old population are of Aboriginal descent.

There is growing demand in some parts of the basin for more water to be used for development, in particular for irrigated agriculture. The Fitzroy Basin has been used for irrigated farming since the 1970s. About 1 500 people are employed in irrigation activities in the basin. The irrigated agriculture production of the basin is worth more than $100 million per year, and the region accounts for 10 per cent of the value of irrigated crops produced in Queensland. However, if more water is allocated to development, there would be environmental and social impacts that need to be considered.

The water reform process in Queensland has been in progress for several years following the 1994 Council of Australian Governments (COAG) agreement on a national agenda for water reform. A key legislative component of the reform process in Queensland is the 'Water Act 2000', which assesses the trade-offs between economic and environmental demands for water and identifies any unallocated water in the river system. If some of the unallocated water (if it is available in a river system) is allocated for development, it will provide economic benefits, but there will also be associated environmental and social impacts. While there may be some more obvious impacts in terms of vegetation clearing and adverse impacts on water quality, there will also be some less obvious social impacts such as the loss of Aboriginal cultural heritage sites.

2.2   Aboriginal Cultural Heritage in the Fitzroy Basin

The long period of Aboriginal occupation of the landscape before white settlement, and the relatively short time period since white settlement, means that a great deal of evidence about that previous occupation still exists. Some 'spectacular' sites such as art sites and burial places exist, and are commonly associated with Aboriginal cultural heritage. However, the bulk of cultural heritage places and items relate to living patterns. These include camp sites, stone tools, stone working sites, marked trees, rock wells and middens along waterholes. There is variable distribution of these sites throughout the landscape. Some areas, such as those along major watercourses, may display a rich cultural heritage history, while other areas may show very little trace of prior occupation.

Information on the identification and distribution of cultural heritage places in the Fitzroy Basin was provided by L'Oste-Brown (2001) and derives largely from work undertaken as part of the Bowen Basin Aboriginal Cultural Heritage Project (L'Oste-Brown et al. 1998). A total of 2 724 places containing Aboriginal heritage values have been identified, including places and values spanning periods prior to European contact to more recent times. While there are a number of sites of high significance, such as 312 rock art places, there are also many sites of lower significance such as 807 isolated stone artefacts and 938 stone artefact scatters (Table 11.1).

In Queensland, the *Cultural Record (Landscapes Queensland and Queensland Estate) Act* 1987 (under review) is the State legislation responsible for the management and protection of indigenous cultural heritage values. All Aboriginal places in Queensland are protected under the Act and penalty provisions may apply for any unauthorised interference with them. However, in reality, the Act is not policed, and the protection of cultural sites is strongly influenced by land tenure. Some historic items may be protected under the *Queensland Heritage Act* 1992, and the *Nature Conservation Act* 1992 provides for the protection of Aboriginal cultural heritage in National Parks and protected areas. All Acts are administered by the Environment Protection Agency; they predate the *Native Title Act* 1993, and all cultural items as defined by the Acts are the property of the Crown.

In the Fitzroy Basin a total of 15.5 per cent of the cultural sites identified by L'Oste-Brown (2001) for this study are located in National Parks (7.7 per cent), and State Forests and Timber Reserves (7.8 per cent), and have some form of protection. All the other sites are located on private property and both access to, and protection of, these sites is at the discretion of the landowners. Many of the heritage items that related to living patterns, such as stone artefacts and stone scatters, are often not recognised as Aboriginal sites by landholders and commercial developers, and hence are susceptible to loss. In the Carnarvon Gorge area, there are many art and burial sites located on private land, some of which are more spectacular and significant than those protected in the National Park.

Table 11.1   Number of Aboriginal cultural heritage place types in the Fitzroy Basin

Cultural Heritage Place Type	No.	Cultural Heritage Place Type	No.
Aboriginal wells	4	Rock art associated with stone artefacts	38
Aboriginal well (historic)	1	Rock art associated with stone artefacts & axe-grinding grooves	10
Axe grinding grooves	21	Rock art places	312
Bird trap (historic)	1	Rockshelters containing rock art	35
Burials	60	Rockshelters containing rock art & stone artefacts	13
Burials (historic)	12	Rockshelters containing stone artefacts	12
Burial with associated axe-grinding grooves	1	Scarred trees	177
Burial with associated cached material	1	Scarred tree (historic)	1
Burials with associated rock art	13	Shell middens	4
Earthen circles	2	Spiritual places	4
Hearths	20	Spiritual/story places	12
Historic camps/Yumbas	36	Stone arrangements	8
Isolated stone artefact/s	807	Stone artefact scatters	938
Isolated stone artefacts with associated source stone	18	Stone artefact scatters containing knapping floors	5
Massacre places	4	Stone artefact scatters with associated quarried stone	35
Ochre sources	3	Stone artefact scatters with associated source stone	37
Other unidentified/unknown cultural places	16	Stone sources	6
Place associated with the Native Mounted Police	1	Story places	26
Resource place	1	Story places associated with rock art	5
Rock Art associated with axe-grinding grooves	23	Travel route	1

Source: L'Oste-Brown 2001, p. 2.

The figures in Table 11.1 must be treated with caution as they are derived from the Bowen Basin study and do not include all places in the Fitzroy catchment. In addition:

- the information principally relates to archaeological sites, and very little information exists on places of historical and/or contemporary importance;
- the majority of the catchment has not been systematically examined; and
- in many areas that have been systematically examined, substantial amounts of the recorded Aboriginal cultural heritage no longer exist due to subsequent development activities. (L'Oste-Brown 2001)

2.3 Aboriginal Cultural Heritage Values

There is a wide variety of cultural heritage places in central Queensland and a complex mix of values associated with them. At Carnarvon Gorge, the Aboriginal rock art sites have high cultural heritage values associated with their archaeological, historical and anthropological importance and are a significant international tourist attraction. As such, the sites have value at a local/regional, national and international level. Other sites may only have significant value for much smaller and specifically defined sections of the local community. Some sites may have spiritual significance to only one Aboriginal clan; other sites may have value to several clan groups in the area.

It is helpful to distinguish the values that Aboriginal people may hold for traditional sites in several ways. At one level, Aboriginal people may hold values for accessing or preserving land and water resources generally within their traditional areas. At another level, particular sites within traditional areas may have spiritual or other significance, and be particularly highly valued. Most of these values will be held only by Aboriginal people with direct links to traditional lands, and will not extend across all Aboriginal people. For the relevant groups, access may be just as important as protection.

Another context of value is where Aboriginal cultural heritage sites and items are important for Aboriginal people, even though they may not have direct links or spiritual relationships to the sites and items. Here, there is a much wider group, comprising most Aboriginal people, likely to place importance on protection of those sites. Values derive from more general cultural heritage and anthropological interests, and access is likely to be less important than the protection issues. In a similar context, the general community may hold values for protecting Aboriginal cultural heritage sites.

In terms of what makes an Aboriginal cultural heritage site important then, there are several overlapping groups of values to consider. At the broad level, there is likely to be some interest from the general community and Aboriginal people about protecting Aboriginal cultural heritage sites. Aboriginal people probably place more importance on protection than does the general community, but there may be a much larger group within society that considers protection of Aboriginal cultural heritage sites to be important. In addition, there are some much smaller groups of Aboriginal people with direct relationships to the site in question, which place importance on such sites. These groups, although relatively small in number, are likely to place very high importance on both access and protection.

The National Aboriginal and Torres Strait Islander Survey 1994 indicates that Aboriginal and Torres Strait Islander culture and identity are not considered to be strong in the central Queensland region. In that survey, 5 440 people aged 13 years and over were consulted. Sixty-seven per cent stated that they did not identify with a clan, tribal or language group, and less than 4 per cent reported that they could speak an Aboriginal and Torres Strait Islander language. Only half of the survey group identified the area as their homeland. However, 64 per cent had attended or were involved in Aboriginal and Torres Strait Islander cultural activities (CQANM, 2001).

Clearly, both use and non-use values are important components of overall value. It is likely that a large proportion of values associated with cultural heritage sites are non-use values rather than use values. These may be held by regional, state, national and international populations. In the survey reported here, only non-use values held by people in Rockhampton (the regional centre) and Brisbane (the state capital) have been assessed.

2.4   Assessing Cultural Heritage Values

There have been relatively few valuations of cultural heritage sites generally, but even fewer of Aboriginal cultural heritage. Market valuation of tangible cultural heritage assets such as buildings and paintings can often be assessed through related market techniques such as hedonic pricing and the travel cost method. In cases where there is direct commercial income and clear property rights, values can be assessed from market data. A small number of valuations of Aboriginal cultural heritage have evaluated commercial benefits, e.g. Janke (1998); Zeppel (2001). There has been little attention paid to valuing the protection of Aboriginal heritage sites. For many cultural heritage sites, an important component of values is non-use values, such as existence values. While the estimation of non-use values provides greater challenges, heritage assets will remain under-valued unless such values are considered alongside use values.

There is a growing number of applications of non-market valuation techniques to assessing non-use values for cultural heritage sites (Navrud and Ready 2002). Many of these have employed the CVM to assess values for historic buildings and art objects in Europe and North America. For example, Bille (2002) used the technique to estimate total value of the Royal Theatre to the Danish population, and Navrud and Strand (2002) used the technique to assess preservation values for the Nidaros Cathedral in Norway. A CM approach was adopted by Morey et al. (2002) to ascertain values for reducing acid deposition on marble monuments in Washington DC.

Adamowicz et al. (1998) have discussed some theoretical issues relating to the non-market assessment of indigenous values, and a subsequent application of CM to value attributes of subsistence hunting by Aboriginal people in Canada is described in Haener et al. (2001). That study found that both age and Aboriginal status (First Nation Vs Metis) may result in different responses to changes in hunting attributes. Boxall et al. (2002) report the use of a stated preference application to assess the recreational values associated with Aboriginal rock paintings in a region of central Canada. They surveyed wilderness canoeists to ascertain the additional values that might be associated with knowledge of, and access to, rock art sites in the region, and showed that increased access had positive values for canoeists.

3   CHOICE MODELLING CASE STUDY

In this section, the results are reported of a CM application that was used to assess values for the protection of Aboriginal cultural heritage sites in the context of water resource development in the Fitzroy Basin. CM is used to describe a particular scenario in terms of different attributes. In the application, the choice set described a scenario based on four attributes, as well as a cost attribute. Three attributes described environmental impacts and the fourth related to the protection of Aboriginal cultural heritage sites. Three separate population groups were sampled in 2001. Aboriginal and general community groups were targeted at the same location (Rockhampton, the main regional centre), and an urban (Brisbane) sample of the general community was also collected. Results have been reported in Rolfe and Windle (2003) and Windle and Rolfe (2002, 2003).

3.1   Survey Design

The first stage of the project was to identify key attributes of the case study of interest. The 'Protection of Aboriginal cultural sites' was one of four attributes along with 'Healthy vegetation left in the floodplain', 'Kilometres of waterways in good health' and 'Unallocated water reserve' used to describe the case study. A key advantage about using three environmental attributes with the cultural heritage attribute was that it helped to frame the cultural heritage trade-offs in a wider context.

A cost attribute (increase in local rates) was also included, so that the trade-offs that respondents were prepared to make could also be assessed in monetary terms. As is standard practice in non-market valuation studies, the monetary attribute was framed in willingness to pay (WTP) terms, even though the case study of interest is focused on assessing the losses that the community might bear if further development proceeds. It was not expected that the WTP format would have been unrealistic, as there is the strong presumption that private property rights are dominant on most issues involving primary production.

The 'cultural heritage' attribute was developed through the use of focus groups. A series of four focus groups was held; three with Aboriginal participants only, and one with a selection from the general community. As both the Aboriginal and general community were being sampled, it was important that the information provided would be acceptable to both communities and not induce any 'non-response' bias. The Aboriginal groups were keen to ensure that their cultural heritage was presented in the right context. From their perspective, one issue that clearly needed to be included was that of native title, an issue that sparks an emotional response from many people in the community. Considerable effort was made to provide sufficient, factual information that would avoid generating any emotional response.

The information to describe the attribute was discussed and refined in the focus groups and the following aspects were highlighted in the survey:

• spiritual and cultural significance;
• historical, anthropological and archaeological importance;
• preserving traditional knowledge;
• recreational activities;
• educational activities; and
• providing Aboriginal people with links back to their country.

The key choice in presenting the cultural heritage attribute to Aboriginal people was to identify whether a protection or an access context should be presented. Many Aboriginal people focus on access to cultural heritage sites as a key aspiration. However, access presents a number of logistical problems. These include questions about who has access, when and how it is available, and how it impacts on the property rights of existing landholders. To minimise these problems, the attribute was presented in terms of the proportion of Aboriginal cultural heritage sites that could be protected. Part of the information presented to survey respondents is shown in Box 11.1.

Box 11.1 Information presented about levels of protection of cultural heritage sites

Using the best information available, 2 724 Aboriginal cultural heritage places are currently recorded in the Fitzroy Basin. This includes places and values spanning periods prior to European contact to more recent times. 15.5% of these sites are located in National Parks (7.7%) and State Forests and Timber Reserves (7.8%), and have some form of protection. An unknown small percentage of the remaining sites, located on private land, are well protected and accessible to traditional owners. Most Aboriginal cultural heritage sites are located on private property and are not well protected. Some may be lost to development in the future.

Current trend:
This survey assumes that 25% of Aboriginal cultural heritage sites will have some form of protection in 15 years time.

Respondents to the survey were presented with the expected level of environmental and cultural heritage factors in 15 years' time under current policy conditions.[1] This constant alternative was presented as the status quo option in each choice, together with two other options where respondents could potentially pay to achieve more desirable outcomes. Increases in local rates were chosen as the payment vehicle. Reasons for choosing local rates over other payment vehicles such as taxes include the direct association between catchment health and water treatment costs, the unsuitability of income tax for respondent groups that have low income levels, and the difficulties involved in using state or national level payment vehicles to achieve a regional outcome.

The levels in the two alternative options varied according to an experimental design process. Levels were chosen to span the range of environmental and policy outcomes possible, and to identify cost trade-offs that would influence choice behaviour. Four of the attributes had four levels, and another one had eight levels. The attribute levels for the survey are outlined in Table 11.2 and an example of the choice set presented to respondents is presented in Figure 11.1.

Table 11.2 Base and attribute levels for the CM survey

Attribute	Base Levels	Choice Set Levels
Payment ($)	0	10; 20; 50; 100
Healthy vegetation in the floodplain (%)	20	20; 30; 40; 50
Kilometres of waterways in good health	1500	1500; 1800; 2100; 2400
Protection of Aboriginal cultural sites (%)	25	25; 35; 45; 55
Unallocated water (%)	0	-15; -10; -5; 0; 5; 10; 15, 20

	Question X: Options A, B and C. Please choose the option you prefer most by ticking ONE box.				
	Fifteen-year effects				
How much I pay each year	Healthy vegetation left in floodplains	Kilometres of waterways in good health	Protection of Aboriginal Cultural sites	Unallocated water	I would choose
Option A					
$0	20%	1500	25%	0%	☐
Option B					
$20	30%	1800	35%	5%	☐
Option C					
$50	40%	2100	45%	10%	☐

Figure 11.1 Example choice set used in the survey

Special consideration was taken over the design of the survey as the Aboriginal community was one sample population. Survey design was discussed in the focus groups, and several techniques were used to minimise problems of comprehension and collection. Icons were used in the survey to help respondents identify the attributes and assimilate complex information. The survey was presented in a large format with text well-spaced and easy to comprehend.

The survey was collected in a drop-off/pick-up format. This allowed respondents to complete the survey in their own homes and without time pressures. The initial face-to-face contact between collector and respondent helped to increase trust and participation. An Aboriginal collector was employed to sample the Aboriginal community to address the problem of trust outlined in Haener et al. (2001). Options of face-to-face interviews were offered for respondents who had difficulties in reading the survey, although these were not taken up. The Aboriginal respondents were selected at random from a compiled list of Aboriginal households in Rockhampton, based on the best available information. Addresses were supplied by various organisations such as the Aboriginal Housing Cooperative, the Fitzroy Basin Elders Committee, and educational institutions. The Aboriginal survey was conducted independently and was not associated with any Aboriginal organisation.

3.2   Survey Collection Details

One hundred and twelve surveys were hand-delivered to an Aboriginal sample of the Rockhampton area. Sixty-three responses were collected, yielding a response rate of 56 per cent. There was a response rate of 83 per cent for the general community sample in Rockhampton where 120 surveys were hand-delivered and 100 were collected. A total of 58 surveys were collected from Brisbane, and collectors reported a general response rate of around 70 per cent.

The socio-economic characteristics indicated that the three sample groups were similar and included a broad cross-section of the population (Table 11.3). It may appear that more Aboriginal respondents are in higher income categories than might be expected. However, extrapolating the 1996 Census data for the average weekly income in the Fitzroy Shire (including Rockhampton), the indigenous community has a higher approximate average annual gross income ($32,000) compared with the general community ($30,000). Eighteen per cent of Aboriginal respondents did not provide information about their income and it is possible that these were from lower income groups. As there was some difficulty in collecting completed surveys from some households, it is possible that these were also from lower income groups, and might indicate a non-response bias. As would be expected in a regional area, both Rockhampton groups had lower education levels than the State average, and Aboriginal education levels were lower than the general community.

Table 11.3 Social demographic details of the survey respondents

Variable	Rockhampton Aboriginal Community	Rockhampton General Community	Brisbane General Community	State Average[a]
Average Age (> 17 years)	38 years	45 years	46 years	42 years
Gender (% Female)	59%	47%	41%	50%
Education (%>year 12)	30%	39%	46%	46%
Income (annual, hsehold)	$42,062[b]	$39,882[b]	$35,308[b]	$27,500 [c]
% agree that environment declined	38%	46%	43%	42%

Notes:
[a] Figures taken from Rolfe, Loch and Bennett (2002, Table 4) and use 1996 Census data.
[b] Before tax.
[c] After tax.

3.3   Results

The orthogonal experimental design generated for the survey had 64 different choice sets. These were blocked into groups of eight so that each respondent was presented with eight choice sets in a survey. This meant that there were 504 choice sets completed by the Aboriginal sample, 800 choice sets completed by the Rockhampton general population sample and 464 choice sets completed by the Brisbane general population sample. The choice data were analysed and multinomial logit models (MNL) were developed using the LIMDEP software program. Each of the variables used in the models is specified in Table 11.4.

Table 11.4   Variables used in the CM application

Variable	Description
Cost	Amount that households would pay in extra rates (or rent) each year to fund improvements
Vegetation	% of healthy vegetation remaining in floodplains
Waterways	Kilometres of waterways in catchment remaining in good health
Cultural Heritage	% of Aboriginal cultural sites protected
Unallocated Water	% of water resources in catchment not committed to the environment or allocated to industry/urban/irrigation uses
ASC	Alternate Specific Constant which reflects the influence of all other factors on choice
Environment	Concern about "Environmental problems" was ranked 1st or 2nd. List included Crime prevention, Education, Health, Interest rates Unemployment
Misunderstood	Asked if understood survey 1= strong agree to 5=strongly disagree
Information	Asked if needed more information 1= strong agree to 5=strongly disagree
Age	Age of respondent (in years)
Gender	Male or female
Children	Respondent has children, Yes or No
Environ Org	Respondent is a member of an organisation associated with environmental conservation
Farming	Respondent's family has close association with farming
Education	Education (ranges from 1=never went to school to 6=tertiary degree)
Income	Gross income of household in dollar terms

Model results for the three data sets are shown in Table 11.5. The models appear robust, with most attributes significant and signed as expected.

Table 11.5 Survey results of multinomial logit models

Variable	Rockhampton Aboriginal Community		Rockhampton General Community		Brisbane General Community	
	Coeff.	S. Error	Coeff.	S. Error	Coeff.	S. Error
Cost	-0.010***	0.002	-0.012***	0.002	-0.012***	0.002
Vegetation	0.005	0.007	0.030***	0.006	0.033***	0.008
Waterways	0.000*	0.000	0.001***	0.000	0.001**	0.000
Cultural Heritage	**0.034***	**0.007**	**-0.025***	**0.006**	**-0.022***	**0.008**
Unallocated Water	0.038***	0.007	0.038***	0.006	0.041***	0.008
ASC	0.297**	0.118	0.159	0.103	0.078	0.140
Environment	0.029	0.327	0.309	0.225	1.138**	0.500
Misunderstood	0.801*	0.472	-1.899***	0.321	0.793**	0.358
More Information	1.660***	0.464	0.145	0.212	-0.783**	0.307
Gender	1.267***	0.262	-0.310*	0.169	1.187***	0.290
Children	0.951***	0.300	-0.220	0.237	-0.298	0.338
Environment Organisation	-1.638***	0.390	-0.488*	0.264	-1.326**	0.611
Farming	0.155	0.383	-0.023	0.215	-0.538	0.372
Education	-0.086	0.095	0.390***	0.080	0.448***	0.110
Income	0.000***	0.000	0.000	0.000	0.000	0.000
Age	-0.045***	0.011	0.000	0.006	0.004	0.009
Model Statistics						
N (Choice Sets)	496 (16 skipped)		768 (64 skipped)		464 (88 skipped)	
Log L	-439.42		-639.53		-338.67	
Adj. Rho-square	0.153		0.154		0.162	

Note: *** Significant at the 1% level; ** Significant at the 5% level;
          * Significant at the 10% level.

The key difference in results between the models is that the cultural heritage attribute is positive for the Aboriginal sample (indicating that probability of choice increased with the increased percentage of sites that would be protected), but negative for both general community samples (indicating that the probability of choice decreased with the increased percentage of sites that would be protected).

Various socio-economic characteristics were significant, but varied across the different population groups in their influence. The significance of these variables relates to their influence on the selection of the status quo option or a preservation option (see Figure 11.1). For example, 'income' was significant and positive in the Rockhampton Aboriginal model, indicating that respondents with higher incomes were more likely to select a preservation option. On the other hand, 'age' was significant and negative, indicating that older people were more likely to select the status quo option.

More evidence about how important the respondents viewed the different attributes used in the application can be gained from another question presented in the survey. In that question, respondents were asked whether or not they had a consistent preference for the different attributes, and if so, what their rankings were. The majority of the Aboriginal (62 per cent) and general population groups (Rockhampton 69 per cent and Brisbane 72 per cent), indicated that they had a consistent ranking for the attributes used. For the Aboriginal sample, the cultural heritage attribute was the most important, and the vegetation attribute was the least important. This is consistent with the vegetation attribute being non-significant in the model. The rankings of the attributes in importance by the three groups are shown in Figure 11.2.

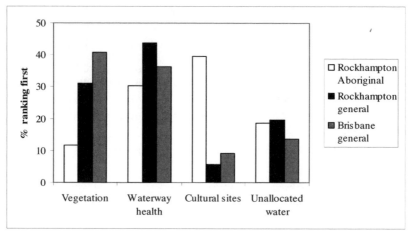

Figure 11.2 Percentage of samples ranking attribute as
'most important'

Further detail on the values that were held for the cultural heritage attribute by the different groups was gained by estimating more specific models. Under this approach, the cultural heritage attribute was split into four separate variables, one for each level. The variables were dummy coded (0,1) to reflect the possibility that respondents may have focused more on the overall direction and position of each level rather than translate the percentage terms to actual sites protected. In other words, the dummy code allowed for tests for differences in value between each separate level for the attribute, as if the attribute was coded in an ordinal manner as:

- current level;
- some more sites protected;
- more sites protected; and
- maximum sites protected.

This compares with the previous models reported, where the cultural heritage variable has been treated as a single continuous variable, with an implicit assumption that there is a linear relationship between the levels and the responses made. By breaking the variable up into separate variables, it allows testing of whether responses have followed some non-linear pattern.

One of the levels (maximum sites protected) had to be dropped from the model for use as a base in the estimation process. The relevant models are reported in Table 11.6. For the Aboriginal sample, the negative coefficients for the three estimated levels indicate that these are less preferred levels, and that these respondents would prefer maximum protection levels. The least preferred level is the current situation, and there was little difference in the impact on choices between the second and third levels of protection. For the general population groups, the positive coefficients means that the maximum protection level is least preferred. Preference ordering for the levels is non-linear for both general populations. In both of these populations the second level of

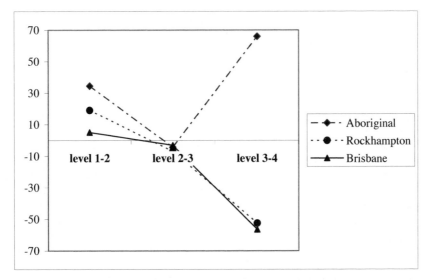

Figure 11.3 Part-worths ($) for changes in protection levels of cultural heritage

protection is most preferred, with both lower and higher levels being less preferred.

It appears that the Aboriginal community preferences for cultural heritage are quite different from those of the general community. However, a closer examination reveals some similarities. In Figure 11.3 the part-worths have been calculated for changes in attribute levels. The values for a change from level two to level three are very similar for all groups and show a similar trend in relation to a level one to two change. It is the change from level three to four that is so notably different between the Aboriginal and general community groups.

Table 11.6   Models with cultural heritage attribute split into levels

Variable	Rockhampton Aboriginal Community		Rockhampton General Community		Brisbane General Community	
	Coeff.	S. Error	Coeff.	S. Error	Coeff.	S. Error
Cost	-0.009***	0.002	-0.013***	0.002	-0.013***	0.003
Vegetation	0.003	0.007	0.028***	0.006	0.030***	0.008
Waterways	0.000	0.000	0.001***	0.000	0.001**	0.000
C Heritage 1 (25%)	**-0.866***	**0.206**	**0.523***	**0.157**	**0.708***	**0.220**
C Heritage 2 (35%)	**-0.555**	**0.267**	**0.772***	**0.230**	**0.774**	**0.318**
C Heritage 3 (45%)	**-0.594**	**0.287**	**0.682***	**0.248**	**0.734**	**0.343**
C Heritage 4 (55%)	**0.000**		**0.000**		**0.000**	
Unallocated Water	0.037***	0.007	0.040***	0.006	0.043***	0.008
ASC	0.550***	0.173	-0.202	0.148	-0.281	0.202
Environment	0.185	0.360	0.319	0.225	1.169**	0.501
Misunderstood	0.643	0.471	-1.974***	0.325	0.794**	0.362
Information	1.592***	0.470	0.111	0.213	-0.824***	0.310
Gender	1.407***	0.276	-0.316*	0.170	1.201***	0.290
Children	0.844***	0.306	-0.210	0.239	-0.284	0.335
Environment Organisation	-1.591***	0.397	-0.451*	0.265	-1.169*	0.600
Farming	0.171	0.387	-0.013	0.216	-0.578	0.374
Education	-0.079	0.101	0.389***	0.081	0.439***	0.110
Income	0.000***	0.000	0.000	0.000	0.000*	0.000
Age	-0.051***	0.011	0.000	0.006	0.004	0.009
Model Statistics						
N (Choice Sets)	496 (16 skipped)		768 (64 skipped)		464 (88 skipped)	
Log L	-417.29		-641.30		-338.67	
Adj. Rho-square	0.150		0.150		0.162	

Note: *** Significant at the 1% level; ** Significant at the 5% level;
* Significant at the 10% level.

4   BENEFIT TRANSFER

Benefit transfer refers to the ability to transfer values from an existing valuation study to a new case study of interest without having to repeat the valuation process. Such transfers may involve different sites, different populations and different framing contexts. The cultural heritage attribute that has been described in this case study has been framed very generally in its application, with changes in protection levels described as percentage changes of the total stock of cultural heritage items. This broad focus, as opposed to trade-offs framed around a particular item, should make it easier to transfer estimated values to other regions.

A key issue though will be whether it is possible to transfer values between different populations. The debate over native title and other Aboriginal issues has been quite heated in Australia in recent years, and there appears to be some political differences generally between Aboriginal, regional and urban communities. Here the question about whether values can be transferred between these groups is tested in some detail.

The two key hypotheses of relevance for benefit transfer are outlined below.

Hypothesis 1: The regional Aboriginal, regional general (Rockhampton) and remote urban (Brisbane) communities hold similar values for the protection of Aboriginal cultural heritage sites, that is:

$$\beta ABch = \beta ROCch = \beta BNEch$$

where βAB, βROC and βBNE are the parameter vectors corresponding to the Rockhampton Aboriginal, Rockhampton general and Brisbane general communities respectively, and *ch* refers to the values held for the protection of Aboriginal cultural heritage sites.

Hypothesis 2: The Aboriginal and general community value resource management trade-offs in the same way, that is:

$$\beta ABrto = \beta ROCrto = \beta BNErto$$

where βAB, βROC and βBNE are the parameter vectors corresponding to the Rockhampton Aboriginal, Rockhampton general and Brisbane general communities respectively, and *rto* refers to the values held for the resource management tradeoffs.

The test for the first hypothesis is focused on whether the part-worths for cultural heritage can be transferred from one case study to another. This is a form of a point benefit transfer, where the marginal values are transferred rather than the full values. A Krinsky and Robb

(1986) procedure is used to draw a vector of 1 000 sets of parameters for each model, and part-worths are calculated for each set of parameters. Differences between part-worths are calculated by taking one vector from another. Following Poe et al. (2001), this process is repeated 100 times by randomly re-ordering one vector of parameters. The 95 per cent confidence interval is approximated by identifying the proportion of differences that fall below zero.

Results of the Poe et al. (2001) procedure are shown in Table 11.7. These show that there is no significant difference between the Rockhampton and Brisbane populations for any of the part-worths. However, there are significant differences between the Aboriginal population and both the Rockhampton and Brisbane populations in terms of the vegetation and cultural heritage attributes. The Aboriginal population had a lower part-worth for vegetation and a higher part-worth for cultural heritage than the two general population groups. The results for vegetation have to be treated with caution because the coefficient for this attribute was not significant in the Aboriginal model.

Table 11.7 Proportion of part-worth differences falling below zero

	Vegetation	Waterways	Cultural Heritage	Unallocated water
Aboriginal – Rockhampton	0.986	0.647	0	0.337
Rockhampton – Brisbane	0.580	0.493	0.613	0.589
Aboriginal – Brisbane	0.984	0.624	0	0.429

These results imply that the hypothesis should be rejected, as there are significant differences in the values held by the Aboriginal and non-Aboriginal communities for cultural heritage, although there is no significant difference in the values held by the local regional and remote urban general communities.

Tests of the second hypothesis are focused on whether overall value functions are equivalent. Although there is evidence (Table 11.7) that it is possible to transfer many part-worth values, it is usually preferable to transfer value functions. This is because (a) differences in marginal values between attributes may cancel out in a value function, and (b) differences in population characteristics may compensate for differences in marginal values. To test whether the value functions can be transferred between the populations of interest, two separate tests are employed.

The first series of tests are log likelihood tests used to identify whether models are significantly different. The standard log likelihood tests take the following form:

$$LR = -2(LogL_{1/2} - (LogL_{X1} + LogL_{X2}))$$ (11.1)

where $LogL_{1/2}$ is the log likelihood value attached to the MNL model of the combined data set, and $LogL_{X1}$ and $LogL_{X2}$ are the log likelihoods of the MNL models for the individual data sets. The resulting likelihood ratio statistic follows an asymptotic chi-square distribution with $(P + 1)$ degrees of freedom, where P is the number of parameters across the models involved. The appropriate log likelihood tests for the three data sets are reported in Table 11.8.

Table 11.8 Log likelihood tests for significant differences between models

Data set	Log likelihood statistic	No. of variables in model	Likelihood ratio statistic
Aboriginal	-439.42	16	
Rockhampton general	-639.53	16	
Brisbane general	-338.67	16	
Rockhampton + Brisbane general	-1010.98	16	65.56
Rockhampton general + Aboriginal	-1149.74	16	141.58
Brisbane general + Aboriginal	-829.60	16	103.02

For each of the three model comparisons, the calculated likelihood ratio statistic is higher than the 5 per cent chi-square statistic at 17 degrees of freedom. As a result, the hypothesis that the models are equivalent must be rejected. From this test, it does not appear appropriate to transfer the value functions between populations.

The second test for transferring value functions is to compare the differences in consumer surplus estimates when a transferred model is adjusted for the characteristics of the target population. For example, the Brisbane model may be applied to the Rockhampton population, with average socio-economic characteristics of the Rockhampton population used to adjust the Brisbane model. A convolutions approach (Poe et al. 2001) can then be used to map the distribution of differences between the model predictions.

To maximise model accuracy, specific models (with only significant variables included) have been calculated. These results are summarised in Table 11.9.

Table 11.9   Multinomial logit models specific to each data set

Variable	Rockh'ton Aboriginal		Rockh'ton General		Brisbane General	
	Coeff	S. Error	Coeff.	S. Error	Coeff.	S. Error
Cost	-0.010***	0.002	-0.012***	0.002	-0.012***	0.002
Vegetation	0.004	0.007	0.027***	0.006	0.033***	0.007
Waterways	0.0005*	0.000	0.001***	0.000	0.001**	0.000
Cultural Heritage	0.033***	0.007	-0.025***	0.006	-0.019**	0.007
Unallocated Water	0.040***	0.007	0.037***	0.006	0.040***	0.008
ASC	0.299**	0.118				
Environment					1.237***	0.473
Misunderstood			-1.919***	0.309	0.651*	0.340
More Information	1.531***	0.443				
Gender	1.123***	0.220	-0.315*	0.161	1.060***	0.253
Children	0.751***	0.267				
Environment Org	-1.461***	0.288	-0.447***	0.163	-1.679***	0.313
Education			0.379***	0.062	0.448***	0.094
Income	0.00003***	0.000				
Age	-0.037***	0.009				
Model Statistics						
N (Choice Sets)	496 (8 skipped)		768 (48 skipped)		464 (64 skipped)	
Log L	-449.82		-669.64		-369.02	
Adj. Rho-square	0.151		0.148		0.150	

Note: *** Significant at the 1% level; ** Significant at the 5% level;
            * Significant at the 10% level.

The indirect utility functions take the following forms:

Aboriginal (Rockhampton):

$V_{ij} = 0.299 - 0.010(Cost) + 0.0005(Waterways) + 0.033(Cultural\ heritage) + 0.040(Unallocated\ water) + 1.531(More\ information) + 1.123(Gender) + 0.751(Children) - 1.461(Env.\ Organisation) + 0.00003(Income) - 0.037(Age)$ (11.2)

Rockhampton (general):

$V_{ij} = -0.012(Cost) + 0.027(Vegetation) + 0.001(Waterways) - 0.025(Cultural\ heritage) + 0.037(Unallocated\ water) - 1.919(Misunderstood) - 0.315(Gender) - 0.447(Env.\ Organisation) + 0.379(Education)$ (11.3)

Brisbane (general):

$V_{ij} = -0.012(Cost) + 0.033(Vegetation) + 0.001(Waterways) - 0.019(Cultural\ heritage) + 0.040(Unallocated\ water) + 1.237(Environment) + 0.651(Misunderstood) + 1.060(Gender) - 1.679(Env.\ Organisation) + 0.448(Education)$ (11.4)

In the following exercise, Equation 11.3 is used to predict results for Equations 11.2 and 11.4, across a representative set of eight choice profiles. These have been selected from the experimental design using an orthogonal process. The eight profiles that are used are shown in Table 11.10.

Table 11.10 Sample of eight choice profiles used to test differences between models

Scenario #	$	Vegetation	Waterways	Cultural heritage	Unallocated water
1	50	40	1 500	35	10
2	100	50	1 800	25	10
3	10	30	2 200	25	5
4	50	20	1 800	55	0
5	100	40	1 500	55	-10
6	20	20	2 000	35	-10
7	50	50	1 800	45	0
8	20	30	2 200	45	-5

In the first case, Equation 11.2 (the Aboriginal model) was used to predict values held by that population for each of the choice profiles across 1 000 draws of model parameters. Then Equation 11.3 (the Rockhampton model) was used to predict values for the same profiles across 1 000 draws, with the means of the relevant socio-economic variables from the Aboriginal data set used where relevant. For each draw, the difference in values was then calculated, and the Poe et al. (2001) procedure used to repeat the process 100 times.

A summary of the results is shown in Table 11.11, and indicate that significant differences existed across several scenarios. For those scenarios, more than 97.5 per cent of the Aboriginal scenario values were higher than the values predicted using the benefit transfer approach. The two scenarios with no significant difference in values were the ones with no potential improvement in the protection of cultural heritage. This indicates that many of the differences in values held by the two populations are focused on that attribute.

In the second case, Equation 11.4 (the Brisbane model) was used to predict values held by the Brisbane population for each of the choice profiles across a vector of 1 000 draws of model parameters. Then Equation 11.3 (the Rockhampton model) was used to predict values for the same profiles across 1 000 draws, with the means of the relevant socio-economic variables from the Brisbane data set used where required. For

Table 11.11 Difference in values from Aboriginal and benefit transfer models

	Mean value from Aboriginal model	Mean value using benefit transfer from Rockhampton model	Proportion of value differences that are less than zero
S1	$249.7	$127.7	0.01476
S2	$232.6	$187.7	0.27945
S3	$233.6	$149.5	0.14389
S4	$291.4	$26.9	0.00011
S5	$233.6	$25.1	0.00004
S6	$193.9	$49.4	0.01132
S7	$258.0	$115.5	0.01432
S8	$258.9	$77.2	0.00601

each draw the difference in values was then calculated, and the Poe et al. (2001) procedure used to repeat the process. The proportions of value differences that fell below zero are shown in Table 11.12.

Table 11.12 Difference in values from Brisbane and benefit transfer models

	Mean value from Brisbane model	Mean value using benefit transfer from Rockhampton model	Proportion of value differences that are less than zero
S1	$137.0	$54.7	0.21901
S2	$201.9	$119.5	0.23967
S3	$154.1	$78.3	0.25872
S4	$28.2	-$51.1	0.23309
S5	$29.7	-$51.4	0.22211
S6	$43.0	-$28.1	0.25512
S7	$129.5	$45.3	0.22610
S8	$81.7	$4.0	0.24972

There were no significant differences between the values calculated from the Brisbane model and the values calculated under the benefit transfer approach.

Two tests have been conducted to test Hypothesis 2. The results of the first, involving log likelihood tests, imply that the hypothesis should be rejected as there are significant differences between the value functions of all population groups. The second test compares differences in consumer surplus and adjusts for socio-economic characteristics of the populations. The results of these more robust tests also imply that the hypothesis should be rejected as there are significant differences between the values of the Aboriginal and non-Aboriginal populations (apart from cases where there was no improvement in the protection of cultural heritage sites). However, there are no significant differences in the values of the local regional and remote urban communities, indicating that some form of benefit transfer would be appropriate between these population groups.

5 DISCUSSION

The case study outlined above explored the values of different population groups for the protection of Aboriginal cultural heritage sites. The valuation was set in the context of water resource development and the potential adverse impacts of further development on both the environment and Aboriginal cultural heritage sites. As the development scenario focused on a variety of factors and involved non-use values, CM was used as the most appropriate valuation technique. This means that the values for the protection of Aboriginal cultural heritage sites were determined in the context of trade-offs with other environmental impacts of development. Had the focus of study been specifically on cultural heritage impacts, the use of CVM may have been more appropriate.

In the first instance, the conditions for benefit transfer were examined in terms of the part-worths of the cultural heritage attribute. The results in Table 11.5 suggest that values held by the Aboriginal and general communities are significantly different, with values for the former being positive and negative for the latter. These results were confirmed (Table 11.7) and imply that any benefit transfer of part-worth values would not be appropriate. This highlights a fundamental difference in the nature of values held by the Aboriginal and general populations. There was no significant difference in the marginal values of the two general populations.

The comparison of the marginal values for different attributes implies a linear relationship between the different attribute levels. However, an examination of the changes in values for different attribute levels (Figure 11.3) indicates that such a linear relationship did not occur in any of the three population groups. In fact, values for changes in attribute levels were similar across the population groups for lower level changes and the real difference in values occurred in preferences to changes from the third (45 per cent) to the highest (55 per cent) level of protection.

In the context of water development trade-offs, the general populations indicated their preferences for lower levels of environmental losses rather than lower levels of cultural protection. They were most concerned about the impacts of development on vegetation and waterways (Figure 11.2). In contrast, the Aboriginal community was most concerned about the impacts on its heritage sites, but also had strong preferences to protect the waterways. Unlike the general population, the Aboriginal community did not have significant values for vegetation protection. The general community might have different values for Aboriginal cultural heritage if it were the only good being valued or if it were being valued along with a different set of attributes to those presented in these studies.

The second test for benefit transfer considered the complete value functions developed in the MNL models for the different population groups. This is a more relevant focus as it examines the values held by the different communities for resource development trade-offs. This is the context in which respondents were presented with the valuation exercise. People were not asked to value the different attributes of development separately, but were required to make trade-offs between certain levels of different attributes. In other words, tests for transferring value functions are focused on whether different population groups would make similar choices between similar choice profiles. It is important to consider complete value functions, rather than the part-worths of the separate attributes, because differences in marginal values for different attributes may cancel out in a value function, and population characteristics may also compensate for differences in marginal values.

The log likelihood tests conducted on the MNL models (Table 11.8) indicate that value functions could not be transferred between any of the populations. A second, more robust test was conducted that compared differences in consumer surplus estimates and adjusted for the socio-economic characteristics of the different populations. In this case, the results indicate that a benefit transfer would not be appropriate between the value function of the Aboriginal and general community populations (Table 11.11), but would be appropriate between the Brisbane and Rockhampton general populations (Table 11.12).

It might have been expected that the local regional and remote urban general communities would have different values for water resource development trade-offs and the protection of Aboriginal cultural heritage sites. People in the remote urban areas may be expected to have higher values for environmental protection as they are unlikely to benefit directly from the economic gains of regional development. In a similar way, urban populations might be expected to have higher values for Aboriginal cultural heritage protection than the local community, because they do not bear the costs of protection (economic loss). As well, development in urban areas means few cultural sites remain in such an environment, and a scarce good is valued more highly.

Although the results of the log likelihood test suggest that some differences do occur between these two population groups (Table 11.8), the more robust consumer surplus tests imply that there are some socio-characteristics differences between the Brisbane and Rockhampton general communities that mitigate differences in marginal values (Table 11.12).

While the values of different Aboriginal populations were not assessed in the study, there are features of the Rockhampton Aboriginal community sample that would suggest some degree of value transfer would be realistic. The Rockhampton Aboriginal community is relatively urbanised (in a regional context) and represents a mix of people and backgrounds. Not all Aboriginal people in Rockhampton come from the region, and many of those that do have not maintained links with their traditional culture or country.

It is likely that the values held by the Aboriginal community for the protection of its cultural heritage sites include both use and non-use values. The proportion of use values is likely to be relatively low because many cultural heritage sites are on private property. In this respect, there may be justification for the transfer of values to another area where non-use values are significant. The more disconnected the population is from its cultural heritage, the more important non-use values are likely to be in maintaining an important link with its traditional culture.

Finally, it should be noted that the cultural heritage attribute was described in terms of the quantity of sites protected, and no mention was made of the quality of different sites. For example, no mention was made of the very famous rock art sites at Carnarvon Gorge. Where benefit transfer also involved differences in site quality, then some benefit adjustment may be necessary. Further research is needed to determine how values for the protection of cultural heritage sites vary with quality differences.

6   CONCLUSION

The research reported here represents one of the first attempts to test how values relating to indigenous issues might be suitable for benefit transfer purposes. There are two important issues that the results have highlighted in the context of benefit transfer. First, it would appear that marginal values for the protection of Aboriginal cultural heritage sites are not transferable between the Aboriginal and general populations, but there do not appear to be demographic differences between the regional and urban samples of the general population, indicating that a transfer of marginal values may be appropriate.

Second, the values the Aboriginal and general communities hold for trade-offs between environmental and cultural impacts of water resource development in the Fitzroy Basin are not transferable. The general community holds stronger preferences for environmental protection rather than cultural protection. The Aboriginal community has stronger preferences for the protection of its cultural heritage sites than environmental protection. To the Aboriginal community, environmental and cultural heritage protection may be interlinked, whereas they appear to be viewed quite separately by the general population. In contrast, there does appear to be evidence to support the transfer of values for water resource development trade-offs between the two general population groups.

NOTE

1. It would also be possible to frame the survey in terms of willingness to pay to achieve greater protection levels from the current situation, or willingness to accept compensation for losses arising from further development (Rolfe and Bennett 2003).

REFERENCES

Adamowicz, W., T. Beckley, D. Hatton MacDonald, L. Just, M. Luckert, E. Murray and W. Phillips (1998), 'In search of forest resource values of Indigenous peoples: are non-market valuation techniques applicable?' *Society and Natural Resources*, **11** (1), 51–66.

Bille T. (2002), 'A Contingent Valuation Study of the Royal Theatre in Copenhagen', in S. Navrud and R.C. Ready (eds), *Valuing Cultural Heritage*, Cheltenham UK and Northampton, MA, USA: Edward Elgar, pp. 200–37.

Boxall, P., J. Englin and W. Adamowicz (2002), 'The Contribution of Aboriginal Rock Paintings to Wilderness Recreation Values in North America', in S. Navrud and R.C. Ready (eds), *Valuing Cultural Heritage*, Cheltenham UK and Northampton, MA, USA: Edward Elgar, pp. 105–17.

CQANM, CQ A New Millennium (2001), *Social and Cultural Development*, Technical Paper, Rockhampton: CQ A New Millennium.

Dore J. and J. Woodhill (1999), *Sustainable Regional Development: Executive Summary of the Final Report*, Canberra: Greening Australia.

Dovers S. and C. Mobbs (1999), 'Towards the Development of Principles for Adaptive Regional Natural Resource Management', paper presented at the International Symposium on Society and Resource Management, 8 July, Brisbane.

Gray, I. and G. Lawrence (2001), *A Future for Regional Australia. Escaping Global Misfortune*, Cambridge: Cambridge University Press.

Haener, M.K., D. Dosman, W.L. Adamowicz and P.C. Boxall (2001), 'Can stated preference methods be used to value attributes of subsistence hunting by Aboriginal peoples? A case study in northern Saskatchewan', *American Journal of Agricultural Economics*, **83** (5), 1334–40.

Janke, T. (1998), *Our Culture: Our future*, Report on Australian Indigenous Cultural and Intellectual Property Rights, prepared for the Australian Institute of Aboriginal and Torres Strait Islander Studies and the Aboriginal and Torres Strait Islander Commission, by Michael Frankel and Company.

Krinsky, I. and A. Robb (1986), 'On approximating the statistical properties of elasticities', *Review of Economics and Statistics*, **68**, 715–19.

L'Oste-Brown, S. (2001), 'A Brief Note Regarding the Distribution of Aboriginal Cultural Heritage Places and Values Within the Fitzroy Catchment, Central Queensland', paper prepared for the Institute for Sustainable Regional Development, Central Queensland University, by Central Queensland Cultural Heritage Management.

L'Oste-Brown, S., L. Godwin and C. Porter (1998), *Towards an Indigenous Social and Cultural Landscape of the Bowen Basin*, Bowen Basin Aboriginal Cultural Heritage Project, Cultural Heritage Monograph Series, Volume 2, Brisbane: Queensland Department of Environment.

Morey, E.R., K.G. Rossmann, L.G. Chestnut and S. Ragland (2002), 'Valuing Reduced Acid Deposition Injuries to Cultural Resources: Marble monuments in Washington D.C.', in S. Navrud and R.C. Ready (eds), *Valuing Cultural Heritage*, Cheltenham UK and Northampton, MA, USA: Edward Elgar, pp. 159–83.

Navrud, S. and R.C. Ready (eds) (2002), *Valuing Cultural Heritage*, Cheltenham UK and Northampton, MA, USA: Edward Elgar.

Navrud, S. and J. Strand (2002), 'Social Costs and Benefits of Preserving and Restoring the Nidaros Cathedral', in S. Navrud and R.C. Ready (eds), *Valuing Cultural Heritage*, Cheltenham UK and Northampton, MA, USA: Edward Elgar, pp. 31–9.

Poe, G.L., K.L. Giraud and J.B. Loomis (2001), *Simple Computational Methods for Measuring the Differences of Empirical Distributions: Application to Internal and External Scope Tests in Contingent Valuation*, Staff Paper 2001–05, Department of Agricultural, Resource and Managerial Economics, Cornell University.

Rolfe, J.C. and J.W. Bennett (2003), 'WTP and WTA in Relation to Irrigation Development in the Fitzroy Basin, Queensland', paper presented at the 47th Annual Conference of the Australian Agricultural and Resource Economics Society, 12-14 February, Fremantle, Western Australia.

Rolfe, J., A. Loch and J. Bennett (2002), *Tests of Benefit Transfer Across Sites and Population in the Fitzroy Basin*, Valuing Floodplain Development in the Fitzroy Basin Research Report No.4, Emerald: Central Queensland University.

Rolfe, J. and J. Windle (2003), 'Valuing the protection of Aboriginal cultural heritage sites', *Economic Record*, **79** (Special Issue), 85–95.

Windle, J. and J. Rolfe (2002), *Natural Resource Management and the Protection of Aboriginal Cultural Heritage*, Institute for Sustainable Regional Development Occasional Paper 5/2002, Rockhampton: Central Queensland University.
Windle, J. and J. Rolfe (2003), 'Valuing Aboriginal cultural heritage sites in central Queensland', *Australian Archaeology*, **56**, 35–41.
Zeppel, H. (2001), 'Indigenous Heritage Tourism and its Economic Value in Australia', in Australian Heritage Commission, *Heritage Economics – Challenges for Heritage Conservation and Sustainable Development in the 21st Century*, conference proceedings, 4 July 2000, Canberra, pp. 108–18.

12. The Significance of Policy Instruments in Benefit Transfer

Paula Horne and Jeff Bennett

1 FRAMING IN STATED PREFERENCE METHODS

The criteria used to assess the viability of benefit transfer exercises normally involve comparisons between the source and target sites in terms of their ecological characteristics, the socio-economic parameters describing the populations of those impacted and the extent of the environmental changes being investigated (Boyle and Bergstrom 1992). The focus of these criteria is on the comparability of value estimates of the outcomes of resource use change. Yet it is apparent from the stated preference literature that the mechanisms used to secure resource use changes are also important in the values that people place on outcomes. Put simply, people value the ways in which outcomes are achieved as well as the outcomes themselves.[1]

The most prevalent evidence of this phenomenom centres on the importance of payment vehicle selection in stated preference methods applications (Mitchell and Carson 1989; Morrison et al. 2000; Windle and Rolfe 2004). Those being asked to pay for environmental improvements consistently demonstrate that their willingness to pay is dependent not only on the extent of the improvement being offered but also on the mechanism being used to collect (albeit hypothetically) the payments. Stated preference method practitioners are therefore advised to select a payment vehicle that is both believable to respondents and appropriate to the policy setting that underpins the valuation study. The 'frame' of the stated preference questioning should therefore replicate as closely as possible the policy setting of the case at hand to avoid so-called 'framing bias' in the value estimates so derived (Boyle 1989).

An implication of this finding is that the source and the target in a benefit transfer exercise should also be compared in terms of their policy settings and hence their 'frame' of value reference.

The goal in this chapter is to elaborate concerns regarding 'frame' comparability by demonstrating that 'payment vehicle' is a term that covers an array of aspects of the implementation of proposed policies. The conclusion drawn is that comparability between source and target cases must be considered across all the key elements of policy measures.

To support this conclusion, the results of two choice experiments are presented. Both studies involve choices between alternative policy measures to promote the protection of biodiversity in forests owned by non-industrial private forest owners in Finland.

In the first, forest owners were asked to choose between alternatively specified voluntary conservation contracts to be offered to forest owners across Finland. Under the contracts, forest owners would be paid on a per-hectare basis for forests that are set aside from logging. Strictly speaking, this is not a study that yields value estimates for benefit transfer because it provides net marginal cost valuations. However, in so far as the values are useful to a process that could establish a common pool of 'standardised' compensation values, the importance of considering the relevant frame gives relevance to the results.

In the second, policy choices for forest biodiversity conservation were presented to a sample of Finnish citizens. The citizens, as taxpayers, would be responsible for covering the cost of additional forest conservation in Finland.

The studies show that the attributes used to describe the terms of the contracts offered have a significant impact on forest conservation consumers' willingness to pay and forest conservation suppliers' willingness to accept payment.

2   FOREST OWNERS' ATTITUDES TO CONSERVATION POLICY MEASURES

The so-called non-industrial private forest (NIPF) owners own 61 per cent of forests in Finland, and almost 75 per cent in the southern part of the country. State ownership in southern Finland is less than 10 per cent. Hence, the economic and social implications of additional forest protection are of concern specifically to this sector of society. Conventionally, Finnish nature conservation policy has been implemented through the government buying areas that have conservation value. The NIPF owners have not always approved these top-down approaches to nature conservation.

Along with the recent international trend in biodiversity governance, there has been a shift toward incentive-based policy mechanisms. In 2002, the Finnish Government accepted a programme for action that introduced pilot projects using incentive mechanisms based on the initiative of forest owners. The new policy measures are aimed at bringing about positive social and economic impacts through improvements in the acceptability of conservation among forest owners, and cost effectiveness for both the state and forest owners.

The study[2] reported here sought to estimate the impacts of attributes of one type of incentive-based mechanism for forest conservation, voluntary contracts, on the amount of money that forest owners would be willing to accept as compensation for changes to their forest management practices that would in turn improve biodiversity protection. It involved the application of choice modelling. A questionnaire was used that contained six choice sets, each involving three alternative policy settings. Two of the options specified contracts between forest owners and the governmental agencies described in terms of five attributes.

1. **Who initiates the contract:** The first level this attribute could take is that the forest owner herself or himself is active in initiating the conservation contract. Conventionally, environmental organisations, the second level, have been active in initiating conservation actions, while forest organisations, the third level, have dealt with timber trading and extension of silvicultural practices. The new policy programme suggests the formation of a conservation trust that would be funded by voluntary payments for biodiversity conservation purposes, which is given as a fourth level of the initiator attribute.
2. **Restrictions on forest use:** About a third of forest owners leave some small patches of forests unmanaged, so the small patches of forest protected would be an attractive level of this attribute for many forest owners. The second level, a nature management plan, would involve a voluntary plan that safeguards and enhances nature values in the forests but also allows harvesting. The third level for the restrictions on forest use attribute is a total ban on silvicultural practices. The most restrictive management level is the creation of a strict nature reserve that would impose restrictions on other uses as well as forestry.
3. **Compensation paid:** The amount of compensation proposed varied between zero and 350 euros per hectare per annum.
4. **Contract duration:** The duration of the contract attribute ranged from five years to 100 years, a period that would cover, on average, three generations of forest owners.
5. **Cancellation policy:** The levels of cancellation policy varied according to who is allowed to cancel the contract. One level was that the forest owner who enters into a contract might cancel it and,

naturally, return the compensation due. Alternatively, the contract would bind the forest owner but a new owner would be allowed to cancel the contract. Lastly, the contract would also bind the new forest owner.

These attributes and their levels are summarised in Table 12.1.

The third option in all the choice sets was the 'status quo' in which the level of conservation in private forests would not be increased. Respondents to the questionnaire were asked to choose their preferred alternative from each choice set for adoption by the government across Finland.

Table 12.1   Attributes and levels: forest owner study

Attribute	Levels
Initiator of the contract	Forest owner him/herself Environmental organisation Forest organisation Conservation trust
Restrictions on forest use	Small patches of forest protected Nature management plan No silvicultural practices allowed Strict nature reserve
Compensation/ha/year	€0; €40; €70; €210; €280; €350
Duration of contract	5 years; 10 years; 30 years; 100 years
Cancellation policy	Forest owner can cancel New owner can cancel Also binds new owner

Choice data were collected by distributing the questionnaire by post to 3 000 private forest owners from across Finland in spring 2003. Forty-two per cent of the questionnaires dispatched were returned completed, providing adequate representation of the population. The average size of forest property owned was 42 hectares with respondents being, on average, 52 years old. Forty-one per cent of respondents were retired, 28 per cent were employees, 22 per cent were farmers and 80 per cent were male.

The model of respondents' choices, estimated using the multinomial logit procedure, is displayed in Table 12.2.

The status quo was assigned the alternative specific constant (ASC). The positive and statistically significant ASC estimate indicates a preference for no additional forest conservation. The compensation parameter estimate is also positive indicating that the higher the compensation offered in a policy alternative, the higher the probability that the option was selected. All the other variables were effects coded.[3] At least one of the levels was statistically significant for all the variables. 'Forest owner' was the most preferred alternative for the initiator of the contract, while the 'environmental organisations' was least favoured. Respondents were more willing to conserve small patches of forest or manage their forest according to a nature management plan, rather than take more restrictive measures. Short contract periods were preferred to longer ones, with the 100-year contract level being a highly unpopular choice. Respondents also preferred flexibility in their forest conservation decision, opting more frequently to have a possibility of withdrawing from the contract at their will.

Table 12.2 Estimated model parameters (and standard errors): forest owners

Variable	Parameter estimate (standard error)
Alternative specific constant (status quo)	1.7385*** (0.0762)
Compensation	0.0033*** (0.0003)
Initiator: Forest owner	0.4626*** (0.0607)
Initiator: Forest organisation	0.0573 (0.0664)
Initiator: Environmental organisation	-0.2503*** (0.0642)
Initiator: Conservation trust	-0.1550 (-)
Restriction: Small patches conserved	0.4601*** (0.0580)
Restriction: Nature management plan	0.2373*** (0.0695)
Restriction: No silviculture	-0.1379** (0.0660)
Restriction: Strict nature reserve	-0.5595 (-)
Duration: 5 years	0.4841*** (0.0592)
Duration: 10 years	0.2865*** (0.0609)
Duration: 30 years	0.0713 (0.0637)
Duration: 100 years	-0.8419 (-)
Cancellation: Present owner can cancel	0.1725*** (0.0497)
Cancellation: New owner can cancel	0.0591 (0.0537)
Cancellation: Binds new owner	-0.2316 (-)
Log-likelihood	-2490.18
$\rho 2$	0.1889

Note: ***significant at $p < 0.01$; **significant at $p < 0.05$.

A number of findings can be drawn from these results, in terms of their relevance to the issue of benefit transfer. First, they demonstrate that the terms of the contracts offered to forest owners are important to them. The claim for compensation increases as the levels of the undesirable contract attributes rise. This is perhaps not unexpected given that some of those attributes relate directly to the expected income that forest owners are being asked to forgo. For instance, the restrictions on forest utilisation under the contracts limit or postpone wood extraction potential. Others are not so straightforward. For instance, the initiator of the contract is shown by the modelling to be important to forest owners, independent of the type of restrictions placed on forest management, the period of the contract and the capacity of the owner to terminate the contract. So even though the contracts to be offered are voluntary for forest owners, there is shown to be a preference for self-initiation. This is a clear demonstration of the importance of 'frame'.

The second point to note from these results is that, in a strict sense, they are not relevant to the process of benefit transfer. That is because they are estimates of the marginal costs of forest owners, net of any private benefit each owner enjoys from the protection of their forest. The value estimates driven by the model are thus willingness to accept compensation from the supply side. This is to be differentiated from willingness to accept compensation by those who consume forest protection benefits. The willingness to accept in that context refers to those consumers' willingness to accept payment to have forest protection values to which they have an explicit or perceived right taken away from them.[4] The forest owner willingness to accept values are, however, relevant for a value transfer process whereby payments to forest owners can be standardised across different conditions. Hence, the conclusion regarding the relevance of frame holds for that type of value transference.[5]

3   CITIZENS' ATTITUDES TO CONSERVATION POLICY MEASURES

Data for this choice modelling application[6] were collected by a mail survey in the early summer of 2002. A simple random sample of 3 000 was selected to represent 15–74 year old Finnish citizens. The response rate achieved was 45 per cent.

Each respondent faced six choice tasks, each having three alternatives in the choice modelling questionnaire designed for this application. One of the alternatives was always the status quo that involved no additional conservation areas. The other two alternatives that involved increases in the amount of forest conservation being provided were described in terms of six attributes. Two attributes represented the percentages of forest area under protection in southern and northern Finland. These attributes were interpreted as representing the numbers of threatened species under each alternative. Socio-economic attributes of the protection alternatives were the number of lost jobs and the annual cost to households through taxes over a 10-year period.

Three policy instrument types were set as levels for the fifth attribute. The first, land acquisition, was explained as presenting a low risk of achieving conservation targets but as giving little consideration for the sovereignty of forest owners. On the other hand, information-based instruments such as counselling by forest owner organisations were described as having high conservation risk but high owner sovereignty. Finally, conservation contracts based on the voluntary actions of forest owners were presented as a middle course instrument. Table 12.3 sets out the attributes and the levels they varied over to create the alternatives.

Table 12.3   Attributes and their levels: citizen study

Attributes	Levels
Percentage of protected forest area in southern Finland	Present: 1.8 % (status quo only) 1.5 x present (2.3%) 2 x present (3.6%) 4 x present (7.2%)
Percentage of protected forest area in northern Finland	Present (17%) 1.25 x present (21%) 1.55 x present (25%) 2 x present (34)
Loss of jobs	-5000; -2000; No change; +1000
Annual cost to households over 10-year period	No change; €10; €30; €100; €150; €300
Policy instrument	Land acquisition Conservation contracts Counselling

The results of the choice modelling undertaken for a sub-sample of the data set – those respondents who were found to stress the importance of forests as a resource in an analysis of preference heterogeneity – are given in Table 12.4. This group comprised 46 per cent of all respondents. This group was characterised by being more often male, rural, forest owners and older than the average of all respondents. The remaining respondents, those who emphasised the non-material and natural values of forests, were found to be ambivalent to the selection of a policy instrument (Horne et al. 2004a). The results were generated through the application of the multinomial logit procedure.

The alternative specific constant was assigned to the status quo alternative. As with the forest owner survey results, it is positive and the statistically significant coefficient reflects the relative preference for the status quo to any additional conservation regime.

The 'forests as a resource' respondents preferred lower forest protection percentages in both the northern and southern regions of Finland. The coefficients estimated for those attribute parameter estimates were both negative and significant. In addition, forest protection options that were harmful to employment prospects were not preferred.

Of specific interest in this chapter is the significance of the effects coded variables relating to the policy instrument. The sub-sample of respondents whose choices were modelled showed a preference for voluntary contracts over the counselling approach, and both were preferred to compulsory acquisition. The latter policy option was associated with a deterioration of welfare for these respondents.

Table 12.4 Estimated model parameters (and standard errors): 'Forests as a resource' respondents

Variable	Parameter estimate (standard error)
Alternative specific constant (status quo)	0.6187*** (0.1310)
Tax	0.0025*** (0.0005)
Southern Finland forest	-0.0468* (0.0236)
Northern Finland forest	-0.0198* (0.0074)
Jobs lost	0.0002*** (0.00002)
Policy instrument: Contract	0.1607** (0.0619)
Policy instrument: Counselling	0.0889* (0.0996)
Policy instrument: Land aquisition	-0.2496 (-)
Log-likelihood	-1483.5
ρ2	0.1873

Note: ***significant at $p < 0.01$; **significant at $p < 0.05$; * significant at $p < 0.10$

The significance and signs of the estimated coefficients for the policy instrument attribute levels demonstrate the importance to respondents who perceived forests as a resource of the way in which forest conservation goals are achieved. For this sector of respondents, more forest conservation is not a priority. Employment is the attribute that is primary in driving their choices. However, if the government proceeds with a forest management strategy that involves more conservation, the negative impacts on this group can be moderated somewhat through the selection of a policy instrument that is based on voluntary measures rather than forced acquisition.

The relevance of this result to the benefit transfer process is that it is not sufficient simply to transfer a value estimate based on the amount of additional forest conservation to be achieved. The relevant willingness to pay value estimate would be different between two areas if the policy instrument to be used in the two areas was different.

4   CONCLUSIONS

Benefit transfer is acknowledged widely as having many pitfalls. Yet for many cases where the net values of welfare change are relatively small in comparison to the costs of a primary data collection exercise, its use in the development of policy is both convenient and low cost (Morrison et al. 2002). Its capacity to provide benchmarks against which 'threshold values' can be assessed is a particular strength. Yet the results presented in this chapter demonstrate another reason for caution in its use. Consistency of policy setting should be added to the list of criteria to be used in determining the efficacy of using a source study in a specific target case.

The results also demonstrate the strength of choice modelling in providing information to be used as source data in a benefit transfer task. The studies reported here both used choice modelling to help untangle the strength of the contributions made to values of numerous attributes. It is because these studies included attributes that related to the way in which policy is implemented that this can now be recognised as a potentially important factor in determining values. It also means that choice modelling results can be used to provide adjustment to raw value estimates in order to reflect these additional complexities. Put simply, because choice modelling breaks down the components of value, the value estimates it produces are more readily applied in a benefit transfer exercise where the circumstances are different between source and target cases.

NOTES

1. This is not to suggest that the consequentialist philosophy underpinning neo-classical economics is flawed given that the means of achieving an outcome can be regarded as an outcome in itself.
2. Full details of the study referred to in this section can be found in Horne et al. (2004b).
3. Effects coding provides a useful way of including qualitative attributes into the analysis. The main effect of an attribute with L levels can be defined by creating L-1 effects coded variables that take values of 1, 0 or -1 depending if the alternative contains the value of the new variable (see e.g. Louviere et al. 2000).
4. The conceptual basis of using stated preference techniques to investigate farmer decision-making is provided by Lusk and Hudson (2004).
5. Government-funded compensation schemes for land owners setting aside areas of remnant vegetation would be informed by such value estimates. In addition, auctions for conservation contracts of the type developed for the BushTender Scheme in

Victoria, Australia (Stoneham, Chaudri, Ha and Strappazzon 2003) can be better formulated and then assessed in terms of economic efficiency with reference to willingness to accept value estimates.

6. Full details of the application referred to here can be found in Horne et al. (2004a).

REFERENCES

Boyle, K. (1989), 'Commodity specification and the framing of contingent valuation questions', *Land Economics*, **65** (1), 57–63.

Boyle, K. and J. Bergstrom (1992), 'Benefit transfer studies: myths, pragmatism and idealism', *Water Resources Research* **28** (3), 657–63.

Horne, P., H. Karppinen and E. Ylinen (2004a), 'Kansalaisten Mielipiteet Metsien Monimuotoisuuden Turvaamisesta', in P. Horne, T. Koskela and V. Ovaskainen (eds), *Metsänomistajien ja Kansalaisten Näkemykset Metsäluonnon Monimuotoisuuden Turvaamisesta*, Metsäntutkimuslaitoksen tiedonantoja 933, Helsinki: Finnish Forest Research Institute, pp. 25–47.

Horne, P., T. Koskela, V. Ovaskainen, H. Karppinen and A. Naskali (2004b), 'Metsänomistajien Suhtautuminen Yksityismetsien Monimuotoisuuden Turvaamiseen ja sen Toteutuskeinoihin', in P. Horne, T. Koskela and V. Ovaskainen (eds), *Metsänomistajien ja Kansalaisten Näkemykset Metsäluonnon Monimuotoisuuden Turvaamisesta*, Metsäntutkimuslaitoksen tiedonantoja 933, Helsinki: Finnish Forest Research Institute, pp. 47–73.

Louviere, J., D. Hensher and J. Swait (2000), *Stated Choice Methods: Analysis and Application*, Cambridge: Cambridge University Press.

Lusk, J.L. and D. Hudson (2004), 'Willingness-to-pay estimates and their relevance to agribusiness decision making', *Review of Agricultural Economics*, **26** (2), 152–69.

Mitchell R. and R. Carson (1989), *Using Public Surveys to Value Public Goods: The Contingent Valuation Method*, Washington DC: Resources for the Future.

Morrison, M., R. Blamey and J. Bennett (2000), 'Payment vehicle bias in contingent valuation studies', *Environmental and Resource Economics*, **16** (4), 407–22.

Morrison, M., J. Bennett, R. Blamey and J. Louviere (2002), 'Choice modelling and tests of benefit transfer', *American Journal of Agricultural Economics* **84** (1), 161–170.

Stoneham, G., V. Chaudri, A. Ha and L. Strappazzon (2003), 'Auctions for conservation contracts: An empirical examination of Victoria's BushTender Scheme', *Australian Journal of Agricultural and Resource Economics*, **47** (4):477–500.

Windle J. and J. Rolfe (2004), 'Assessing Values for Estuary Protection with Choice Modelling Using Different Payment Mechanisms', paper presented at the 48th Annual Conference of the Australian Agricultural and Resource Economics Society, 11–14 February, Melbourne.

Index